Great Web Architecture

CLAY ANDRES

GREAT WEB
ARCHITECTURE

IDG BOOKS WORLDWIDE, INC.

AN INTERNATIONAL DATA GROUP COMPANY

FOSTER CITY, CA ▲ CHICAGO, IL ◆ INDIANAPOLIS, IN ▼ NEW YORK, NY

Great Web Architecture

Published by

IDG Books Worldwide, Inc.

An International Data Group Company
919 E. Hillsdale Blvd., Suite 400
Foster City, CA 94404
www.idgbooks.com (IDG Books Worldwide Web site)

ISBN: 0-7645-3246-4

Printed in the United States of America

10 9 8 7 6 5 4 3

1K/RV/QZ/ZZ/FC

Distributed in the United States by IDG Books Worldwide, Inc.

Distributed by CDG Books Canada Inc. for Canada; by Transworld Publishers Limited in the United Kingdom; by IDG Norge Books for Norway; by IDG Sweden Books for Sweden; by IDG Books Australia Publishing Corporation Pty. Ltd. for Australia and New Zealand; by TransQuest Publishers Pte Ltd. for Singapore, Malaysia, Thailand, Indonesia, and Hong Kong; by Gotop Information Inc. for Taiwan; by ICG Muse, Inc. for Japan; by Norma Comunicaciones S.A. for Colombia; by Intersoft for South Africa; by Eyrolles for France; by International Thomson Publishing for Germany, Austria and Switzerland; by Distribuidora Cuspide for Argentina; by LR International for Brazil; by Galileo Libros for Chile; by Ediciones ZETA S.C.R. Ltda. for Peru; by WS Computer Publishing Corporation, Inc., for the Philippines; by Contemporanea de Ediciones for Venezuela; by Express Computer Distributors for the Caribbean and West Indies; by Micronesia Media Distributor, Inc. for Micronesia; by Grupo Editorial Norma S.A. for Guatemala; by Chips Computadoras S.A. de C.V. for Mexico; by Editorial Norma de Panama S.A. for Panama; by American Bookshops for Finland.

For general information on IDG Books Worldwide's books in the U.S., please call our Consumer Customer Service department at 800-762-2974. For reseller information, including discounts and premium sales, please call our Reseller Customer Service department at 800-434-3422.

For information on where to purchase IDG Books Worldwide's books outside the U.S., please contact our International Sales department at 317-596-5530 or fax 317-596-5692.

For consumer information on foreign language translations, please contact our Customer Service department at 800-434-3422, fax 317-596-5692, or e-mail rights@idgbooks.com.

For information on licensing foreign or domestic rights, please phone +1-650-655-3109.

For sales inquiries and special prices for bulk quantities, please contact our Sales department at 650-655-3200 or write to the address above.

For information on using IDG Books Worldwide's books in the classroom or for ordering examination copies, please contact our Educational Sales department at 800-434-2086 or fax 317-596-5499.

For press review copies, author interviews, or other publicity information, please contact our Public Relations department at 650-655-3000 or fax 650-655-3299.

For authorization to photocopy items for corporate, personal, or educational use, please contact Copyright Clearance Center, 222 Rosewood Drive, Danvers, MA 01923, or fax 978-750-4470.

Library of Congress Cataloging-in-Publication Data

Andres, Clay.
    Great web architecture / Clay Andres.
       p.   cm.
    ISBN 0-7645-3246-4 (alk. paper)
    1. Web sites--Design.   I. Title.
    TK5105.888.A53   1999
    005.7'2--dc21   99-28480
                                      CIP

 is a registered trademark or trademark under exclusive license to IDG Books Worldwide, Inc. from International Data Group, Inc. in the United States and/or other countries.

ABOUT IDG BOOKS WORLDWIDE

Welcome to the world of IDG Books Worldwide.

IDG Books Worldwide, Inc., is a subsidiary of International Data Group, the world's largest publisher of computer-related information and the leading global provider of information services on information technology. IDG was founded more than 30 years ago by Patrick J. McGovern and now employs more than 9,000 people worldwide. IDG publishes more than 290 computer publications in over 75 countries. More than 90 million people read one or more IDG publications each month.

Launched in 1990, IDG Books Worldwide is today the #1 publisher of best-selling computer books in the United States. We are proud to have received eight awards from the Computer Press Association in recognition of editorial excellence and three from Computer Currents' First Annual Readers' Choice Awards. Our best-selling ...For Dummies® series has more than 50 million copies in print with translations in 31 languages. IDG Books Worldwide, through a joint venture with IDG's Hi-Tech Beijing, became the first U.S. publisher to publish a computer book in the People's Republic of China. In record time, IDG Books Worldwide has become the first choice for millions of readers around the world who want to learn how to better manage their businesses.

Our mission is simple: Every one of our books is designed to bring extra value and skill-building instructions to the reader. Our books are written by experts who understand and care about our readers. The knowledge base of our editorial staff comes from years of experience in publishing, education, and journalism — experience we use to produce books to carry us into the new millennium. In short, we care about books, so we attract the best people. We devote special attention to details such as audience, interior design, use of icons, and illustrations. And because we use an efficient process of authoring, editing, and desktop publishing our books electronically, we can spend more time ensuring superior content and less time on the technicalities of making books.

You can count on our commitment to deliver high-quality books at competitive prices on topics you want to read about. At IDG Books Worldwide, we continue in the IDG tradition of delivering quality for more than 30 years. You'll find no better book on a subject than one from IDG Books Worldwide.

John Kilcullen
Chairman and CEO
IDG Books Worldwide, Inc.

Steven Berkowitz
President and Publisher
IDG Books Worldwide, Inc.

Eighth Annual Computer Press Awards ⟫1992

Ninth Annual Computer Press Awards ⟫1993

Tenth Annual Computer Press Awards ⟫1994

Eleventh Annual Computer Press Awards ⟫1995

IDG is the world's leading IT media, research and exposition company. Founded in 1964, IDG had 1997 revenues of $2.05 billion and has more than 9,000 employees worldwide. IDG offers the widest range of media options that reach IT buyers in 75 countries representing 95% of worldwide IT spending. IDG's diverse product and services portfolio spans six key areas including print publishing, online publishing, expositions and conferences, market research, education and training, and global marketing services. More than 90 million people read one or more of IDG's 290 magazines and newspapers, including IDG's leading global brands — Computerworld, PC World, Network World, Macworld and the Channel World family of publications. IDG Books Worldwide is one of the fastest-growing computer book publishers in the world, with more than 700 titles in 36 languages. The "...For Dummies®" series alone has more than 50 million copies in print. IDG offers online users the largest network of technology-specific Web sites around the world through IDG.net (http://www.idg.net), which comprises more than 225 targeted Web sites in 55 countries worldwide. International Data Corporation (IDC) is the world's largest provider of information technology data, analysis and consulting, with research centers in over 41 countries and more than 400 research analysts worldwide. IDG World Expo is a leading producer of more than 168 globally branded conferences and expositions in 35 countries including E3 (Electronic Entertainment Expo), Macworld Expo, ComNet, Windows World Expo, ICE (Internet Commerce Expo), Agenda, DEMO, and Spotlight. IDG's training subsidiary, ExecuTrain, is the world's largest computer training company, with more than 230 locations worldwide and 785 training courses. IDG Marketing Services helps industry-leading IT companies build international brand recognition by developing global integrated marketing programs via IDG's print, online and exposition products worldwide. Further information about the company can be found at www.idg.com. 1/24/99

To the memory of Garson Kanin: a dear friend, a writer, and a true inspiration. I'm still learning from you.

FOREWORD

As editor in chief of *Publish* magazine, I've seen a lot of Web sites. I can't begin to count how many of them opted for flashy graphics instead of understated visual guidance, or chose gimmicky metaphors over intuitive navigation. All too often Web graphics are confused with Web design — superficial elements take precedence over structural integrity. In *Great Web Architecture*, Clay Andres shows us how it should be done.

Andres pointedly uses the word *architecture* in this title, because designing a Web site is much like constructing a building. You need site analysis and structural blueprints. You need skilled masons to lay the foundation, carpenters to build the framework, and electricians to connect the wiring. You need to consider whether visitors will enter your building directly through the front door — the home page, if you will — or if they'll pause briefly in a vestibule — a splash screen that welcomes people to the site. Is your site a portal through which visitors access other businesses, much like the lobby of an office building? Or is it a shopping mall in which people buy a variety of goods? As you can see, there's a great deal of planning that must occur before you call in the interior designers who paint the walls and decorate the rooms.

At *Publish* magazine, we've been pondering these ideas long before the Web entered mainstream consciousness. Our business is the design and production of communications that are created with personal computers. *Publish* began in 1986, along with the then-nascent desktop publishing revolution. Those early years were a whirlwind of ever-improving software and hardware, released almost as fast as publishing geeks could think up ways to apply technology to the problems of information design and production workflows. Today, we're seeing the same kind of passion, creativity, and excitement around publishing on the World Wide Web, as individuals and corporations revel in the onslaught of ever-better technologies and off-the-shelf tools to communicate their messages. But the thread that ties together these two seemingly diverse disciplines is the flow of information, the architecture of communication.

Like *Publish*, Clay Andres began with desktop publishing and made the transition to the Web several years ago. As an author, he's written books about such mission-critical software as Adobe Photoshop, an application that lives as much in the Web world as in the print one. In addition to his clear and engaging writing style, Andres brings to his books his first-hand perspective as a Web site designer for clients such as International Paper. He uses plenty of real-world case studies to make sense of complex design principles. You'll find him a valuable guide to understanding the secrets of successful Web architecture.

Serena Herr
Editor in chief, *Publish*

PREFACE

Available technology both enhances and limits what you can do with architecture.

When you look at a Web site and browse among its pages, you are seeing the solution to a specific set of business and design problems. But things look very different when you begin to work on a Web site. In most cases, the problem isn't well defined, which makes the process of site development one of mutual discovery for clients and designers. It is this aspect, in addition to rapidly changing technology, that makes each project different from another, and explains why it is necessary to spend so much time gathering information about your clients — their products and services, their customers and employees, the way they do business, and their goals — before you can start to design or build a site.

In *Great Web Architecture,* you get a chance to look at Web sites representing many architectural solutions and explore the different aspects of each. For example, various parts of the book discuss how problems of navigation, identity, familiarity, and image are solved in each site; and how information is presented, made accessible, useful, and kept current. In addition to design issues, business issues are addressed and solved. But the order of exploration does not follow a standard project design workflow. Instead, the hierarchical plans that support a Web site mark the starting point, and the discussion continues through the structural elements of sites and pages.

Each chapter provides an opportunity to look at techniques used to solve problems and create strongly coherent Web sites. You are taken through more familiar HTML constructs, such as those used for tables and frames, into the various components of Dynamic HTML, including JavaScript and Cascading Style Sheets. You also learn about opportunities to use Java. (Be sure to check out the Web site that accompanies this book, `www.idgbooks.com/extras/webarch.html`, for code samples.)

The approach to *Great Web Architecture* is architectural, not in the sense of information architecture, which concerns the classification, ordering, and presentation of data, but in a structural sense. What are the elements of a site? How are these elements assembled into a coherent, useful, and compelling whole that can stand up even under the most adverse conditions? It is this post-and-beam approach to solving the problems of Web site design that proves to be the best metaphor for the design and construction of really great Web sites.

ACKNOWLEDGMENTS

I did not write this book by myself, and there are many people whose help was invaluable and untiring. Without the encouragement and patience of Mike Roney and Katie Dvorak, this book would not exist. I am grateful to both for going beyond the call of duty (and the fine print of contract) to help turn some very fallow periods into truly productive ones. I'd also like to thank my friend and intern, Jesse Simko, who took on the seemingly thankless task of tracking down permissions from all the companies and design firms discussed in these pages. And, as always, nothing is written without passing the critical, yet loving, eye of my wife, Katharine, who makes it all worthwhile.

I would be remiss if I didn't give special thanks to all the people behind the Web sites included in this book. It was wonderful to be in contact with so many talented, creative people so willing to take time to discuss the pleasures and travails of Web site design. I have learned much from all of you and am grateful to have been a part of this active, exciting community.

There are also several companies that supplied me with software and hardware that made the writing of this book possible. Both Adobe Systems and Macromedia were very generous in supplying me with the latest editions of their applications. Apple Computer helped me through the loan of Macintosh systems, as did Sony Electronics with the loan of a Vaio Windows system and Agfa with the loan of one of their SnapScan scanners. I am deeply grateful for all of this support.

CONTENTS AT A GLANCE

CONTENTS

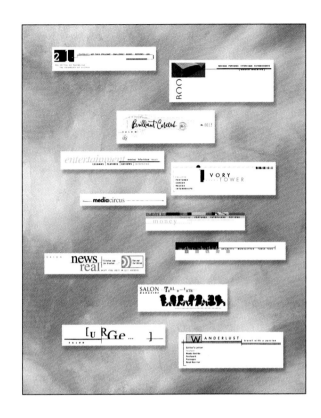

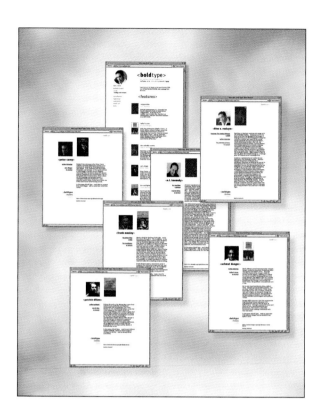

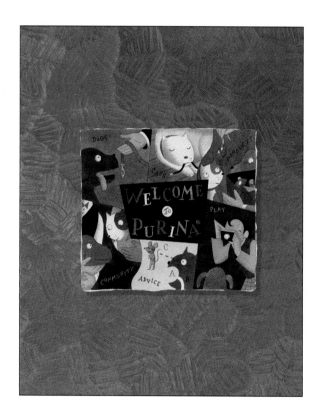

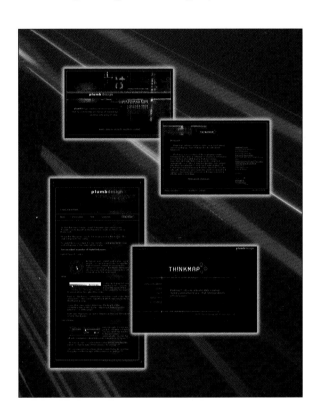

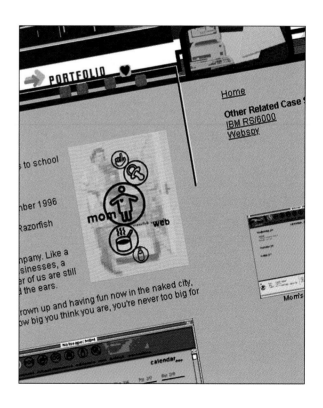

PART I
SECRETS OF WEB ARCHITECTURE

CRANE & CO. INCORPORATED

Welcome to Crane & Company. Since 1801, we've been making fine cotton papers for business and social correspondence as well as specialty papers for banknotes and industrial use. Follow this link to find out more about the company and our tradition of papermaking.

From formal to fun-loving, Crane produces luxurious stationery products for every occasion. Crane's pure cotton paper will add considerable distinction to every word you write. Click now to see what we have to offer.

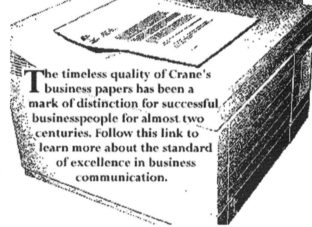

The timeless quality of Crane's business papers has been a mark of distinction for successful businesspeople for almost two centuries. Follow this link to learn more about the standard of excellence in business communication.

Crane's most famous paper is used by the US Treasury. Since 1842, we have been a world leader in the production of durable and secure papers for banknotes and official documents. Follow this link to learn more.

An outgrowth of Crane's papermaking expertise is the production of nonwoven webs. From surfboards to automobiles, Crane Nonwovens are used in a spectrum of products. For more information, please continue.

Crane's historic Pioneer Mill produces papers to serve communications, engineering, industry and art. Pioneer, America's premier long-fiber paper mill now crafts papers

A division of Crane & Co., Inc., Excelsior provides

CHAPTER 1
BUILDING HIERARCHICALLY STRUCTURED SITE PLANS

I n this chapter, we look at the backbone of Web architecture: the hierarchical site plan. A Web site's hierarchy is evident regardless of the language, program, or platform used to build pages and the links that hold the pages together as a site. Architecturally, this backbone forms the structure upon which we build our sites and is therefore the logical place to begin a site design. The creation of a strong yet flexible site plan is as much an exercise in engineering as in design, but remember, the discipline of architecture is a cross between design *and* engineering. And even though the *look* of a building is what we first admire, it is the combination of form and function in equal measure that enables us to say whether that building is well designed. In the same way, good Web architecture combines a strong aesthetic sense with clean, flexible site planning.

Hierarchies provide both form and elasticity, but deciding what makes a *good* site is very much a matter of personal taste. For instance, when in search of good design on the Web, I tend to judge sites quickly, fleeing to other domains before an ugly page has even finished loading. If I'm looking for information, I'm more likely to tolerate long load times or click through numerous links to get to my destination. But I'm also quick to look elsewhere if a path seems to be going nowhere. First impressions are important, but successful Web sites need more than quick, attention-grabbing elements.

The structure that holds up a site is its plan, and even though it's possible to use links to jump from page to page almost at random, all site plans are

A site without hierarchy is like a jellyfish — an amorphous mass with a bunch of tentacles leading nowhere.

RAYMOND GARGAN, INTERACTIVE ARTS & ENGINEERING

From formal to fun-loving, Crane produces luxurious stationery products for every occasion. Crane's pure cotton paper will add considerable distinction to every word you write. Click now to see what we have to offer.

organized hierarchically. The hierarchy needn't be rigid, but a clearly delineated structure makes it possible to facilitate stream-of-consciousness browsing.

YOU CAN'T JUDGE A WEB SITE BY ITS HOME PAGE

To begin, take a look at an example home page and the site it covers. TAG Heuer is a well-known brand with a carefully crafted image as a manufacturer of high-end sports watches. Its home page (www.tagheuer.com) reflects this (1.1). Graphically, this page looks like a TAG Heuer ad: sport plus watch equal man/woman of action. The addition of a list of links turns this ad into a simple but effective site entry point. Image and the promise of information—the basic elements of a home page.

But a home page does not constitute a site plan. Instead, it is a portal into the site that reflects the overall design of the site. TAG Heuer's site plan, designed by Adjacency, has a straightforward two-level hierarchy: home page, first-level divisions, and second-level category pages (1.2). Each entry on the home page leads to a division page, each of which is subdivided into categories. This basic structure, reflected in the navigation bars of the site, makes it easy to find information and also know at all times where you are within the site. Easy navigation combined with a sense of place is the hallmark of a well-structured Web site.

There is much more to Web architecture than pretty pages and hierarchical links, but these two elements are the design and engineering basis of good sites—they are our elevations and plans.

FINDING YOUR FOOTINGS: HIERARCHICAL FOUNDATIONS

It is the nature of the human mind to categorize, order, and sort information. Thus, it is no surprise that given a collection of Web pages, we naturally create hierarchies. Or to put it another way, most subjects can easily and naturally be broken down into subsets to create a hierarchy of information.

Take a look at any Web site. Some will have relatively broad or flat hierarchies, whereas others may be quite deep, with many levels of detail. Neither is inherently better, but they serve different purposes. Most obviously, a site with a lot of information will require greater depth simply to accommodate all of its pages.

Smaller sites tend to have flatter hierarchies, which makes it easier to get to details more quickly. As you can see immediately on his home page, designer Rob Day's site (www.evansday.com) is divided into three

1.1   *© Copyright Adjacency, Inc.*

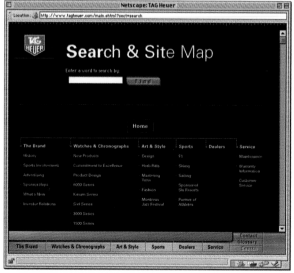

1.2   *© Copyright Adjacency, Inc.*

functional categories: *Our Work*, *Photoshop*, and *About Us* (1.3). The site map shows that no category goes beyond the next level of detail (1.4). You don't need much more than this to organize a couple dozen pages and allow for modest growth.

This site can grow in two directions: Day can deepen the site by adding more subcategories or detail, or broaden the site by adding whole new categories. This site will deepen naturally as more examples are added to the subsections of the *Our Work* division. If the business were to expand to include a retail division selling Rob Day's Iris prints, it could easily be added as a new division to the site. It might well end up being the largest division, but a simple hierarchical plan can accommodate this kind of change and growth.

The Web site produced by Impact Design for Absinthe, a restaurant in San Francisco, uses the same structure as Day's site: four divisions off a home page, each with a few or no subdivisions and detail pages (1.5). A Web site for a *belle époque* restaurant in San Francisco might seem to have very little in common with a designer's personal showcase, but in plan, they are remarkably similar (www.absinthe.com).

NOTE

The two-level hierarchy is quite flexible and is easily expanded. If you think about the mathematical possibilities, a site with four categories, each with four subcategories, has 16 physical divisions for storing detail pages. Any category can have more than four subcategories, and it's also easy to create additional first-level categories. You can see that this simple arrangement of pages can quickly expand to 25 or 36 categories, each with numerous detail pages.

1.3

1.4

1.5

DIGGING DEEPER: BIGGER BASEMENTS FOR BIGGER SITES

Crane & Co., Inc., a paper manufacturer in Dalton, Massachusetts, has a moderate-sized site designed by Interactive Arts and Engineering—over 100 pages (www.crane.com). It appears to be organized on the same basic two-level hierarchy with seven primary categories that reflect the business divisions of this international corporation (1.6). But there's a twist here. When you click on any of the divisions, you are

still within the Crane & Co. domain, but the larger divisions have their own two-level hierarchy of pages.

When you enter the *Business Papers* division, you are one level down in the Crane site hierarchy, but you are also at the top level of the Business Papers subsite (1.7). This page acts as another home page. It conveys a strong image and the promise of information through seven additional links. Frequent business visitors to Crane's site would be more likely to bookmark this page than the corporate home page, because it is the logical entry point for them. Going

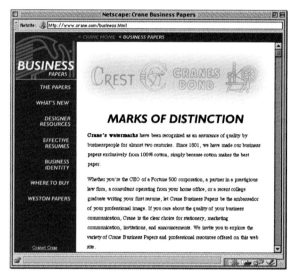

1.6   1.7

HIERARCHY TELLS ALL

Raymond Gargan, Interactive Arts & Engineering

Q: How does the process of defining a site hierarchy work?
RG: It's like any research project. What you want to know is: How does this company do what it does? You start by collecting information. In the case of a Web site, you talk to the client — talk to everyone you can, executives, managers, sales, and marketing people. Read everything they have available — annual reports, sales brochures, company newsletters. If you're lucky, you might even find some letters from customers. With this mass of information, you get to

know the company and can see beyond the standard corporate organizational charts.

In addition, we always look at what our clients' competitors are doing both on and off the Internet. It's also very important that both the developer and the client agree on the objectives for the site. For example, does the company want to have e-commerce or online customer service immediately, sometime in the future, or never?

With all this knowledge, you can begin to categorize and order the information

down this hierarchy another level, you find the lowest organizing level leading to the detail pages (1.8).

The Crane site can also be seen as a collection of nested sites, with each corporate division as a closely related but independent site. If Crane acquired a new company with its own Web site, it would not be difficult to incorporate it as a subsite like any of the existing divisions. When Crane creates a new product line, the division's subsite can broaden to include it without affecting any of the other divisions.

It's as though your filing system not only had document and file drawers, but also rooms of file drawers. You can see that adding a new room expands the capacity of the system without affecting anything that came before it. On the other hand, you could spend your life in a single room and never know that other rooms existed.

Nested sites like Crane's also allow for a division of Web responsibility. Corporate PR handles the home page and one category, while product managers within each of Crane's divisions are responsible for the content of their own section of the site.

1.8

BREAKING HIERARCHIES

Just as we're beginning to feel comfortable with a purely hierarchical organizing scheme, something comes along to remind us that ours isn't a purely hierarchical world. Not all subjects can be neatly

you've gathered. Inevitably, this leads to a hierarchy. Sometimes you have to make compromises. Or there are times when you might want to put the same thing in two categories, but that's what the Web is great for. You can have the same thing in multiple places just by linking across whatever hierarchy you've created.

Q: What happens if you need to change the hierarchy?
RG: We originally designed the Crane site with only its two most prominent di-

visions in mind — Social Papers and Business Papers. But then Crane decided all seven divisions, including their engraving and currency papers divisions, should be added. The hierarchical plan easily expanded to accommodate this. Of course we had to redesign the home page to include all seven links, but that was easy. The real trick was to keep the look consistent across all of these very disparate entities. Maintaining a very well-structured hierarchy is what made this possible.

categorized. There are too many extenuating circumstances, interruptions, and leaps of the imagination. As we strive to achieve a harmonious site plan, something sticks out and upsets the balance. Our goal is to incorporate these elements without destabilizing the site structure.

We start with order. We divide and subdivide like Linnaeus with the living world until we get down to the species level. But what do we do with the platypus? Even worse, what if our system of knowledge is imperfect? What if we started with only two kingdoms: plants and animals? Where do we put bacteria and algae?

The Braun site (www.braun.com), for example, is a model of clean design (as are its appliances). The home page is devoid of extra decoration; the logo is the image (1.9). On the left is a column of seven links that constitute the two-level hierarchy of the site, plus a site map link for quick navigation. On the right, more links, but outside of the standard order. (Notice also the Braun-designed switch that is used as a navi-

gational element throughout the site. These elements are discussed in more detail in Chapter 4.)

When you look at Braun's site map, it doesn't look hierarchical (1.10) But if we take this graphic and straighten out the hierarchy, we can see that it's a classic two-level design (1.11). Now where do we put the elements from the right column of the home page?

1.9

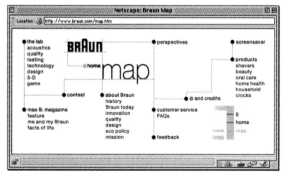

1.10

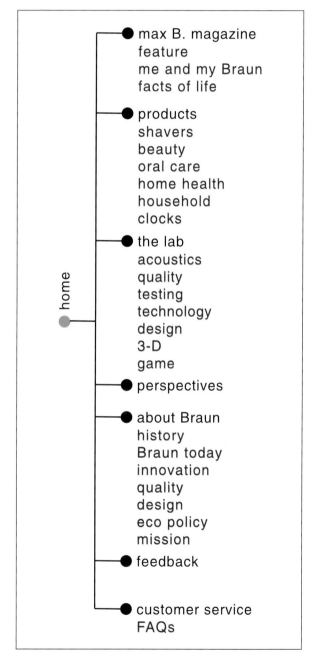

1.11

The Contest and Screensaver links can easily be thought of as separate categories that fall under the home page. We might like all categories at this level of the hierarchy to be of equal importance. Logically, this would make sense, and by moving them off to the side of the home page, the designers of this site are making the statement that these links are different. But structurally, they fit right in.

Braun's World Cup site has special significance. Intended to attract attention to Braun during the world's largest sporting event, it is both timely and temporary. The designers have made it of equal importance to the home page itself by creating a unique domain for it, www.worldcup.braun.com (1.12). Hierarchically, this has created two linked and equal sites. It's as if Linnaeus had discovered a whole new life form.

GROWING BIGGER

You may be thinking that it's easy for a site like Braun's to remain clean and uncluttered. It's relatively small, it has a well-defined clientele and product line, and it doesn't try to do too much. Even the addition of its World Cup feature doesn't make the site seem much more complex. After all, Braun is not an appliance giant. But it is a small part of the consumer giant The Gillette Company, which has its own Web site that points to Braun's domain. This is not unlike the situation at Crane & Co., where there are several divisions. But it's a matter of scale; The Gillette Company is made up of several companies, and its Web site (www.gillette.com) reflects this (1.13).

The Gillette Company is so big that Braun, one of its major entities, barely shows up on the home page. You have to click down a level through the Brands button to get to a Braun link (1.14). You can see what the designers of The Gillette Company's site are up to

1.12

1.13

1.14

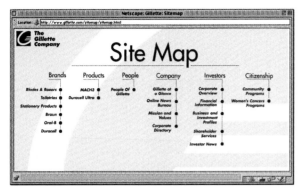

1.15

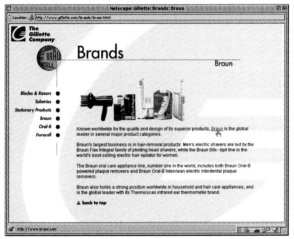

1.16

when you look at the site map (1.15). This looks like any other two-level hierarchy, but it only represents the very top of Gillette's deep domain — the tip of the iceberg.

From the Brands page, you can access Braun, Oral-B, or Duracell, each of which had its own site before The Gillette Company's corporate domain went online. Actually, there is a detail page for each brand with links to the brand's domain (1.16). It's a bit hidden, but you can see that the word *Braun* in the text is a link that takes you to the Braun site. This isn't really nested, because you have to leave The Gillette Company domain to enter the Braun domain, but the effect is similar. And I would guess that, in the future, there will be links added from Braun's site back to Gillette's.

One of the most powerful aspects of hierarchical organization is that it allows for the creation of hierarchies independent of one another. These can be plugged in together without the need to change either one. You can see how Braun was able to link across at the topmost level to add its World Cup feature. Crane was able to do this from the top down with its divisions, and Gillette was able to incorporate entire pre-existing sites for its independent brands.

BALANCING SITES

As you explore the structure of the site for The Gillette Company (which was relatively new and still expanding as of this writing), you find that the depth varies considerably according to category. *People*, *Company*, *Investors*, and *Citizenship* are obviously important subjects The Gillette Company wants to highlight. But even though they represent two-thirds of the first-level hierarchy, they contain less than one-third of the site's pages. Yet the site does not appear unbalanced.

If balance were achieved by sheer weight of pages, Gillette could have organized its site differently into Brands, Products, and Company Information, with People, Investors, and Citizenship moving down a level under this last category. The site plan would have looked more balanced, but the editorial aspects of this site would not have been as well served.

NOTE

Throughout this chapter, the discussion has moved from smaller to larger sites, with the focus on how size affects site organization and structure. But we have not examined the process of gathering information and ordering it by importance, because this is not within the scope of this book. The Gillette name, for example, is practically synonymous with shaving, and with one of the bigger advertising budgets in the world, this is likely to remain so. But a Web site enables The Gillette Company to promote other important, if less obvious, aspects of the company. The fact that it is "people-oriented" and a good world citizen rarely gets mentioned in 30-second spots, but on the Web, the story can be featured right up front (1.17).

This first-level hierarchy presents what The Gillette Company sees as a balanced view of the company. They've essentially tilted a typical product-oriented view (1.18) up on one side to show a more corporate-oriented view. By doing this, they rotate the categories that might have been the first-level hierarchy downward to the second and third levels, and they become the underwater two-thirds of the iceberg.

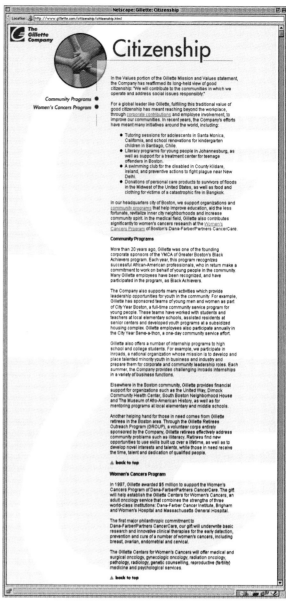

1.17

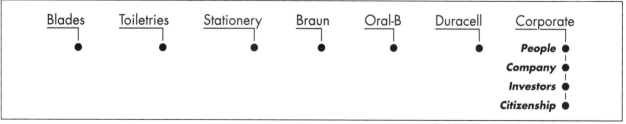

1.18

This points out another aspect of hierarchies. Imagine that your site plan is constructed like an Alexander Calder mobile with each sculptural element hanging from the top by a wire and balanced along a rod with other elements of equal prominence (1.19). It's possible to pick any element and rotate the mobile so that it all hangs from this new top element. Gravity may wreak havoc with your wires and rods, but a site plan on paper can always be rotated this way.

Don't forget that even though a site is designed from a home page downward, sites can be entered at any page. The home page is the formal entry point, but not the only one. The preponderance of search engines almost ensures that a large percentage of a site's visitors will not come in through the front door. A balanced site is one that can welcome browsers at any point. As detailed later in this book, this has as much to do with navigational elements as with a site's structure.

LEAPING OVER HIERARCHIES

I have touted hierarchies as the only way to organize Web sites. With a physical collection of printed pages, there's no other way. But truly large sites, and sites that change frequently, must present what is important up front, regardless of where this information lies in the hierarchy. Newspapers have always used organizing schemes that include rules for laying out the front page, as well as multiple sections that make it easy to find things like sports and business news. *The New York Times* adapted this technique for its Web-based front page, and it almost looks like a "real" newspaper (www.nytimes.com). There are no articles on this page, however, only headlines, brief summaries, and links . . . lots of links (1.20).

In an electronic newspaper, headlines remain important elements, but the stories themselves are banished to the inner pages, replaced on the front page by short summaries. Without the physical sections of paper folded inside each other, section links become

1.19

1.20

Reprinted by Permission. ©1998 The New York Times Company.

more important. The sections remain the same from day to day, whereas the headlines and summaries change with the news. So there is a familiar structure that you can use to go straight to the Technology news (1.21), and there are linked items of greater importance (in the eyes of *The New York Times*) that let you skip over the hierarchy and go right to the lead story (1.22).

The way we *read* a printed newspaper is very different from browsing through an on-line newspaper, but in *The New York Times*' version some similarities remain. We can browse the front page headlines, but we can't read more than the first sentence or two of any article. We've got to click to link to the full text and link back if we want to continue browsing the headlines. Going directly to a story this way is very different from browsing through one of the sections.

As with the printed paper, sections are organized with a front page and following articles, but in the electronic version, there is greater emphasis on linking to the articles. To put this another way, there's a greater reliance on the structural hierarchies provided by site links. The home page sets up an initial hierarchy that includes numerous sections or subsites, each with its own hierarchy established on its own home page.

1.21

Reprinted by Permission. ©1998 The New York Times Company.

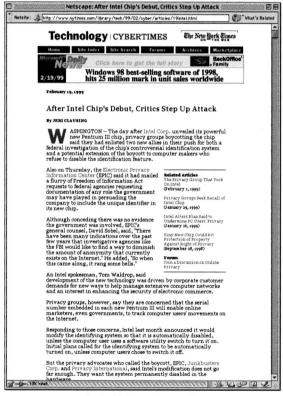

1.22

Reprinted by Permission. ©1998 The New York Times Company.

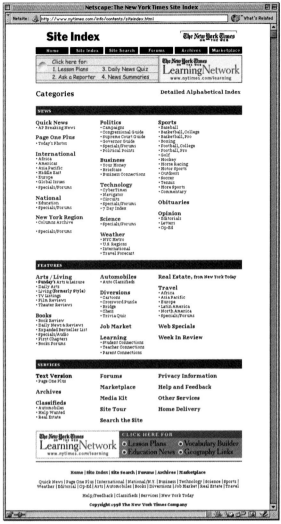

For example, the *Technology* sections includes navigation bars that clearly delineate a hierarchy, and the section is further divided into regular subcategories with the day's items highlighted for direct linking. This demonstrates the independence of sections within the paper and the overall site. Once again, we have a situation where complex relationships are simplified by nesting a subsite within a larger domain.

Although it isn't immediately obvious on first viewing, *The New York Times'* site is a multilevel hierarchy that is both broad and deep. The full hierarchy is presented as a site map (1.23). The publication has taken advantage of the Web to let its readers avoid the multilevel path and go directly to items that interest them. The hierarchical plan cannot be avoided, but the long path to stories can.

Changing links to highlight new features or important items within a strongly delineated structure is a basic tool for designers of larger sites or sites that change regularly. There are a number of ways to give the appearance of familiarity so that regular browsers feel comfortable when they return to your site. Establishing a recognizable structure is primary. Once this is done, it's possible to create links that cross all the boundaries of the hierarchy without losing track of where you are.

In other words, once you have a structure for organizing the pages of your site, you can deal with content issues. What's new, different, timely, or of special interest? A hierarchy may not include these categories, but items like these can exist within your hierarchy. It's a matter of linking across the hierarchy to highlight them.

TIP

It's important to remember that the site hierarchy is a low-level tool used to create and maintain order among the site's pages. Once a structure is established, the site can grow or be reordered along hierarchical lines, but the flow of information is more like a game of Chutes and Ladders. You want browsers to be able to climb all over your site in any way they can. In other words, don't let the structure restrict the links.

OBSCURING HIERARCHIES FOR THE GREATER GOOD

Look at any online periodical. Current stories are available right from the home page, whereas regular sections are arranged hierarchically. Salon Magazine's site (www.salonmagazine.com) is a good example of content driving the home page, but existing within a clear structure (1.24). You can follow a regular browsing pattern through such sites or pick and choose as the mood suits you. The same is true for many other sites that serve a community of frequent visitors. Links to what's new follow the familiar structural layout of sections or categories.

Web indexes and search sites present an opposite picture. Their main purpose is to give the user search capabilities that ignore all site hierarchy. But all these sites include categorical searches that provide an orderly means to navigate through a subjective hierarchy and narrow a search. Yahoo! got its start as the ultimate hierarchical Web index, and although one could argue whether this is still true, Yahoo! remains the largest single point of entry for people in search of Web content—the ultimate home page perhaps (1.25).

Search fields are the most obvious tool for finding information buried in the depths of site hierarchies, but search engines are not really architectural elements. You can't organize a site around a search engine, as sites like Yahoo! clearly demonstrate. They are instead a user-directed linking device, which we'll examine in Chapter 4.

I'm often tempted to do away with a hierarchical plan and search for something more free flowing. But I've never succeeded. I've come to realize that the ability to browse by following a train of thought is purely a function of links that have nothing to do with site structure. Links and structure are separate concerns, but by starting with a sturdy hierarchical base, a stronger system of links can be built on top of it.

1.24

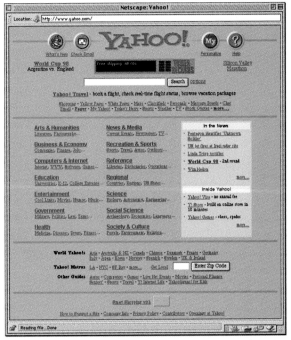

1.25

Courtesy of Yahoo! Inc.

2 1st

features | GET THIS STRAIGHT | CHALLENGE | BOOKS | REVIEWS | LOG

THE CULTURE OF TECHNOLOGY
THE TECHNOLOGY OF CULTURE

BOOKS

REVIEWS FEATURES INTERVIEWS AUTHOR EVENTS

[BOOKS ARCHIVE]

Brilliant Careers

SALON

No. 0013

entertainment

movies television music

COLUMNS | FEATURES | REVIEWS | INTERVIEWS

COLUMNS
FEATURES
CAREER
RECESS
INTERNSHIPS

IVORY TOWER

media circus

money

COLUMNS | FEATURES | INTERVIEWS | REVIEWS

mothers who think

ARCHIVES NEWSLETTER TABLE TALK

SALON

news
real

"Clinton can
be trusted ..."

The war
for Wired

▶ OFF YOUR CHEST   ▶ 21ST ARCHIVE

SALON
MAGAZINE

Table talk

[uRGe...]

SALON

WANDERLUST

travel with a passion

Editor's Letter
Feature
Mondo Weirdo
Postmark
Passages
Road Warrior

CHAPTER 2
NAVIGATING SITES:
THE FLOW OF PAGES

T he collection of pages that make up a Web site does not float randomly in hyperspace. As discussed in Chapter 1, the pages are ordered in a hierarchical structure that firmly establishes their relationship to one another and to the site as a whole. From a site builder's point of view, it's crucial to understand the flow of pages. But such information is superfluous to the browsers who visit a site. These browsers are mostly concerned with how they get from page A to page B and find their way back again, and so from their perspective, links are more important. The site solution (the system of links) is navigational and not necessarily structural.

The definition of a structural hierarchy is an essential part of designing and maintaining a site. But the elements of site navigation can exist apart from this. In most cases, navigation will proceed along the hierarchies you've defined, but it needn't. This becomes more important as sites get bigger and the number of pages increases. You don't want to force browsers to traverse a long hierarchy to find the information they're looking for.

If you think of the page hierarchy as a site's structure, the navigational system is the floor plan that leads browsers through the structure from page to page. Our navigational systems can follow a carefully ordered sequence, or, because we are dealing with hyperstructures, it can transport us to the farthest edges of the site in a single bound.

The simpler the navigation, the more people will read and the deeper they will delve into the site.

KAREN TEMPLAR, SALON MAGAZINE

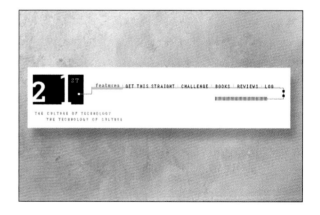

2.1   *GetSmart is a registered trademark of BFC Enterprises.*

2.2   *GetSmart is a registered trademark of BFC Enterprises.*

FOLLOWING A PATH

Even though we refer to HTML documents as *pages*, they are not like pages in a book. HTML pages do not have a clearly defined sequence, as do the pages of a book, magazine, or any other printed document. The sequence must be defined with links. The individual user decides the viewing order, but it is the Web architect who defines the choices available.

In the formal study of architecture, there is a phenomenon known as *architecturale promenade,* which refers to the sequential flow of spaces or rooms that one walks through to get to a certain point. You have experienced this kind of planned sequence of spaces when you walk through the galleries of a museum or even when you ride a roller coaster at an amusement park.

You can't ensure that everyone will enter your site at the beginning and proceed through it in orderly fashion, but this doesn't mean that you can ignore page sequence altogether. *Architecturale promenade* can be a powerful site design tool, especially for process-oriented sites or sections of sites. For instance, the GetSmart Web site (www.GetSmart.com) provides information to consumers on borrowing money. The site is divided into categories by loan type, home loans, debt consolidation, credit cards, and so forth (2.1). This provides a logical, straightforward hierarchy that is mirrored in the navigational scheme.

The GetSmart home page contains six loan categories, plus a resource link that is clearly differentiated as less important by its smaller size and placement at the bottom of the list. Clicking one of the major links leads you down a loan-type-specific path. In fact, each of the loan-type links opens what could be considered a subsite headed by its own home page. The navigational scheme is similar to the top-level home page and therefore familiar, but there is no back option or home button (2.2). If you click the *Home Loans* link, you will be sent to the MortgageFinder subsite — the beginning of a goal-centered journey.

Each subsite home page has it own set of loan-type links. You can continue the journey by clicking one of these, or you can click one of the more general informational buttons — About Us, Privacy/Security, For Lenders, Why Should I Use GetSmart? These links are shared across the subsites. If you click the Business Financing button on the GetSmart home page, you'll see three of these same links at the BusinessFinanceCenter subsite (2.3). These buttons represent global links, and if you were to diagram this site, they would exist under the home page, but outside the second-level hierarchy of subsites.

Just as these tangential links take you away from the information-gathering process, so, too, have I digressed. Let's return to our path. As you follow the loan-type links deeper into the site, GetSmart builds a personal loan profile for you. You are essentially filling out a loan application without realizing it, and it's not even painful. The navigational scheme to this point is based on simple sequential links — virtually a Next button.

Well, it looks simple, but actually each page is being built on the fly by GetSmart's back-end database from the answers you supply. Consistent design and clean navigation were the underlying considerations and all that we, as browsers of this site, are aware of. When you finish the process, you're given additional options (links) to choose from. "It was important to keep the pages consistent throughout the information-gathering process. We had to assure an uninterrupted flow to avoid programming errors, so that the site takes you through the sequence and then brings you out again when you're finished," said Percy Wang, Senior Art Director/Developer at Elliot|Dickens Advertising, GetSmart's designers.

2.3   *GetSmart is a registered trademark of BFC Enterprises.*

FANCY TRICKS, SIMPLE SOLUTIONS

When you view the GetSmart home page online, the red arrows pointing to the six subsite buttons flash in sequence. This draws your attention to the all-important site links. At first glance, this looks as if it might be a fancy JavaScript trick, but in fact it is a simple animated GIF inserted as a single vertical image and positioned using a table.

However, the labeled buttons do use the JavaScript event triggers, onmouseover and onmouseout, to highlight a link when the cursor is over it. (Code segments for the animated GIF and JavaScript rollovers can be viewed at the Web site that accompanies this book, at www.idgbooks.com/extras/webarch.html).

ESTABLISHING ROUTES

It's easy to stay on a designated path when there's only one choice. (Your only choice is to continue on or to leave.) But Web site navigation is all about making choices. If you take a top-down view, you see the site hierarchy (discussed in Chapter 1), and each branch taken is a step deeper into the hierarchy. But we know that people can and will enter a site at any point and that it's often more useful to jump around a site than to follow a path. So we must both create the paths of hierarchy and allow navigation that ignores hierarchy. It's like a world where gravity and weightlessness coexist.

The GetSmart site is firmly rooted in the gravitational world, where navigational options are closely bound to the underlying site hierarchy. There is very little opportunity to leap across subject or site boundaries, but there's also very little need to do so. At the opposite end of the gravitational spectrum are search sites, such as Excite, AltaVista, or Lycos, where information is stored in a database and the query is the navigational tool. The norm is somewhere between GetSmart's highly directional paths and the great leaps of a search site.

For most sites, the ideal navigational scheme is one that matches the hierarchy and provides some cross-hierarchical linkages. This enables visitors to the site to follow a path from the top, change their minds and their direction through the site, or enter in the middle of the site and still be able to find their way around. In the seemingly chaotic environment of the World Wide Web, this last capability is a crucial part of good navigational design.

A typical site hierarchy might have from three to ten top-level subject headings that appear as links on the home page. Take a look at Novo Nordisk's 1997 Environmental Report (2.4), which is comprised entirely of links to the chapters of the report. (Novo Nordisk is a large pharmaceutical firm headquartered in Denmark.) Although the home page (www.novo.dk) is only the formal entry point for the site, it is used to establish the site's hierarchy.

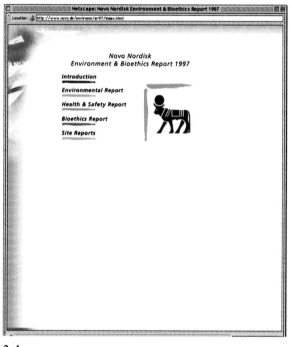

2.4

Because we are all experienced browsers of the Web (as opposed to being Web browsers), we at once recognize the six headings on this page as a title and five links. What else could they be? But not everyone interested in reading this report is likely to realize this immediately. So the designer of this site, Tim Clements, project manager of the Danish design firm Araneum A/S, has made the navigation simple by using JavaScript rollovers for each of the links. But unlike the rollovers of the GetSmart site that highlight the text, these change the single illustration on the page (2.5).

Although the rollover may be one of the more overused Web techniques, in this instance, it does its job: It adds graphic interest to the page and clearly identifies the links through imagery. But this is just more tip-of-the-iceberg stuff. The real navigation of this site doesn't begin until you click down a layer, at which point you are presented with a tour de force of navigational elements.

ELEMENTAL NAVIGATION

Navigational elements exist throughout all sites, on every page. These elements can be simple text links, buttons, bars, imagemaps, or any combination of these rolled into a JavaScript. The actual element is important, because it directs the action of the person browsing your site. But at the same time, navigational elements are secondary to the course a browser takes through your site. Which is more important: the road or the journey? We'll leave this conundrum unanswered and examine some totems of navigation.

Not long ago, the rollover buttons on Novo Nordisk's Environmental Report home page would have been simple buttons arranged in a table or perhaps even a single client-side imagemap with the links defined as hot spots on the page — merely implementation details for the site's entry point. But within the site, navigational elements had to be much more carefully considered. This is a content-driven site, and it's important that browsers be able to find

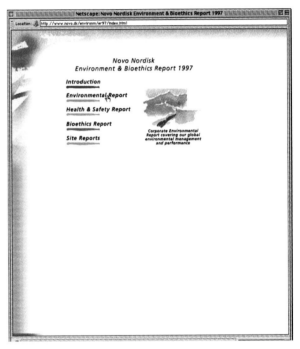

2.5

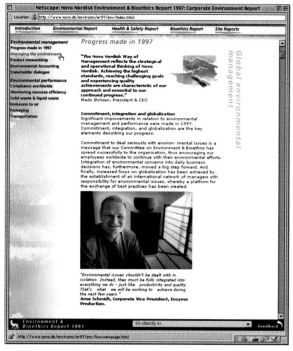

2.6

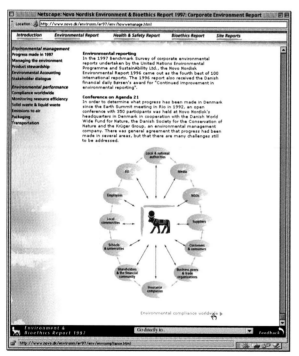

2.7

pertinent material and read it without sloppy navigational planning getting in the way.

Each section of the Novo Nordisk Web-based report is divided into subsections — a simple two-level hierarchy. In fact, this is a collection of four related reports in a single site tied together with an introductory section. But these are not subsites. This second level of the hierarchy goes straight to the text of the report. Each report is identified by its title and the familiar graphic from the home page rollovers. These pages are characterized by clean layout that is matched by clearly delineated navigational elements (2.6).

Hierarchically, each section of the report is a separate page. In the printed version, each section follows the one before it sequentially. In the Web version, you can follow this sequence by clicking on the link at the bottom of each section. It's a simple link identified by a right-pointing arrow and the name of the next section (2.7). This allows the report to be read sequentially, just as you would read it in printed form.

Each report in this site also has a table of contents arranged as a list of links. Putting this list in a frame makes it a navigational column that is always available, no matter where you are within the report. For various legitimate reasons, frames have acquired a bad name. From a navigational standpoint, frames can cause real problems for the person browsing a site. Some Web browsers don't keep a history of frame pages, which means that you can't find your way back to the exact framed page you want to revisit.

Although this can make it difficult to jump between pages of different sites, the persistent navigational frame makes it easy to move around the sections of each report in Novo Nordisk's site. The long textual frames can be scrolled, or you can move on to further sections without losing this table of contents. Once again, rollovers are used to highlight the actual links, which simply change from black to red text.

We can isolate the contents of this frame to examine its construction details (2.8). What appears as text over a background image actually consists of text images arranged in a table over the background. Rolling over the area of a table cell reloads the cell with the corresponding red text image. Clicking the rollover text links to the appropriate section of the report, which is loaded into the text frame of the page without changing the navigational table.

Table of contents–style navigation makes it easy to click back and forth or jump around in what would otherwise be a sequential report. But this site is comprised of several reports. To avoid getting buried too deeply in any single report, there is an additional level of navigation that appears as a horizontal frame across the top of every page. The five links of this frame correspond to the five links of the home page and the first-level hierarchy of the site (2.9).

This top-level navigation bar indicates the current section (the active link) with a colored underline swash. The other four swashes are gray. The color used is the same as that on the site's home page, but there is no "back to home page" link. None is needed; the navigation provided by the home page is completely accomplished by this horizontal frame. Essentially, it's an ever-present home page. Click a link to change reports.

With these two navigational frames, we can move across the hierarchy (horizontal frame at top) and up and down within sections of the hierarchy (vertical frame at left). What about jumping from a section of one report to a specific section of another report? For this there is a third navigation bar across the bottom of each page.

Because of its location on the page, the bottom bar is the least obtrusive of the three navigational frames, yet it contains more links. It displays the title of the site at the left and a feedback button at the right with links to an e-mail form for sending comments to Novo Nordisk. (It's essential to be able to do this from every page of the site.)

An important navigational component is contained within a drop-down menu entitled "Go directly to." The little down-pointing arrow attached to this field has become the universal symbol for the instruction "Hold down the mouse button here to make the drop-down menu appear." And this is some drop-down menu. Featuring direct links to every page of the site arranged in order by report, the menu fills an entire 21″ monitor screen from top to bottom (2.10).

2.8

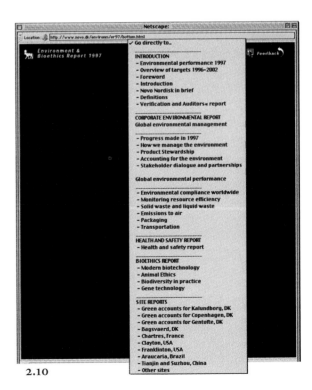

2.10

Introduction   Environmental Report   Health & Safety Report   Bioethics Report   Site Reports

2.9

On smaller monitors, the list scrolls so you can link from any page to any other page on the site in a single mouse action. (The code for this drop-down menu can be viewed on the Web site that accompanies this book, www.idgbooks.com/extras/webarch.html.)

You can see that the general layout of pages for this site surrounds the content (text and graphics) on three sides with navigational elements. Yet each of the three navigational frames provides a different navigational tool: intra-hierarchy links at the top, inter-hierarchy links on the left, and direct links to all pages at the bottom. The consistent implementation of this scheme across the site makes it a straightforward matter to get from one report, section, or page to any other in a single bound.

It would seem that this is enough, but it is not all. There are also contextual links within the content of each page. Some of these links lead directly to content on other pages, whereas others open a new glossary window to explain technical or less familiar terms (2.11). These links have nothing to do with the hierarchy of the site.

How many designers would put so much effort into the navigation of a site with no more than a few dozen pages? For this site, the added value is clear, especially when you compare the Web version of the report to what a more traditional printed one would be like. A table of contents, chapters, section headings, even page numbers help the reader navigate a printed document, but they don't come close to providing the kind of easy access that the four layers of navigation in Novo Nordisk's site do.

We can even generalize and say that this four-layered navigational approach is a good model for many sites: inter-level links, intra-level links, direct page links, and contextual links. In fact, the environmental report is merely a subsite within Novo Nordisk's larger corporate site that uses similar navigational constructs (2.12). Note the link to the environmental report (it happens to be an animated GIF) and the navigation bar on the right. Where you put the different link types and how you implement them will vary by site, but won't alter the effectiveness of these techniques.

2.11

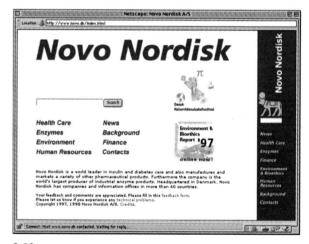

2.12

THINK LOCALLY, NAVIGATE GLOBALLY

Although the four-layered navigation employed by Novo Nordisk can be used in various ways and in many kinds of sites—the Crane site shown in the preceding chapter uses a multilayered frames-based navigational scheme—it also has a number of short-comings, especially for larger sites. A navigational scheme that depends on frames locks the designer into a very rigid layout and restricts the amount of navigational information that can be displayed for the entire site. For a site that changes frequently, this can be a limitation and a burden.

As users, we expect to find navigational elements at the top, sides, and bottom of pages. It's simply a question of clearly identifying links using such graphic elements as buttons, tables, or frames. As Web architects, we must consider navigation from several angles, not just from the front door or home page. Let's say we enter a site by linking to a page from a search engine. We have been suddenly plunked down in the middle of the site as if transported from an alien spaceship. Where are we?

We have landed at a feature article within the domain of Salon Magazine (2.13). We may or may not be familiar with Salon (www.salonmagazine.com), but the layout and typography make it obvious that this is an electronic magazine (e-zine). The name *Salon* is an understated link in the upper-left corner, and there are headline links to other recent articles and columnists. There's a banner ad at the top (animated GIF), but the emphasis is on the article. There's not even an accompanying image.

The elements of this page are arranged as an HTML table, with headline links in a column on the left and the article in a wider column filling two thirds of the page. The article is of more than passing interest, so we read it to the bottom, scrolling the browser window as we do so. Salon's designers have given us many choices for what to do next. (They've captured our attention and will do anything to keep it.) Where do we go from here?

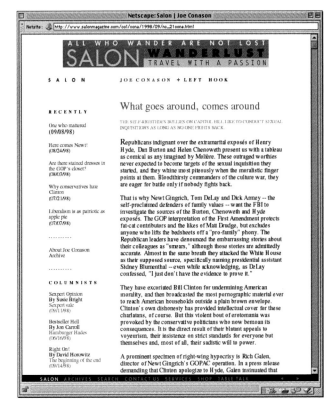

2.13

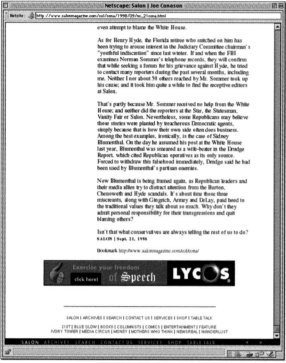

2.14

We came to this page for its content, and Salon provides it. In other words, people come to read the articles, and there are lots of them. To satisfy its large and hungry browsing audience, Salon publishes new articles daily on a wide variety of topics. You can see in the simple navigation bar at the bottom of this article that Salon is divided into 13 topical sections (2.14). You can also search the site, view the archives, or go to Salon's front page.

This is a no-nonsense navigation bar of HTML text, all capital letters separated by vertical slashes. Every version of every browser can display these links. It's the lowest common denominator for navigational elements. (The HTML for this navigational element can be viewed on the Web site that accompanies this book, at www.idgbooks.com/extras/webarch.html.)

The only thing Salon's designers have done to make this footer navigation more attractive is to add the `<font face>` tag and specify Futura Medium, Arial, or Helvetica. This tag looks for the specified font on the browser's system. If found, it becomes the display face for the designated text. If it isn't found, the next font will be used, and so on, until a matching font is found or the default is used.

I happen to have Futura on my machine, so this is what you see in the screen shot. Arial and Helvetica are the Windows and Mac OS system sans serif typefaces, so it's likely that most people browsing the Salon site will see the footer navigation displayed in a sans serif face.

And there's more here. Salon is actually a framed site. There's a single horizontal frame at the bottom of the window with Salon's most basic links. Even as we scroll past all the tempting links to other articles, we can break away from the text by clicking one of the links in the bottom frame. You'll notice that this frame appears in both Figures 2.13 and 2.14.

This bottom frame is color-coded to match the Salon section we happen to be reading. And in addition to the labeled links, there are two arrows, which constitute back and forward buttons. Click one or the other to go to the previous or next section. The sections are listed in alphabetical order, and from the Columnists section we can go back to Books or forward to Comics. I think these arrows serve the random browser better than goal-directed visitors.

Because we are goal oriented, let's click the Entertainment link in the footer and look for movie reviews. Notice how we can't go straight from any section to movies. But then again, our mind is making a leap that a Web site can't anticipate. Let's see how quickly we can get to movie reviews.

We know right away that we're in a different section of Salon. Not only is the bottom navigational frame a different color, but it says Entertainment right at the top. The featured article du jour is a music interview; we can tell this by the way these words are highlighted in the same orange shade as the navigation frame. There are links to other timely entertainment articles and to the subsections within Entertainment, Salon's largest department.

So where are the movie reviews? Should we click on Movies or Reviews at the top of the page? A quick pass over these words with the cursor reveals JavaScript rollovers, including drop-down menus for reviews. Voilá! Here is the link we seek, and an additional JavaScript puts a selection cursor next to the

movie reviews when we roll over it (2.15). Click, and we're there.

The featured movie review is laid out on a page identical to the music interview page we just came from — the navigational elements are the same, only the content (including the banner ad) changes (2.16). We can read the review or choose from a number of other recent reviews in the table column on the left. And down at the bottom of the column is a link to Salon's movie articles archive.

We arrived at our destination in two clicks, thanks to a simple text link and a clever rollover linked to a pair of scripts. From the latest news to the movie archives only took three clicks. We were able to do this because of two things the designers did when establishing Salon's navigational elements. First, they set up basic links that match the structure of the site — 13 sections with 13 direct links from every page. The navigational footer made this possible.

Second, within Entertainment, their most complex section, they provided some navigational choice, and

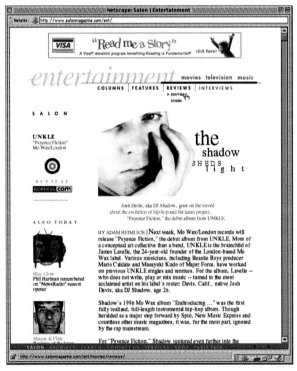

2.15

2.16

they did it with a brilliant bit of graphic design. The top slug across the pages of the Entertainment section appears to be a single graphical element comprised of a few lines and some nicely set typography (2.17).

This might have been implemented as a single HTML imagemap. After all, the image was first created in Photoshop. But then the navigational flexibility would have been lost. Instead, the art director, Karen Templar, sliced up the image into multiple image elements to be reassembled in HTML as a two-row by one-column table. The images are placed next to each other in rows and given fixed sizes using the Height and Width attributes of the `<image>` tag.

To indicate the current subsection of the site, an orange version of the text image is loaded into the table. Remember, orange is the key color of the current section, Entertainment. For the rollover effect in the top row, gray text is replaced with black.

The second row rollovers trigger the menu and pointer scripts. Here's the cleverest part: The links for the drop-down menu items are implemented as

imagemaps. You can see the imagemap areas defined in this screen shot taken in Adobe GoLive (2.18). Each image in the second row of the table is subdivided into rectangular areas that show up with dotted borders.

Using imagemaps within table cells accurately reflects the navigation on these pages. Clicking the section logotype, Entertainment, takes you to the top of the section. When you choose *Movies*, *Television*, or *Music* directly from the top row, you're linked across this level in the hierarchy. Choosing one of the imagemap links from the second row leaps over this hierarchy right down to a lower layer of content. You've essentially rebalanced the hierarchical mobile to get at information in another direction.

This bit of navigational layering was necessary, because Salon's other sections contain direct links to interviews and reviews. But the Entertainment section is subdivided into three categories. This keeps it consistent with Salon's other departments.

2.17

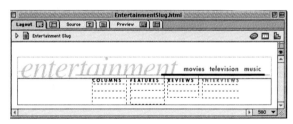

2.18

CLEAN HTML = CLEAN DESIGN = SATISFIED USERS

**Karen Templar,
Salon Magazine**

Q: Salon Magazine is graphically very clean. You don't seem to go in for the "cool" aesthetic that dominates much of Web design.

KT: We're not impressed by "neat-looking" stuff. We like to see what HTML can do. When you surpass the rote limitations of HTML, that's really great. Also, we try to keep the pages as [graphically] light as we can to improve the responsiveness of the site. We get a lot of feedback from people saying they like it like that.

Q: Is any of the site automated for the daily updates?

KT: We're looking into automation to run the site off of a database, but we do so much customization that it isn't practical. We need to see the code.

Q: Have you considered publishing a print version of Salon?

KT: All the time. But print just isn't cost effective. That's why we're on the Web.

FINDING THE TOP

Every site on the Web has a home page, and most sites have a "back to home page" button on each interior page (although two of the sites discussed in this chapter don't). This is not navigation; this is common sense. We've been browsing around in the interior of Salon Magazine for a while now. At any time, we could have clicked the Salon button at the top corner, in the bottom navigational frame, or in the footer of each page. Because Salon's home page changes daily (at least on business days), it's worth expending some effort to make sure users can get back home (2.19).

Salon's home page is a collection of its latest links — the headline news in a way. Not a lot of content appears on this page, but we know there's lots of text to go with these headlines. There's a single, eye-catching image and one banner ad. The hierarchical links are all squeezed into the Departments drop-down menu. There's also a second drop-down menu with special offers and contests — presenting a lot of information in a fairly fast load time. This seems to be Salon's overriding principle for Web site organization.

This is not an uncommon organizing principle for Web sites; cram in as many links at the top level as possible and set them up with a consistent navigational scheme. The key to good navigation is clearly directed links and a choice of linking methods. It makes no difference if the structure is deep or flat, topical or linear; you've got to allow browsers to get to pages the way they want to. You can suggest a preferred route, but there should be alternatives.

Additionally, consistent navigation across a site helps create a sense of place, and familiarity is important to encourage return visits. The elements of navigation are important, too, in that they make links obvious and help to establish the identity of the site.

2.19

CHAPTER 3
DEFINING DESIGN ELEMENTS

There are three things to remember about Web site design: *Content is king, content is king, content is king.* But in order to ensure its primacy, we must present the content in a way that is attractive, orderly, and, if possible, original. All of the hierarchical and navigational work discussed in the previous two chapters is content driven, but these organization elements do not constitute content in and of themselves. These are ways to make content accessible, to present it logically, and to maximize its usability.

The Web is a visual medium. From an informational point of view, how do we present content so that it is seen, understood, and used most effectively? With a hierarchy and navigational framework established, how do we package any ordinary content and make it look good enough to eat?

All the elements are designed to do the same thing— convey the mission of the entire site.

DAN OLSON, DUFFY DESIGN AND INTERACTIVE

VISUAL PRESENTATION:
CHOOSING ELEMENTS

Take dog food. Out of the bag, it's not very appetizing to most people. This is why Purina, the self-proclaimed world's leading manufacturer of dry dog food, puts the stuff in such attractively designed bags. The savvy marketers at Purina know how to present unappetizing content in its best light. This makes dog owners happy when they put that big bag of kibble in the grocery cart.

3.1

3.2

3.4

Dan Olson, senior designer at Duffy Design in Minneapolis, Minnesota, faced a similar quandary in choosing design elements for Purina's Web site (www.purina.com). You can show one bag or you can show forklift palettes heaped high with bags. But however good-looking a bag of kibble may be, it is not the stuff of a compelling Web site. For Purina's site, the content is not kibble, but talk *about* kibble — informational text about pets and pet care. Rather than bags of kibble, this site features people and their pets (3.1).

THE ELEMENTS OF PLAYFULNESS

Why is Purina's home page good? First of all, it looks good. The illustration is skillfully drawn and humorous. It is well chosen and interesting, features good use of color, and is well placed in the frames-based layout. Also, this home page contains the elements of good navigation that reflect the kind of carefully conceived hierarchy discussed in Chapters 1 and 2. The top navigation bar provides access to the first-level site hierarchy, and the left-hand navigation column gives direct access to the Purina Store, news, and product-specific sites.

Let's take a look at the images used to assemble this composition. The primary image is actually a collage consisting of pieces of each of the first-level links (3.2). For each link in the top navigation bar, there is a corresponding portion in the image. More specifically, the composition is a JPEG imagemap, which provides visual focus and clearly defined navigation, and sets the illustration style for other pages of the site.

There are other less significant, but no less important, images on the page as well. The Purina checkerboard appears in the upper-left corner of every page of this site, and the Purina logotype appears as a graphic image at the bottom right of each page. Both are linked to the home page. All of the navigational text is in graphic form. The typesetting of the text across the top is lighthearted and includes JavaScript rollovers (3.3), and playful shapes and color highlights distinguish the type down the left (3.4). Used on a single page, these elements function well together without overwhelming the layout and the main informational text.

TABLE 3.1	CATALOG (DOGALOG?) OF PURINA SITE DESIGN ELEMENTS		
DESIGN ELEMENT	IMAGE TYPE	ANIMATION	LINK
Primary image	JPEG	No	Imagemap
Checkerboard logo	GIF	No	To home page
Top navigation text	GIF	JavaScript rollover	Second-level hierarchy
Left navigation text	GIF	No	Nonhierarchical, subsite links*
Left pet food package image	GIF	Animated GIF	To product pages
Purina logotype	GIF	No	To home page

* The product-specific site links are included in the left-hand navigation bar as an imagemap.

But these images were not chosen to create a single page. The images are design elements for the site. They establish the play-with-your-pet feeling for the site, while at the same time differentiating between the two distinct tiers of navigation available. These elements can even be cataloged, as shown in Table 3.1.

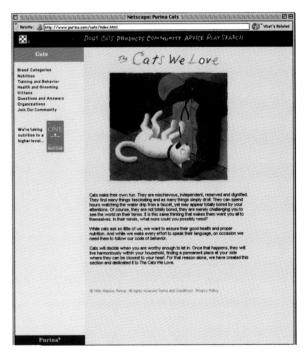

3.5

ESTABLISHING THE COLORS OF CONTINUITY

Purina uses the design elements listed in Table 3.1 to give its site visual continuity. For instance, each second-level hierarchy has a different thematic color — sage for dogs, mustard for cats, and so forth. The colors are taken from the primary illustration and used as highlight colors for the rollover links. These are subtle effects, but they work.

Take a look at the Cats section of the site (3.5). The primary JPEG illustration matches the home page illustration. The mustard color of the couch has been picked and used for the background color of the page's title and also for the rollover color of the primary navigation bar. Notice how the colors of the illustration and the typography of the navigation are both picked up and used in the GIF text of the title, "The Cats We Love" (3.6).

Also note that the framed layout remains constant throughout the main portion of the site — top and left navigation frames with primary images and text frame covering the rest of the page.

3.6

3·7

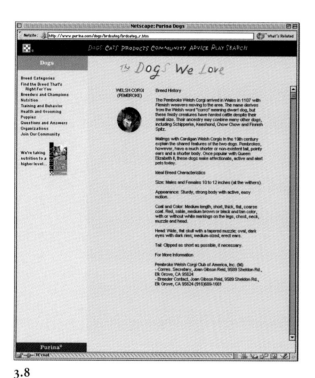

3.8

With so many design elements remaining constant, what's changing across Purina's pages? Even with a strongly harmonious design, it's easy to alter the content by adding new images and new text. In fact, these elements set up a framework as strong as any hierarchical structure for changing content.

The content of the left-hand navigational column also changes as we move down a level in the hierarchy (3.7). The links no longer take the browser to subsites, but to the "meat and potatoes" at the lower levels of the hierarchy. (The animated bag of pet food remains, but it is not a linking element.) When we reach the second level of the site, this design element becomes a strictly navigational tool, allowing the browser to look over the information within each section.

FEEDING THE PET FANCIERS

There is a lot of information in this site — enough to keep pet fanciers occupied for a good long browsing session. And it's not all about shiny bags of crude protein. The site features descriptions of every dog and cat breed, tips on health and behavior, advice on pets and community awareness — in short, this site sets out to make Purina a valuable resource for all kinds of pet information (3.8). And since you're having so much fun, perhaps you'll buy their pet food, too.

ELEMENTS AND TEAMWORK

A conversation with Dan Olson, Design Director; Nhan Nguyen, Designer; and Debbie Gold, Senior Writer at Duffy Design and Interactive

Q: When you look for the elements that create the design continuity of a site, do you start with the content or the plan?
DO: With Purina, we started with the content and then came up with a schematic that outlined the various content areas of the site. Once we identified the areas to portray, we digested each section down to the single scenario. These are reflected in the illustrations, which have a look and feel based on interactions that we have with our pets.

We wanted to keep the whole experience very inviting, warm, friendly, and endearing — with a real caring feel to it.

That's where the whole color palette came from. The warm earth tones, creams, and browns give the site an overall feeling of warmth and respect for caring for animals. We want the consumer to know that Purina has a site full of great information, and it's created by people who love pets. Our object was to build a community or family of pet lovers and pet owners.

It's easy to recognize good graphic design in Purina's pages: well-chosen images, clean, clear layout, careful typography, and good use of color. These elements establish strong navigational links and design continuity and constitute the glue that holds the individual pages together and makes this a compelling Web site.

IMAGE AND TEXT AS MOSAIC ELEMENTS

There is a recent trend toward the exclusive use of graphics and away from any HTML text in home page design. Creating a strong initial image is so important that designers are leaving nothing to the vagaries of HTML. They're concentrating on image and navigation, and saving all true content for other pages.

Yet Web pages do not lend themselves conveniently to monolithic images. Big images take too long to load, and imagemaps alone limit dynamic design possibilities. For these reasons, there is currently a proliferation of Web sites that feature mosaic images. The whole presents a unified graphical appearance, whereas the smaller pieces maximize flexibility and minimize load times.

THE BYZANTINE ART OF WEB MOSAICS

The Web site for the Getty Center in Los Angeles shows this technique used to full effect. When we look at the home page (www.getty.edu), the combination of text swirling around a central animated GIF of changing images from the museum is beautifully composed (3.9). But if we were to take this composition apart, we'd see it's actually over 40 separate images. An image of the Getty home page in the early stages of loading in a browser window shows the

3.9

Q: Are these design decisions based on input from the client, content they've already created for other media, or something else?

DO: We approach most sites in a similar fashion. We hear from a client what their hopes and aspirations and needs are. Then we ask ourselves, what is the consumer going to find in this medium that they can't find in a traditional medium or from a retailer? Like the breed finder [a feature of Purina's site that helps find the "right" breed of dog or cat], it's something wholly unique to what users can do on the Web. That comes from understanding the consumer. Our planning department is really good at getting to the heart and soul of what that consumer is so we can get their attention. Planning is a big part of the whole creative process.

We had consumer focus groups testing content information and user functionality throughout the development of the site. We allowed users to play with the site to make sure they could find their way through it. Out of that consumer research, we developed a schematic that focuses the linking structure and identifies all content. It gets very specific about the architecture and includes a creative strategy and spec along with it.

Q: Does this take into consideration possible changes or additional material that may be added in the future, and how does this affect the navigational elements?

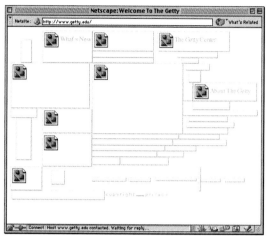

3.10

3.11

rectangular spaces Netscape Navigator has reserved for all of the image files (3.10).

There are really two element types used on this page — linking images and contextual images. The context here is the spiral design of the buildings of the Getty Center itself. The physical appearance of the museum is used as an architectural icon on which to hang the hierarchy of this site. (Think of the Calder mobiles mentioned in Chapter 1.) The graphical arrangement of elements not only catches the eye, but also provides an excellent organizing scheme.

At the center of this vortex is the image of the main entrance to the Getty Museum. The façade is dominated by a circular tower that is reflected in a rectangular pool. Notice how the arrangement of the circular graphics and the text "Welcome to the Getty" mimics the configuration of the Museum and its reflecting pool and entranceway (3.11). These page elements create the context around which the linking elements are positioned.

NN: We pick keywords that summarize the site, and build it so that whenever new content comes up there are areas for it in the future. We create a structure for the navigation [established by the development team], so that you only jump where it's appropriate: main navigation on top, secondary navigation on left. Even though you can jump around, you have to constrain the user, because you don't want to lose the navigational elements. On the home page, we want it to feature ongoing, most current things on the left with content on the right.

Eventually we can add more current content, and direct every month's issue to interesting areas for the user.

DO: We've found that all the new content that we've added has a place to live. We haven't had to rethink primary navigation — it's easy to add to secondary navigation. It's a very deep site, but it's simple enough, there are some easy choices you can make, it's not overwhelming.

We had to work with existing content and considered content we would need to create. Now we're thinking about

what we'd like to add to support the user's need. Like having more presence in the community. Pet friendly hotels, parks in cities, and so forth.

Q: How did you go about incorporating the textual content with the design elements?

DG: We worked closely together with the design team to capture in words what the illustrator was able to capture in pictures. To bring each section to life on a very visual level, we wrote short paragraphs about each section on a kind

The photographic element at the center is actually an animated GIF of four images, one for each of the Center's major divisions (3.12, 3.13, 3.14, 3.15). It's as if the circular elements of the site were actually housing these works, and to learn more about them, we must enter this metaphorical museum. (More about metaphorical design in Chapter 4.)

3.12

3.13

3.14

3.15

TEXT ELEMENTS BECOME LINKS

The linking text elements, all two dozen of them, are JavaScript rollovers (3.16). This is where color comes into play as an organizing element. The word *Getty* is always the same golden glow of the lighted museum in the center photo. Notice how the two major circular elements are green and red. Green is used as *the Getty Center* links' color, and red is the color of *about the Getty* links. Roll over the gray text, and it is highlighted in either green or red. The titles actually

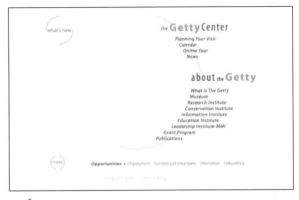

3.16

of emotional level and then went back and forth with the illustrator.

DO: Early on, we decided never to show a face of a pet owner, just arms and legs. We really focus on showing the emotion of the dog or cat to the owner. We wanted to make sure that we focused not so much on distracting the consumer by showing owners but by showing the pets.

DG: The site as a whole is about loving your pet. It's understood that your pet does all these things for you and it's about what you can do for your pet in appreciation. It's a very emotional site. Cat owners have very different feelings than dog owners. There's an overriding feeling that owners want to do the very best for their pets. We tap into that both in the copy and illustrations. The illustrations give it warmth. It's a 1,200–1,500 page site, but in the architectural design, through the use of frames, the content is organized and very accessible.

DO: Image is important to Web design, and this is one of the key components that sets us apart: We conceptualize, we differentiate. We use our planning department to help us find exactly what it is that sets a brand apart, and we carry those components to the Web site — design, copy, branding, everything.

reverse colors so *Getty* becomes either green or red, while *the Center* and *about the* become golden (3.16, 3.17, 3.18).

The narrower blue circular element lends its color to the less important, more general rollover links across the bottom, whereas the orange is picked up in the *what's new* and *index* links that stand like gateposts to the west, guarding the path to all other links. The designers of this site have identified a hierarchy of linking elements and balanced them with the same colored wires used to surround the images at the site's core.

Looking at this page more practically, we see a somewhat complex HTML table containing the many GIF images that make up this mosaic. We can see the table boundaries in this screen shot taken of the page in Adobe GoLive (3.19). This composition, designed as a single image in Photoshop, has been sliced into rows and columns, the individual elements kept in position using spacer cells.

The painstakingly designed graphic elements of this page have almost nothing to do with the underlying HTML. When you examine the Body code for this page, it's all table cells and images with JavaScripts. (Code listings can be viewed at www.idgbooks.com/extras/webarch.html.) There's a disconnect between design and implementation. This might upset an HTML purist, but there will likely be few of these among the visitors browsing this site. Visitors will be struck by the graphically powerful arrangement of elements, the clear-cut distinction between pure imagery, and the linking text elements with their JavaScript rollovers.

MAKING THE MOST OF METAPHOR

In the larger, more conventional setting of the Web, the architectural metaphor and consistent color cues of the Getty site are subtle almost to the point of obscurity. Yet they provide strong, consistent design elements for the rest of the site. This close attention to design, structure, and carefully integrated elements pays off as we move through the site. When we look down one hierarchical level to the two major divisions of the site, these elements are obviously still at work. The combination of image, linking rollover

3.17

3.18

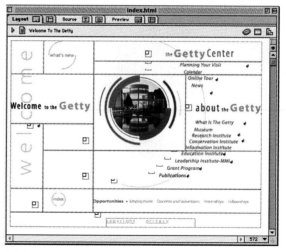

3.19

text, and layout is very similar to the home page (3.20, 3.21). The single paragraphs set on a swirl seem to belong more to the image than to the English language, but they do provide the first element of textual content.

More important, these pages introduce top and bottom navigation bars that are used throughout the rest of the site. These navigational elements have the same architectural quality as the other graphic elements,

but in a strictly linear instead of circular form. They provide more than navigation; they are the frame for the content to come.

Now look at a page with some real content, the Getty online tour (3.22). All the design elements established in the first pages are still in evidence. The iconic circular image has been turned into a site logo. The typographic link has been joined with the logo to become the column header for the tour's text. Although the photo in this image shows the circular entryway that has been the focus of so many of this site's elements, we're now dealing with rectangular images. The colored swirls of the home page have become rectilinear decorations, framing elements for the photos hanging on this metaphorical wall.

This is actually a frames-based page. The 17 stages of the tour scroll in the right-side frame, and the two navigation bars frame the top and bottom. Now the framing element is both literal and figurative. We could look at other pages in the site and see the same elements used sometimes the same way, sometimes modified to suit the content of the page better. But at all times, the design elements define the workings of the site to enhance the content. They are an integral part of the total user experience of this site.

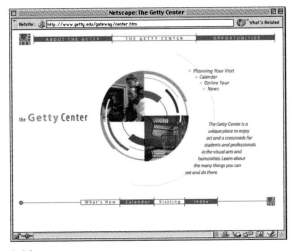

3.20

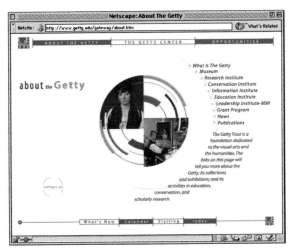

3.21

3.22

INTERACTIVE DESIGN ELEMENTS

When you're done creating navigational elements, graphical elements, layout elements, and the other little pieces that give a Web site its continuity and fluidity, there's still one more element to consider: interactive elements. We've seen a little of this with animated GIFs: Purina's pet food bag and the Getty's photo-filled central image. There have also been plenty of JavaScript rollovers in this and previous chapters. These elements, though effective, are now so commonplace that even the most casual Internet user has come to expect them.

EXERCISING THE URGE TO CLICK

For eye-catching novelty, savvy Web surfers demand more. These impatient surfers, whom I call the *Click Generation*, constitute both an important segment of the browsing populace and an attractive audience for marketers of all that's "cool" and current. It is this group that Casio is trying to attract with its G-Shock site (www.gshock.com), a tour de force of Shockwave animation, quick image refreshes, and games-like navigation.

Peter Seidler, Chief Creative Officer at New York–based Razorfish, a global interactive design firm, was specifically charged by Casio to push the capabilities of the Web. (See Chapter 10 for a feature on the Razorfish Web site.) He responded with this high-bandwidth, not-for-the-faint-of-heart, roller coaster of a wave. For this discussion, the use of classic design elements that make up the underpinnings of this thrill ride are most important.

In Seidler's words: "We used to start with the idea of a Web site, but we don't talk about that anymore. It's about understanding the appropriate taxonomy and bringing together the visual look and feel with the experiential heuristic." This doesn't sound like the semiliterate argot of the Click Generation. What's Seidler talking about? We'll get to this in a bit.

The G-Shock home page looks innocent enough, although the colors and layout might clue you in to the fact that there's something different about to happen (3.23). Like the Getty's home page, the G-Shock home page (www.gshock.com) cum instrument panel is a single image that has been sliced up and loaded as a complex table. You can see this in the screen shot of the G-Shock home page taken in Adobe GoLive (3.24). Note the three small dashed rectangles. These are imagemap areas, the only links to the rest of the site.

This is merely the portal to the site, which is launched by clicking the "enter here" button. How can we resist? This is no ordinary link. Instead, clicking the button launches a JavaScript that checks to make sure we are using the correct browsers and that the Shockwave plug-in is present. If all systems are go, a pop-up window is launched and the journey begins. (Code for this JavaScript function can be viewed at www.idgbooks.com/extras/webarch.html.)

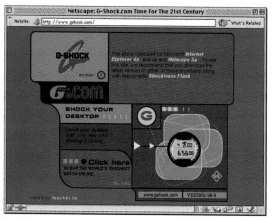

3.23

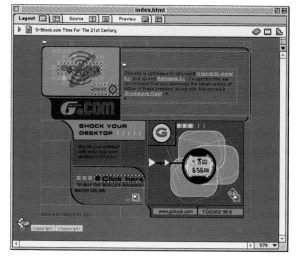

3.24

MAKING A GAME OF IT

Now where are we? The pulsing images of this virtual video wall constitute not so much a page as an experience. We're not in Kansas anymore. This new window is filled with a grid of six square frames, and there's something different happening in each (3.25, 3.26). The top row consists of three continually refreshing panes of G-Shock images — edgy logos and highly stylized photos of young button clickers in action. The colors are all decidedly offbeat. (Surfing, skateboarding, and skiing seem to be the favored activities of the target audience.)

From the very beginning, Seidler has established look and feel through color and imagery, and we're about to begin the experiential heuristic through this navigational board game.

The bottom-left square contains an array of small letters and symbols in circles. These turn out to be JavaScript rollover buttons, and this pane is the navigational element. The game is to figure out what each of these buttons does and where it leads you. The rollovers give you the clues.

The right-hand two squares on the bottom are joined into one double-width Shockwave animated pane. The image of a G-Shock watch lies between a floating background image and a ticker tape marching across the foreground, announcing the site features.

There are two key elements in this composition: the 2 × 3 grid and the single navigation pane. These are the constants for the entire G-Shock Web experience. The grid is executed as HTML frames, but you might not know this to look at it. Although the size of the window remains constant, the frames are rearranged to create double-width or double-height panes. This is simply a matter of turning off all frame borders so that two images can be abutted side by side to give the appearance of a single pane.

Click the big G button to look at the G-Shock product line. (The little g button links to the Baby-G product line.) The entire window is redrawn, but the grid returns, and at the same frenetic pace (3.27). One of the panes lets you pick a watch model. Clicking here changes the two double-width panes, adding additional links to the upper image, while

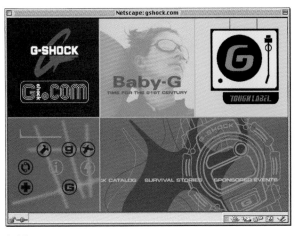

3.25

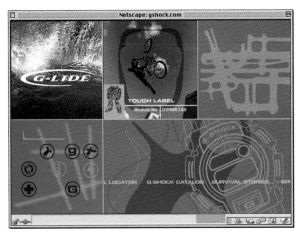

3.26

3.27

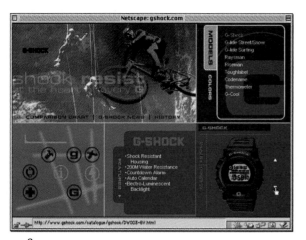

3.28

swapping out the Shockwave animation in the bottom for hard-core watch data and a completely straightforward photo of the selected watch model (3.28).

The watch lines and feature lists are all HTML text formatted using the `<fonts>` tag as either Helvetica or Arial, the Mac OS and Windows System default sans serif typefaces. Lest we be fooled by the high activity level, we've reached the actual content of the site in just a few clicks — two frames of watch information, one textual, one an image.

But the game doesn't end here. We can change both the features list and/or the photograph by clicking in these panes. Don't know which watch you like best? Click the Comparison Chart link and look at the features of three watches side by side (3.29). We know we're having fun, because we're doing a lot of clicking. To put this more philosophically, we are engaged in active Web-based interaction, an experience quite different from the mainly static exercise of most Web site information gathering experiences.

The fact is, Seidler's framed grid is a perfect presentation device for both the game aspects and taxonomy of the site — the hierarchical organization of the information, the G-Shock content. And he's not finished yet. Like all well-designed sites, this one accommodates change and expansion.

The button pane, the key navigational element, already has two grayed-out buttons waiting to link to new features. As product lines change, the content can be updated without changing the taxonomy. And there's no limit to the images that could flash across the matrix of this site's window. Who knows? Perhaps this site will have to serve aging button clickers of the future, when action sports have been replaced by shuffleboard and horseshoes.

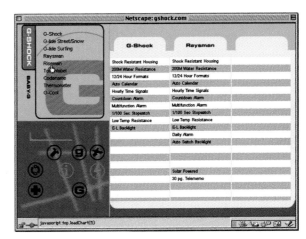

3.29

Aptargroup

PUMPS

VALVES

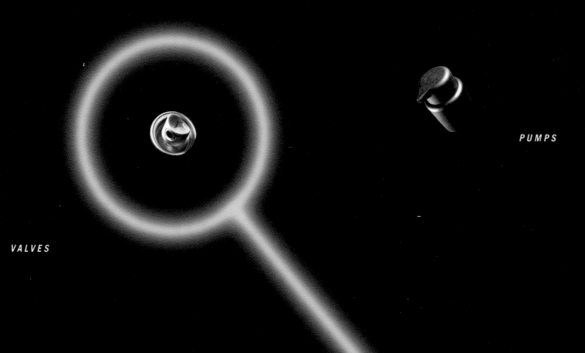

CLOSURES

CHAPTER 4
ENVISIONING INFORMATION

C hapter 3 discussed the elements of design as discrete entities. Now you will see the effect of these elements combined to create the mood, atmosphere, and general feeling that is the overriding vision of a site. But because HTML was not created to be a design language, using it to create compelling designs turns out to be one of the more difficult challenges for Web architects.

From an historical perspective, designers and marketers joined forces to hijack the Web from the scientific community that created it. It is the design community that is pushing the World Wide Web Committee (W3C) to make HTML and the Web more visual and dynamic. We seek a new outlet for the visual display of information and the communication of this information to a global audience; it is our new medium.

CREATING A SENSE OF PLACE

Like the Paleolithic cave painters at Lascaux, early HTML designers have had relatively few tools to work with. We have had to use our ingenuity to build sites that convey information in a graphically pleasing way. It's as if we have been drawing on the cave walls of the Internet. But these limitations have not stifled creative expression. A simple cave painting (4.1), besides being beautiful, conveys to us the speed of pursuit, the tension of the hunt, and the wildness of the horse. We can begin to understand Paleolithic life — keeping warm in cold caves, venturing out to hunt, stone weapons in hand.

You have a message and a look, and they are the same whether you're creating the company's identity in print or on the Web.
KEVIN KRUEGER, SAMATAMASON DESIGN

4.1

Life for late twentieth century humans may not be as elemental as it was for cave dwellers 17 millennia ago, but we share the same thread of creative expression with our prehistoric forebears, if not the same means of communication. The point is that life on the Internet still requires attention to expressive detail. It's not only what we say, but how we say it.

For example, look at Carnegie Hall, one of the great caves of modern civilization. One hundred years old, but young in our historical continuum, it represents the ultimate stage for classical and jazz musicians. Is it possible to convey this sense in our most modern medium?

Peter Seidler, who designed Carnegie Hall's Web site (www.carnegiehall.org), asked the question differently. "How do you capture the spaciousness of the hall, the warmth of its architectural detail, the spirit and tradition of Carnegie Hall in this cold, silicon, binary environment?" As you can see, he simply lit a fire in the center of the cavern (4.2).

First, the design of Carnegie Hall's home page is one of simplicity and elegance, featuring purposefully arranged photographs, minimal, cleanly typeset text, and a single entry link to the rest of the site. It's an invitation to come inside and get warm. This page says almost nothing. Yet even if we'd never heard of it,

we'd know Carnegie Hall was something special and important.

The main atmospheric element is the background JPEG image, a photograph of Carnegie Hall's sweeping loggia and balconies in a deep, cool blue with a large script C (as if from an invitation) superimposed on top. The counterbalance to this image is the small animated GIF placed slightly off-center on the page. The three photographs that make up this animation have an orange glow (4.3, 4.4, 4.5), which makes the interior of Carnegie Hall look particularly warm and welcoming.

Now add the heading text, "Welcome to Carnegie Hall," which also picks up the warm orange color to contrast with the background blue. Seidler does something brilliant here; it seems almost counterintuitive, but it works. The script C, which I would expect to be the warmer element, is frozen in the background, while the headline, set in Futura, an icon of cool modernity, is actually the warmer element in this composition.

In fact, when you view this text image separately from the page's background, its elements of warmth and elegance are lost (4.6). The orange letters look as though they were borrowed from a high school football poster. *Go Carnegie Tigers!* It's just as my

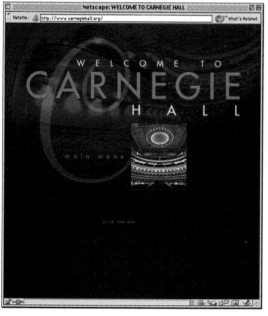

4.2

4.3   4.4   4.5

4.6

intuition predicted, the antithesis of Carnegie Hall sophistication.

But this headline is transformed when integrated into the page. Futura is like pasta; it takes on the flavor of the sauce you give it. The sauce here is warm elegance, and it thoroughly coats every letterform. Futura, although it was designed by Paul Renner in 1930, also gives this page a contemporary look and feel without sacrificing any of the traditional qualities we associate with grand scale nineteenth century architecture.

What might have been as snooty as engraved stationery from Tiffany's (see sidebar) becomes light and airy. The contemporary-looking typography is as spacious as the opulently restored hall, and appeals to the younger audience who is the target of this Web site.

Let's enter the site and look at the main menu (4.7). The elements have changed and are arranged slightly differently, but they're set in exactly the same way as the home page: deep blue background image with a script letter, an M in this case, that is a warm, slightly off-center photograph. Futura text is used with important highlights in orange. All of the navigation for this site is contained in the GIF text images, a simple list.

4.7

A STRONG IMAGE IN ANY MEDIUM

It's not the fault of Tiffany & Co., but its products have great snob appeal (this goes beyond mere brand recognition). Therefore, the company closely guards its image. The name, the Tiffany typeface, and even the Tiffany blue used in all of their advertising and gift wrapping have seemingly remained unchanged for centuries. All of these elements were used by Tiffany to create a home page that says, well, Tiffany. Talk about understatement — this page is pure image, and anyone familiar with the brand will feel right at home (www.tiffany.com). We'll end our discussion of Tiffany's here, because the rest of this site is rather simple and some may say not up to Tiffany's sophisticated design standards.

TIP

There are a number of implementation details that must be addressed when placing a text image over a background photograph. Because the alignment of background and foreground elements varies from browser to browser and platform to platform, the text must be set in a transparent rectangle. But because GIF only supports a single level of transparency, it's impossible to anti-alias text. A common solution is to use a background that matches the overall tone of the photograph. In this instance, Seidler used the deep blue shade. When you set anti-aliased text over this background, then turn the original blue hue transparent, the anti-aliased blue around the letters remains. You can see this halo of blue very clearly in Figure 4.7. When the text image is placed over the photograph, you perceive neither the jaggies of aliased text nor the white halo of improperly anti-aliased text. The foreground and background blend to create the appearance of a single image.

4.8

4.9

Some of the interior pages of the site follow this for-
mula as well (4.8), but as variations on a theme. The
Intro to the Classics page introduces a column of narrative text over a background that is lighter blue for
readability. This is a frames-based format that allows
longer text entries to scroll or the frame content to
change without other page elements changing. There
are no graphics in the light blue frame, just HTML text.

Other pages repeat some of the same elements so
that new themes blend harmoniously with the site
design. The *98/99 Season*, the most recently added
section of the site, uses terra cotta, the color of the
exterior of the hall, instead of cool blue (4.9). (This
section is treated as a subsite and introduces a local
navigational element, as we'll see.) Familiar typography, the script S in the background, the Futura headings, and the quality of the photography clearly link
this section to all that precede it.

As we follow this link in further, we're getting
deeper into the business side of the site. Here the
heavy emphasis on image appropriately gives way to
content, but without losing the carefully created
atmosphere — the Web essence of Carnegie Hall.
The *Season Spotlight* page (4.10) emphasizes concert

4.10

information and contains links to "order tickets." But it's bracketed by vestiges of image elements — photographs of the hall and graphical text headings typeset in Futura. Navigational elements have been added to the top of the page so that you don't get lost in the content.

As this page loads, you get a quick glimpse of the frames-based layout (4.11). All you see is the black background of the left frame with HTML text. The background image that fills this frame includes all the atmospheric elements first established on the home page, yet appears to be sliced off from the rest of the page (4.12). Once the borderless frames are loaded in the browser window, you lose all sense of the frames, because the background colors and foreground elements blend together to create a continuous backdrop for the page (4.13).

The skill with which this page has been put together and then cut up into frames is truly remarkable. If it weren't for the scroll bar on the main content frame, the frames would be practically invisible. Yet the frames make it easy to update the content of this section without changing the layouts.

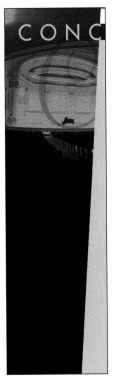

4.12

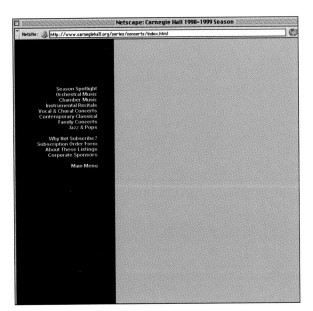

4.11

4.13

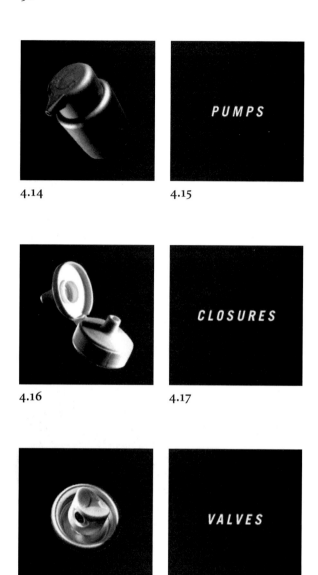

4.14   4.15

4.16   4.17

4.18   4.19

4.20

DEFINING AN IDENTITY

Carnegie Hall's image is a known quantity. Translating it into a digital medium was the challenge, and Peter Seidler and his group of designers at Razorfish managed the task with skill and subtlety. Asked "How do you get to Carnegie Hall?" Seidler has given us a fresh new answer.

But what do you do when a company's image is less clear or even totally amorphous? Where do you find the stuff of compelling Web sites? If asked to identify the "caps and closures" market, I might have said "hats and coats." This was the problem faced by SamataMason Design in putting AptarGroup on the Web.

Whereas Carnegie Hall needs no introduction, AptarGroup is known only to industry insiders. This is a problem not just of image, but of all-encompassing lack of identity. Who are these guys?

SamataMason uses a 19-frame animated GIF to introduce outsiders to the wonderful world of dispensing systems (4.14–4.20). Before we even see the catch phrases, these naked images of spray, pump, and snap-on tops make it abundantly clear what we're dealing with. And the high-contrast, black-and-white macro photography, combined with simple typography, present the AptarGroup as a sophisticated, high-tech leader in their business.

The animation sequence leads to the AptarGroup home page (www.aptar.com). Everything, text and images, is white on black, with the addition of bright green highlights to identify the current page and JavaScript rollover links (4.21). This page is con-

4.21

structed of GIF images arranged in a table. The navigational element is sliced into sections that are fit together as borderless table cells. This is another example of a page that could have been implemented as an imagemap. But it loads faster and works more smoothly as a collection of images and links. It also makes the JavaScript rollovers easier to implement.

After only two pages, what was the unknown turns out to be the familiar. We've seen these "caps and closures" before. They are one of the unconsidered details of our contemporary existence. Presented this way, as disembodied heads, these mundane objects aren't immediately recognizable. But suddenly we realize what they are and see that there's a kind of beauty and elegance in their everyday simplicity. Somehow, this recognition creates a kind of respect and admiration for the previously unheard of AptarGroup and their highly specialized craft.

We hear a lot about the importance of "branding" for the success of products. For a Web site, the company is the product. AptarGroup has the advantage of a clearly defined market within the packaging industry, and this site makes them look like a leader, a company you'd want to do business with. And it's all because the identity of this site is as clearly defined as AptarGroup's product niche.

The Welcome page says it all (4.22). "You probably have at least ten of our products in your home right now and have used a couple of them in the last 24 hours. Our success has been based upon a combination of unique product innovation, outstanding

quality, and superior customer service." Translate this into HTML, and you've got a Web site.

You can see from the site map that the scope of the site is modest (4.23). The hierarchy is straightforward and the navigation simple. But the strong identity of the site has been carried over even to the spray nozzle nodes of this cleverly designed map, which provides quick navigation from and to all pages of the site. It does double duty as a once-removed navigational element.

Even the pages without images are closely tied to the identity of the site. The text is as clear and concise as the spare photographs (4.24). The introductory page to the corporate section of the site consists of a paragraph of GIF text and the bottom navigational element. In this case, the image has been established and the identity is in the text itself.

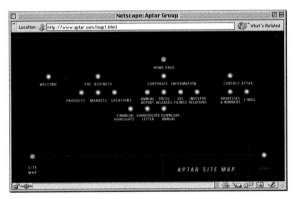

4.23

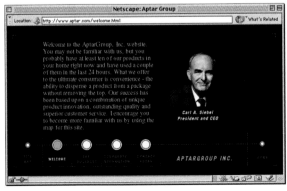

4.22

4.24

INTEGRATING THE CONTENT

Want imagery? How about tight-calved cyclists whizzing through nearly inaccessible, beautiful scenery? Want identity? The Specialized name and logo have become universally recognized among mountain biking and racing enthusiasts for technological innovation and design audacity. Specialized invented the mountain bike, and Adjacency, one of the most-awarded Web design groups around, has brought some of the excitement that defines Specialized to a self-proclaimed "World Ride Web." Let's jump on and see where the breathless ride lands us.

No mud slinging happening on the home page (www.specialized.com): Here we encounter clean imagery, clean typography, and a clean bike heading off into the wilderness (4.25). This home page is one big borderless table. The logo, photograph, title, links, and headings all pull together as one cohesive image. The text images are all set in lowercase Helvetica Black, mostly in white on black, which has plenty of punch. There's nothing shy about this page.

But there's more than imagery and atmosphere going on here. There's actually something a little bit unusual for a high-concept site these days — paragraphs of text. A left column of orange text talks about the site, and a right column of white text highlights what's new and noteworthy at Specialized. Dare we call this content?

In fact, Specialized has one of those rare sites that presents lots of content in a well-designed environment. The textual content is all formatted as sans serif type, Geneva, Arial, or Helvetica, using the HTML `<font, face>` tag. With consistent color choices and typography, the headings and text aren't left to fight each other as they do on the pages of many other sites.

This site uses a straightforward organizational scheme with textual headings for the hierarchical links highlighted by JavaScript rollovers. One layer down in the hierarchy, the links are arranged into a navigation bar across the top of every page — the same white-on-black text used on the home page, with a red Specialized logo to indicate the link back to

---

THE ESSENCE OF IDENTITY

**Kevin Krueger,
SamataMason Design**

Q: What's the first thing you try to establish when designing a company's site?
KK: Basically, to give them a look. For instance, most people think of Aptar as a caps company, but we want to show that they are also a strong company with a strong message and a strong product line. For their annual report, we took an elegant design, made it clean, straightforward, easy to read, but also powerful. So we featured the caps and closures and focused attention on them rather than on bottles of perfume. For their Web site, we wanted the same thing.

Q: What's different about designing for print and Web?
KK: The way people are going to view it and see it. We wanted it to look different from other Web sites. Clean and sophisticated, and so you can follow it like a book. We knew people would be jumping around the Web site, but we didn't want them getting lost or confused in it. We show the product right up front and

4.25

establish the simple black-and-white look with green for emphasis. The simplicity of the navigation and the ability to click on the site map to get anywhere, the clarity of where you are, keeps people browsing the site without getting frustrated. Everything kind of fell into place once we got the strong identity.

Q: Why is that identity so important?
KK: The company's going to be identified by it. Who are they, what are they doing, where they are doing it — that's the content. How you want to convey their message and how you want it to look — that's the identity.

the home page. Second-level hierarchical links are integrated into the content (4.26).

You don't see content used as a hierarchical organizer very often. But integrating these elements keeps the design clean and uncluttered, allows the images to show clearly, and keeps the message of the site strong and undiluted. And it's not a bad idea to have each link described before you set off down the wrong trail.

Every second-level page uses a background image and an aggressively bright background color. Move down another layer in the hierarchy and the second-level links move to a column on the left with the same bright color as the page above (4.27). There's a lot of energetic design consistency in this site.

4.27

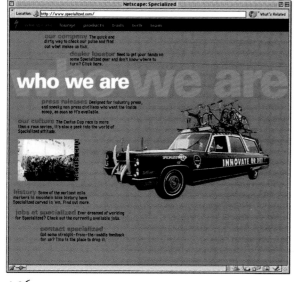

4.26

These third-level pages rely on their content. The narrative text in the *Who We Are* section is about what you'd expect, but Adjacency has been creative in finding other forms of content for other sections. In the Lounge is a chat room, discussion list, diary, downloadable screensaver (Mac OS and Windows), and an e-mail post card feature (4.28).

Clicking through this site is like pedaling in a Criterion; you can't stop. The *Trails* section is composed entirely of bike trail descriptions sent in by Specialized's loyal Web followers (4.29). Descriptions are arranged geographically and now cover three continents.

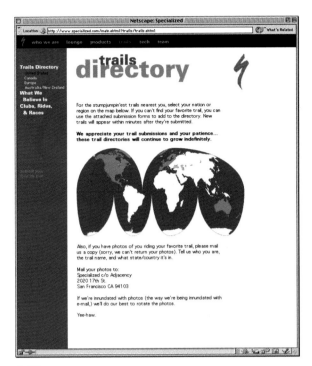

4.29

4.28

4.30

Adjacency has worked hard to make this site fun and engaging, and the heart of the site is in the products section. This is where the mud starts flying (4.30). Specialized makes a lot of bike lines with several models in each line, and every one is fully described and specified on its own page. The emphasis on detail requires extra levels of hierarchy in this section, yet we don't lose the sense of thrills or spills around every bend.

First of all, it's obvious that the dirtier you get, the more fun you're having, and all the minutiae of this site is just so much mud to wallow in. Bikers revel in arcane specifications — it is the stuff that bikes are made of, just as content is the stuff that Web sites are made of (4.31). The content here is full of dash and vigor. Every page, from the most content-rich to the image-establishing pages at the top of the hierarchy, is designed with close attention to the impression it's going to create.

Clearly, the chain-and-spoke set is not going to stick around long if the terrain is tepid. So everything has been cranked up a notch. The imagery gives a feeling of constant motion, the typography is bold, the colors vibrant, and the language of the text equally vivid. It works because this site was designed and executed with a consistent vision of who's looking at it. Specialized shows that not only do they know their stuff, but they know their customers as well. And Adjacency (who probably include a few Specialized customers among its staff) has found ways to bring the followers together on the Web. It certainly makes me want to go out, buy a StumpJumper, and get dirty.

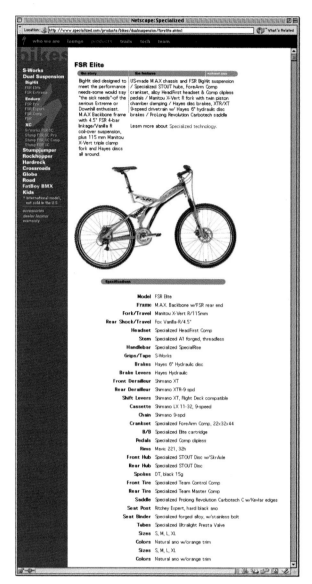

4.31

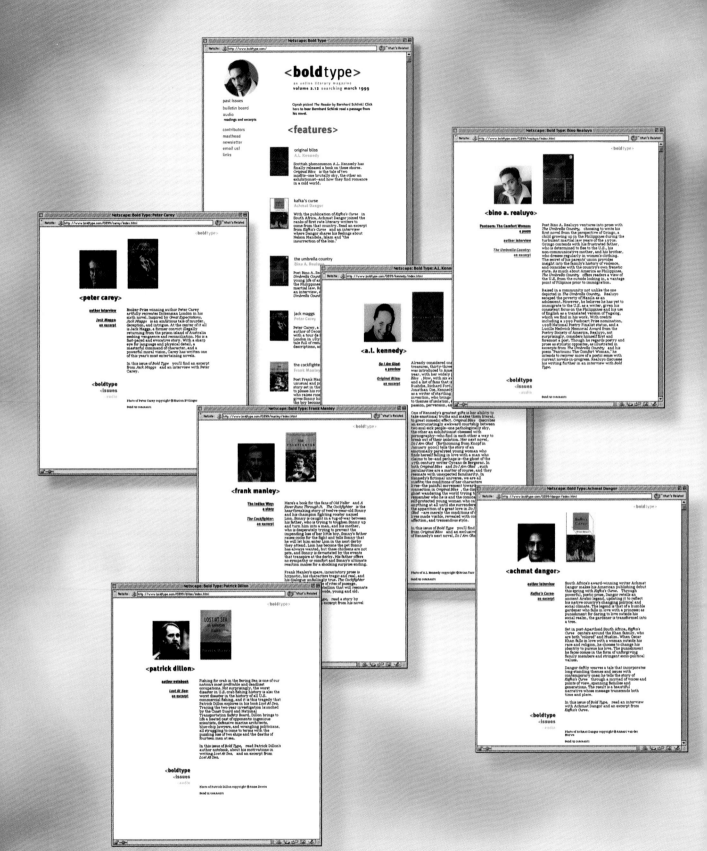

CHAPTER 5
READING IS BELIEVING

We all know that the Web is a visual medium, thus successful Web sites depend on making a positive first impression, and then maintaining a consistent image. This is why so many Web sites revolve around eye-catching graphics. We see color and form first, so it is natural to assume using big, splashy images is the best way to initially capture Web surfers' attention. But it ain't necessarily so.

As easily as our eye is attracted to bold images, it is drawn in by details. We recognize shapes we are familiar with and latch onto them. For instance, we don't just see letterforms, we instantly read words and sentences without having any conscious awareness of the individual letters.

The alphabet and the written word, being so completely familiar, are potent elements of our daily communication. Let us not forget that Internet communication was entirely text-based until the Web came along, and that the first version of HTML added not only protocols for transmitting images, but also constructs for formatting text.

The basics of traditional graphic design and layout are sometimes at odds with the realities of the Web.

MILES MCMANUS, OVEN DIGITAL

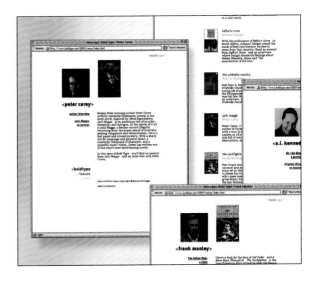

BASIC TEXTUAL MESSAGES

In addition to the impression created by the arrangement of graphic elements on a Web page, there is a message. In the first four chapters of this book, we've looked at a lot of sites in terms of graphic design, yet every one of these sites exists for its textual information. This is not true of every Web site, and certainly not of every Web page, but most sites depend on text.

You might think that a site devoted to the arts was an obvious candidate for a mainly visual, nearly wordless site. But such is not the case with The Business Committee for the Arts (BCA) Web site (www.bcainc.org)—it's pure business (5.1). To be sure, there are images on this home page, the organization's logo and an abstraction of the logo used as a background image. But most important, most telling, and most memorable in this background is the Einstein quotation, "Imagination is more important than knowledge."

The designers of this site, Waters Design Associates, Inc., of New York, have helped draw our eyes to this quotation by placing it at the top of the page, using the elegant Adobe Garamond Italic typeface, and by highlighting the words *imagination* and *knowledge.* But this typesetting and layout effort would be wasted if the quotation weren't an apt and memorable one from a recognizable source. In other words, the carefully selected quote is most important. And it works on this page because of skillful typesetting and layout.

But, you say, "There's no real text here, no HTML text. It's all graphic text and GIF images in tables." True enough. My point is that we're talking about the *message.* And in the case of BCA, it is a message conveyed almost entirely by text. They've chosen to strengthen this textual message by typesetting it all in Photoshop, a legitimate choice for pages with small amounts of text.

BRANDING WITH WORDS

In addition to the quotation, the BCA home page includes a brief statement of purpose. This single paragraph of GIF text tells the uninformed browser what the BCA is all about. The BCA is not a "name brand" item and has no easily recognizable product, so these few words tell us more than any image can.

The horizontal navigation bar is also an all-text device, without cute little icons to suggest an artistic site. Business comes first here. The navigation bar uses JavaScript rollovers to show the third level of hierarchy for the site, but you can't skip over to these links. You have to link to the second-level pages and go on from there (5.2). Repeat visitors to the site might find it easier to skip levels and go right to more detailed content, but that's not how the rollovers are implemented.

This BCA home page even goes a step further into the realms of textual messages and text-based navigation. The *window.open* JavaScript method is executed

5.1

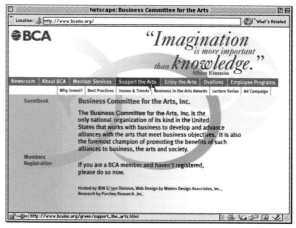

5.2

with this home page to open a second browser window — a so-called "pop-up" window (5.3). The simple JavaScript for this pop-up window is included here:

```
function openWin() {
        this.name="home"
        remote =
window.open("bca_popup.html",
"remote","width=340,height=265")
```

This window, which pops to the front of the screen, is exactly 340 × 265 pixels, and has no browser directory buttons or scroll bars. All of this is part of the JavaScript method. Waters has created this small, squarish window in obvious contrast to the home page. The design uses the same elements and is also heavily reliant on text, this time in the form of two directives and a question:

"Give me some examples of successful business investments in the arts."

"Tell me about recent investments businesses have made in the arts."

"How can my company make an investment in the arts?"

It's all a clever ruse, because these are actually navigational devices. For interested businesspeople wondering about corporate sponsorship of the arts, these questions are likely to be foremost. Sure, images of ballerinas, divas, and elegant halls (like those featured in the Carnegie Hall Web site discussed in Chapter 4) could be used to sell what the BCA has to offer, but they've chosen the bottom line approach instead. The answers to these leading questions are all found at the subsequent levels of this site.

Clicking one of these three lines of text takes you through the hierarchy directly to the pertinent information. Examples of successful business investments are found in the *Support the Arts* section (5.4). Notice that the green background for the related question on the pop-up window is the color for the section. Each section has its own color and is headed by a pithy quotation. Undoubtedly, every would-be industrialist wants to emulate Henry Ford, who said, "A business that makes nothing but money is a poor kind of business."

NAVIGATING WITH WORDS

All of the second-level pages — the section home pages — are laid out like the top-level home page. They have a similar background image, with GIF text providing all of the foreground content. A home icon has been added and the navigation bar has been moved to a bottom frame, where the next level of navigation is also revealed. Once again, they're getting maximum use out of the text.

5.3

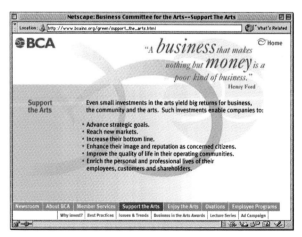

5.4

Click down a level, and all the familiar elements remain consistent (5.5). But now the background image becomes a narrow column on the left, and a wide column is filled with narrative text, the bulk of the site's content. Because this text often is lengthy, filling several screens, it is no longer presented as a GIF image.

This narrative is HTML text. It has been formatted using the `<font face>` tag to set the text to a sans serif typeface, Arial or Helvetica. The site designers have even used the `<ul>` and `<li>` list tags to create unnumbered and bulleted lists of points. This is not brilliant or even vaguely creative typesetting, but it's workmanlike.

Another important aspect of text rarely discussed in design books is whether it is literate and well-written text, as is the text of this site. (We'll have to forgive them a couple of typos.) The points are well chosen and direct. There's nothing florid or exaggerated. And the navigation works with this direct approach, making it easy to find your way around and know where you are when you get there.

It's likely that if the BCA had had a larger budget for their site, images from the arts would have crept in. But images exact a price, both for their creation and in the responsiveness of a site. Yes, this could have been a slick, impressive site, but would it have served

its audience any better for all the added glamour? I think not.

The *Ovations* section of the site, a section devoted to speeches and great quotations, sums it up pretty succinctly: "Words are powerful" (5.6).

STOP BROWSING AND START READING

By its very nature, the act of browsing is more like window shopping than like cozying up to read a book. Therefore, the elements that make a successful browsing site tend to be more visual. Even the text elements emphasize visual qualities (see Chapter 3). Quick visual stimulus is what the Click Generation demands. Fortunately, the Web is a wide-open frontier that attracts a far wider audience than the youth culture so fervently wooed by TV.

When we explore the Web, we are in an ever-expanding universe. Perhaps it will collapse upon itself someday, but for now, we can revel in the luxury of boundlessness. If we want to linger on a single page long enough to read an entire short story, we're sure to find a site to indulge this old-fashioned whim. The question is, why we would want to do this instead of reading it in print?

This is the basic conflict for the sites of all publishers. Is the business of publishing entirely print-based, or

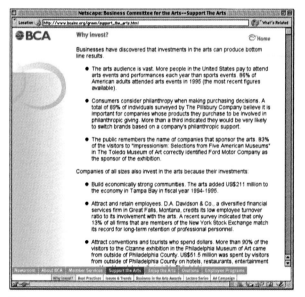

5.5

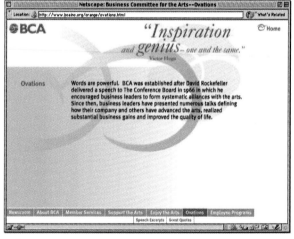

5.6

has it become a multimedia industry? Did any publisher ever see a conflict of interest in publishing
books on tape? I doubt it, but at least tapes are as easy
to stock and sell as books.

But what about books online? In a business as competitive as book publishing, there isn't even time to
consider the question. All the big publishers seem to
be moving quickly into online marketing with high-
design, content-heavy sites. There's lots of talk about
new titles and their authors on these sites, but the real
grabbers are the extended book excerpts.

READ ALL ABOUT IT!

Look at the site of Bantam Doubleday Dell (BDD),
designed by OVEN Digital of New York. As "one of
the largest publishers of general interest consumer
books in North America," you would expect BDD to
have a large, active site, with lots of new books to feature (5.7). For a home page with so many links, BDD
maintains a quiet orderliness (www.bdd.com). It is a
prime example of the hierarchical division of information on a page that could be taken straight from a
textbook on graphic design.

Before we dissect this page, with all its columns of
graphic and textual elements, I want to emphasize the
dominance of the text over the images. Even the
graphic text elements are kept small and subservient
to the bulk of the text here, which is the HTML text.
Also, I want to dwell on this page because it is the
template for most of the site.

BDD's home page is comprised of three columns
with a navigation bar across the bottom (5.8). This
frame provides search by category and keyword
access to a functional table of contents in the form of
a *browse categories* link. The links are presented
as graphical with small arrows (actually right-
facing triangles). There's also a drop-down menu of
site categories and a form field for entering search
keywords. The yellow fill color with lighter yellow
stripe across the top is implemented as a simple background image. There's not much in the way of image
here, not even a BDD logo.

The leftmost column is also a navigational frame
with hierarchical links to the various sections of the

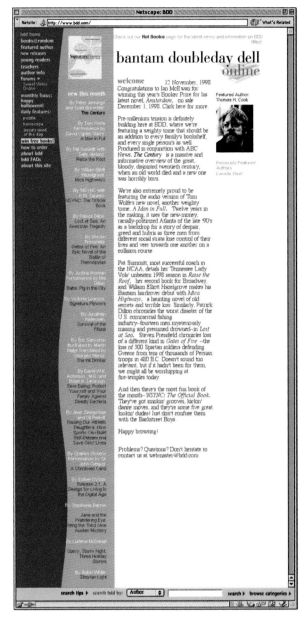

5.7

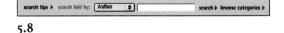

5.8

site. The background is a medium gray, with all links displayed as graphic text, mostly white against the gray. Yellow (the dominant color of the bottom frame) is used to highlight headings linked to changing features. The home link is peach-colored text, the background color of the next column. There's also an animated GIF in this frame.

In keeping with this site's emphasis on words, the animated GIF is purely textual, consisting of a list of BDD's forums. The down-pointing orange arrow is the understated clue and the only picture element in this frame. Rather than list all 15 forums, the link merely suggests the scope of this section by cycling through the forum names. The animation is set at 1.3 seconds per frame, enough time so that each title is readable, but not so much that you can't see the whole list in under 20 seconds. And the whole animated image is tiny, only 2.4K, so it loads fast.

This is a classic navigational scheme utilizing left and bottom frames to provide consistent universal navigation. Content can be browsed by stepping down through or cutting directly across the site's hierarchy. These links are all buttons stripped to their bare minimum, a word or two.

WORD-BASED CONTENT

We're finished with the generalized navigation of this site. Most of this page is dedicated to what's current. A few very small images appear in this, the main frame, but it is mostly dominated by word-based content. It may look as if there are two more vertical frames, but this is actually a single frame with content arranged in a complex HTML table (5.9). The left edge of the

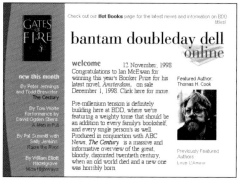

5.9

frame picks up the gray of the hierarchical navigation frame next to it and turns the hard division between it and the left-side navigations frame into a wave-like interchange between the two columns.

This is a long frame that scrolls (so you can read it all), and it's the only place that mentions Bantam Doubleday Dell. It's not really a logo, just the company name and the word "online" typeset in understated lowercase letters. This typographical image is actually cut in half and placed in adjoining table cells to fit the HTML layout of the page, as shown here laid out in Adobe GoLive (5.10). The Bodoni typeface used contrasts nicely with all the text on this page, but this could hardly be called a major focal point. It's more of a simple site identifier.

Where's the branding here, the all-important emphasis on image? The modern book industry is a story of conglomeration. BDD, which used to be three separate publishers, is just a part of the Bertelsmann Book Group of Germany, which recently acquired Random House and includes numerous other imprints. The fact is, practically nobody buys a book these days because a certain publisher's name is on the spine. Each book and author is its own brand vying for shelf space, and herein lies the unique challenge of book marketing.

TEXT FOR READING AND FOR CLICKING

As we scan from left to right across the page, the text moves from words for buttons, to simple headlines, to narrative text. It's interesting that at the same time the text also progresses from GIF text, to styled text, to pure default HTML text. What makes this welcome letter readable is the use of a relatively narrow table cell and placement of a <br> break tag between paragraphs. Book titles are italicized, but there's no other typesetting used here. If I happen to have my browser default set to Agfa Rotis Serif instead of Times (or New York), the readability of this page is

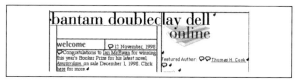

5.10

greatly improved (5.11). And what a fortuitous font choice, as all of the GIF text on this page just happens to be typeset in Agfa Rotis Semisans. Too bad Rotis and a thousand other typefaces aren't installed in everyone's systems.

There's a fourth column in the overall page layout, which is used for a picture of the month's featured author. Under this element is one more tiny animated GIF of the names of previously featured authors. Among all the information on this home page is a single book image element and one author picture. Yet we would never dismiss this page as unsophisticated or overly simple and dull. Exactly the opposite. Simple typography for headlines and links, a layout based on a carefully proportioned table of columns, and a subtle but comfortable and well-implemented color scheme give the user the feeling of a cozy reading nook by the fire rather than a ramshackle street-corner newsstand. (Notice how cozy the big chain bookstores try to make their outlets and how similar the color scheme is, at least in feeling if not in hue, to this one.)

As we descend the hierarchy of this site, we see the same navigational and structural elements used with straightforward HTML text and a few small picture elements. The same Rotis Semisans font is used for the understated section heading at the top of the page, *bdd forums*. Each of the 15 listed forums has a small image, heading title set as GIF text, and a single descriptive paragraph set as HTML text (5.12). (I've left the browser variable width font set to Rotis Serif, because it's the harmonious choice for this page.)

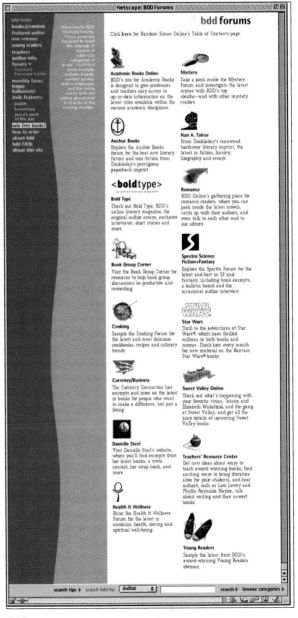

5.11

5.12

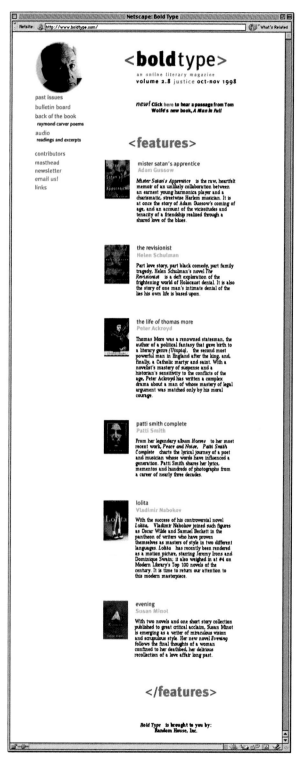

5.13

SUBSITE FORUMS, A VOICE FOR READERS

By clicking on the *boldtype* link, we actually leave the BDD site and enter a new domain (www. boldtype.com). This is a self-proclaimed "online literary magazine." It happens to feature books published by BDD and Random House (5.13). The background color scheme has changed, the navigational elements are gone, and we're no longer looking at Rotis letterforms. But the abstract elements, the avoidance of overwhelming or large images, the reliance on text, and the gridded layout are still here.

The Boldtype domain relies on lowercase FF Meta (designed by Erik Spiekermann) for all its GIF text. Meta is not altogether unlike Rotis in character — nicely informal and very readable — but it gives these pages their own voice. Hierarchical navigation is a simple list of words on the left. There are no frames. Color is used for headings, but most of the color on this page comes from the small book jacket illustrations that accompany each paragraph of text. Even the animated GIF of author portraits that heads the page includes only black-and-white photographs. This page is meant to be read, so let's read on.

Each of the featured works on the home page links to an author's page (5.14). Again, photographs of the author and the book jacket provide all the imagery. Linking words are in a column on the left and text is on the right. When you scroll down to the bottom of the page, additional links to navigate back in the hierarchy are listed on the left. This is a sparse, fast-loading layout.

Author's pages include a review of the book, and there are two links for further reading: one usually author-related, an interview or notes by the author, and the other an extended excerpt. Because Nabokov wasn't around for the interview, there's a RealAudio clip of Jeremy Irons reading an excerpt from *Lolita*, which has just been reissued (5.15). (I talk more about incorporating multimedia into a Web site in Chapter 6.) Or you can read the opening of this book, which remains as brilliantly outrageous as it was in

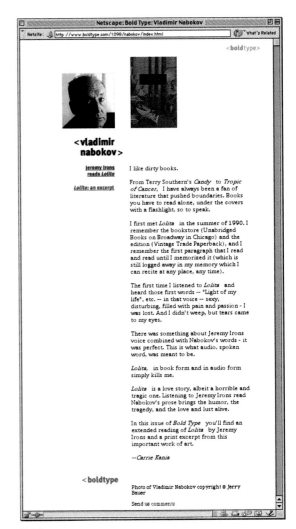

5.14

5.15

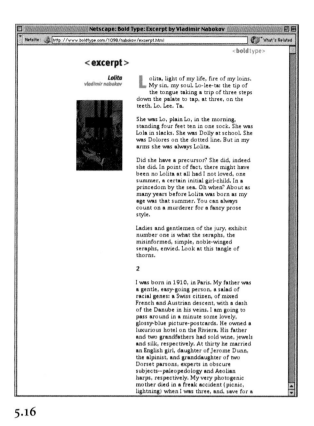

5.16

1956 when American publishers refused to have anything to do with it (5.16).

Just putting it in a relatively narrow table cell makes this text fairly readable. There's a nice drop cap inserted as a GIF image, and there are a couple of pull quotes, also GIF images, along the left column to add interest. But this is plain, unadulterated HTML text. Two `<br>` break tags are used to create the paragraphs, but there's no formatting in this very long passage. "Light of my life, fire of my loins" indeed!

THE LOST WORLD OF TYPOGRAPHY

Almost all of the fancy typeset text on the Web exists as images, not words. With all of our favorite tools and fonts available for the task, we have complete design freedom when converting words into Web images. This is great for typesetting headlines or single paragraphs, or for creating typographic effects. But the bulk of text must be typeset within the limitations of HTML's tag set and the widespread availability of fonts on client machines. (Or the paucity of universal font installation aside from those supplied with operating systems.)

We've looked at a number of sites that use the `<font face>` tag (more properly referred to as the *face* attribute of the `<font>` tag) to specify a typeface for blocks of text on a page. But because it's difficult to predict what typefaces users will have on their

BROWSERS CAN BE READERS

Interview with Miles McManus, Chief Executive Officer and Partner of OVEN Digital

Q: Everyone says Web surfers don't read, yet the Bantam Doubleday Dell and BoldType sites are dominated by words. Aren't you afraid of losing your audience?

MM: As we worked with BDD, we came to the realization that this is a site for readers, and readers are comfortable with text. They don't need to be sold with big, splashy images. The content of this site is text, yet this isn't just a place to read a book. So the question became how much and in what order should you receive the text of the articles and excerpts? We wanted to show the broad

general nature of their offerings and make it clear from the top that this is a brand that encompasses something for everyone. We used an animation of the current offerings and let the content bubble up as much as possible so that you get a very quick idea of what's going on with this site.

Q: Even though these sites were for the same client, they are different domains and were executed as separate projects. How do you account for their similarity?

MM: The constraints of Web design, branding, and the reality of text on the

machines, this specification is usually not particularly precise. More often than not, designers just look for any sans serif font and will specify a list of faces, including Arial (for Windows) and Helvetica (for Mac OS).

It's as if the face attribute exists only to supplement the standard proportional (usually serif) and mono-space font designations already supported by HTML and browsers. There's just not much hope of finding other faces installed across the vast international cross-platform world of the World Wide Web.

There are numerous typographical tags, but they don't do much more than change the size or color, or boldface or italicize text. This isn't real typographic control. The special nonbreaking space character ( ) can be used as a crude spacing device for text and image elements.

A more flexible device, the so-called "single-pixel" GIF trick, can be used like printer's lead to push text around on the page. A GIF image containing a single transparent pixel can be inserted anywhere and sized using the height and width or hspace and vspace attributes of the `<img>` image tag. When inserted in text, it allows you to create the effect of leading by specifying a vspace larger than the font size. An alternative method for adding space between lines of text is to use the `<font size>` tag on a space character and simply specify a larger size. Of course, the effect is relative to the browser setting on a given user's machine.

TIP

Helvetica is the most frequently specified sans serif typeface for Mac-bound Web pages. But, as mentioned earlier, Geneva is a better choice, and, as mentioned later in this chapter, Verdana is really the best for both Mac and Windows.

NOTE

You can also use the *size* and *color* attributes of the `<font>` tag to indicate scale or color type. Size is specified from 1 to 7, relative to the browser setting of the user's machine. 3 is the default setting, 1 is smallest, and 7 the largest. Color is specified using hexadecimal values, so black is 000000 (the equivalent of RGB 0, 0, 0) and white is FFFFFF (the equivalent of RGB 255, 255, 255). The details of HTML tags are not really in the realm of this book, but there are numerous HTML references online. The official reference is kept by the World Wide Web committee at www.w3c.org.

Web account for the similarities. Also, these two sites are for readers and reading on screen. We used similar grids to constrain the text to specific column widths. You never want to design text to fill the measure of a page. It's not arbitrary that books tend not to be extremely wide. Since these are not printed pages, they need navigational elements, as well. The sidebar navigation approach is almost a hackneyed standard on the Web now. It's such an obvious solution. But the good thing about it is that it allows for the type of modularity that our clients need. They can just add on down

the page, and the design won't break after a certain amount of expansion.

Q: Will you be using Cascading Style Sheets (CSS) to do different things in your Web designs?
MM: For us, CSS's greatest advantage is in giving us more control to do more of the same. It also allows us to do different things like adjust leading, but the reality of the Web is that more leading equates to more scrolling. You can get interesting layouts using that type of thing, but we do it in a very restrained way. Leading may improve legibility, but we know

users don't like to scroll. So if users object, what's the point?

Q: What's the biggest argument in favor of text as a design element?
MM: It's a medium with limited bandwidth, and we believe that doing things as efficiently as possible improves the user experience. It's the best way to ensure repeat visitors.

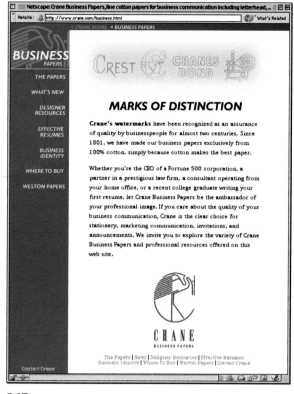

5.17

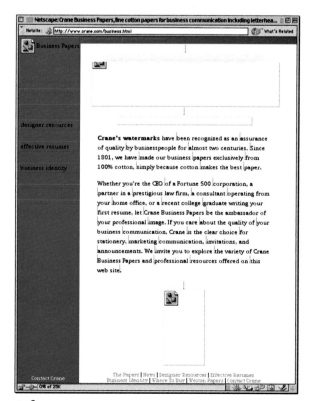

5.18

This page from the Crane & Co. Web site (5.17) uses the single-pixel GIF trick to create the effect of leading in these two paragraphs (www.crane.com/business.html). It's necessary to insert the transparent GIF frequently, because you never know where line endings will fall. (The source code for this page is available from the companion Web site for this book at www.idgbooks.com/extras/webarch.html.) As you can see, while the page loads, the placeholders for the GIF spacers are briefly visible (5.18). The fact is, all those spacers clutter up the HTML, making it difficult to go back and edit the text if you ever need to. But if you don't mind the work, the effect is both sophisticated and distinctive.

Most sites, even those by serious designers, don't do much more than bracket text inside a table cell. As we've seen, the shorter line length this creates does a huge amount for readability. Simply defining a line length creates a text block that is immediately easier to read. These text blocks also take on graphic qualities that can be used to add color or shading and to balance the layout of a page. Even though text is for reading, it has basic graphic qualities just like any other element you put on a page.

MAKING TYPOGRAPHY DYNAMIC

All the typographic tricks discussed in the previous section are just that — tricks. They are ways of getting around the limitations of HTML 3.2 and earlier. And even with these work-arounds, *The New York Times* doesn't look substantially different from *Lolita*. (But please don't tell them I said so.)

In fact, the <font> tag, along with several other type-related tags, has been *deprecated* by HTML 4.0. In other words, browsers will continue to support these tags, but their use in creating Web pages is officially and strongly discouraged. In case you were wondering, the World Wide Web Consortium's (W3C) site (www.w3c.com) points to the following article, "What's Wrong with the FONT Element?" by Warren Steel (www.mcsr.olemiss.edu/~mudws/font.html):

"The font tag is a hindrance to communication over the World Wide Web because it makes too many assumptions about the user's system, browser, and configuration. Cascading Style Sheets, on the other

hand, negotiate between author and viewer to create a carefully-designed appearance that is accessible to all. People create Web documents for many reasons. If you have something to say, information to provide, a message to preach, feelings to express, a product to sell, then it's in your interest to make your work accessible. Smart Web authors, who want to get their message across, stay far away from the FONT element."

CASCADING STYLE SHEETS

Despite official negativity, the `<font>` tag has become extremely popular, whereas Cascading Style Sheets (CSS) have yet to catch on in a significant way. In practice, both are used only to typeset sans serif text—this despite the fact that HTML 4, the standard as of this writing, has made great advances in providing typographic control. CSS give us controls similar to those we've become used to in word processing and page layout programs. CSS make type officially *dynamic*. And although there is no official standard for the collection of new technologies known as Dynamic HTML, every unofficial guide to DHTML includes CSS as a part of the standard—one of the few things about which Netscape and Microsoft fully agree.

In brief, CSS allow for the creation of structured documents by providing a mechanism for describing the way documents look on screen and in print. To put it another way, CSS facilitate the separation of structure and content in the creation of Web pages. This is very important for Web architects, but more important in concept than practice, at least so far.

The same typographical limitations that existed before CSS continue to tie our hands as designers. First, beyond a certain few, you never know what typefaces users will have installed on their machines, and second, Navigator and Internet Explorer have not implemented CSS in the same way. Version 5 browsers, which should be out about the same time as this book, will improve matters considerably, but for now, there just aren't very many compelling examples of CSS in action.

So what do CSS look like? We need to turn to the World Wide Web Consortium's own site to find a styled example (5.19). Not only can you find the

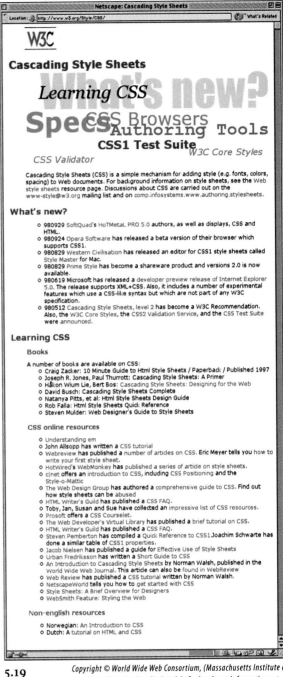

5.19

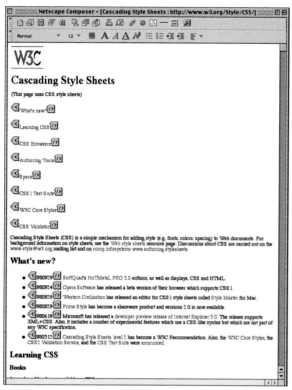

5.20

Copyright © World Wide Web Consortium, (Massachusetts Institute of Technology, Institut National de Recherche en Informatique et en Automatique, Keio University).
http://www.w3.org/Consortium/Legal/copyright-documents.html

5.21

complete CSS1 and CSS2 specifications (and they're talking about CSS3), but here is a section devoted to style sheets—not only in its content, but also in its design.

Look at this page again previewed in Netscape Composer (5.20). Where are the text images? There aren't any. The only image to be found is the W3C logo at the top of the page. Everything here, including the montage of variously typeset headings, is CSS-styled text. CSS have been used to redefine most of the standard HTML styles and add nearly a dozen additional styles. The author of this document, Håkon Lie, has used styles not only to define typographic and color information, but also to set positioning—thus the collection of overlaid text elements, each a different style, that make up the main graphic element of this page. (The HTML for this page, including the style sheet definitions, is available at the companion Web site for this book at www.idgbooks.com/extras/webarch.html.)

The structure provided by HTML is augmented by CSS to give the site creator consistent tools to define the site's look. But even Lie, who works for the W3C, admits that it's difficult to find many designers who are using CSS. "CSS isn't well supported in current browsers, and it's hard for designers to depend on style sheets."

PUTTING TYPE TO WORK

Of course, using CSS doesn't guarantee a compelling design. This isn't really the primary concern of the W3C. Instead, CSS facilitate consistent design across platforms and browsers. Take the site for Caterpillar Tractors (www.CAT.com). This is a heavy-duty site that befits the image of the company—big trucks, big company, big site. All the hallmarks of a well-designed site are evident from the first page (5.21): excellent use of imagery, clear, thorough navigation, and plenty of worthwhile content. And why shouldn't a blue-collar site be well constructed?

Although most of the text on the home page consists of GIF text, the Highlights (the changing features) use HTML text. But this is HTML with a difference. Instead of using the `<font face>` tag, this type is set in Helvetica using CSS. This isn't a big deal for a single page with very little text, but when you multiply this across a large site, CSS begin to show their usefulness.

As is evident from the Company Information page, the Caterpillar site has a very clearly defined page template (5.22). A band of navigational elements divided into hierarchical sections runs across the top. These links are all GIF text. The page and column titles are also GIF text, but the rest of the text is formatted using CSS. There is more to the typesetting here than a simple Helvetica specification. The leading, the positioning, the color, and the bold headlines have all been specified using CSS. Even the Company Information–specific column of links has been typeset using CSS.

Notice the similarity that exists between the Company Information page and this News page. The strong template ensures familiarity, and although the type is not set identically on these two pages (the leading is more generous here), it too is familiar (5.23). This page still uses CSS, but it is a different style sheet. Numerous style sheets are defined for the Caterpillar site, but they don't need to be redefined for every page. Instead, the style sheets are saved with the site like any document or image, and pages refer to sheets as needed.

This has two chief advantages. First, once a style sheet is defined, it can be reused across a site without the need to define the style on every page. Second, if you want to change a style sheet, the changes are immediately reflected on every page that references the sheet. For a site the size of Caterpillar's, one that is updated frequently, this can greatly simplify site maintenance.

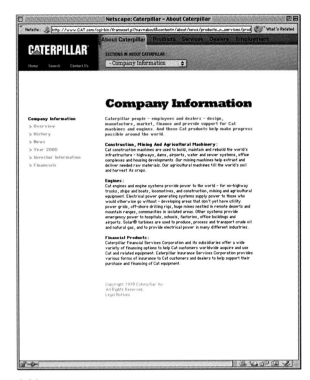

5.22

5.23

FINDING STYLES

If you really want to see what CSS are capable of, you should try out the Styleserver Development Interface at http://style.verso.com/styleserver/ (5.24). Here you can experiment with a matrix of six style parameters predefined by Todd Fahrner, design technologist at Verso Design and a contributor to W3C's CSS standards. There are from three to eight choices for each parameter. Make a selection from the drop-down boxes (there's no indication yet of what any of the choices does), select a sample document, and click the Show Me button. A new window pops up formatted using the CSS you just defined. You can even generate the CSS itself, in case you want to use or modify it for your own pages.

Here are three Styleserver examples: The first is formatted using vanilla HTML, no CSS (5.25). You might even say it was unformatted. The second and

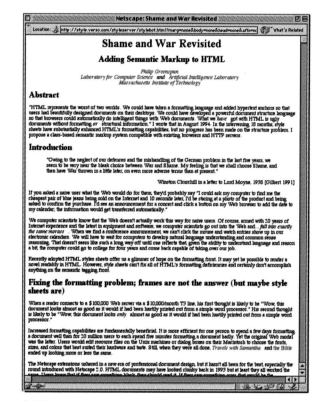

5.24

5.25

third use different combinations of settings from the Styleserver (5.26, 5.27). This first image looks familiar, like many other Web pages we've seen. To put it kindly, it's neither attractive nor easy to read. The formats created with CSS may not be your idea of perfect typography, but you can see that there's dramatic improvement over standard HTML. The beauty of CSS is that the tags stay the same. Only the CSS stylesheet has changed. And you can imagine that once you divide the work of creating a single stylesheet over an entire site, the amount of work per page becomes insignificant compared to the benefits.

If you're sharp-eyed, you will have noticed that some of the text in the two CSS examples is overprinted and not easily readable. This points out one of the design problems with CSS. In this case, the Communicator 4.5 implementation of CSS isn't handling this style properly. This, of course, is why many designers aren't ready to design sites using CSS. This will change, just as tables and then frames became standard design tools.

Here are a couple of "real world," if somewhat esoteric, examples of CSS on the Web. They indicate both that CSS can be used to create sophisticated

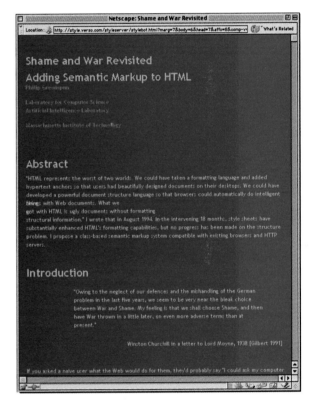

5.26   5.27

5.28

designs and that the world of CSS is still rather insular. The first site was designed for Dave Siegel, one of the leaders in pushing for CSS and Todd Fahmer's boss (5.28). This truly is Siegel's vision: simple, elegant typography, striking use of color, and a dryly sophisticated sense of humor. This is all HTML text. The only image is used for the background. There are no frames, and the columns are created using tables.

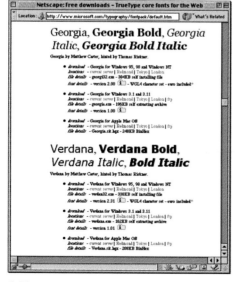

5.29

NOTE

The typeface specified in Dave Siegel's CSS is Verdana, a humanist sans serif design by master typographer Matthew Carter. Microsoft commissioned Carter to create two faces specifically for Web use, and the results are Verdana and Georgia (a serif face), probably the finest general-purpose faces available for the low-resolution displays of the Web. Both Windows 98 and Mac OS 8.5 include these faces, and they are available for free download from Microsoft's typography site (5.29): http://www.microsoft.com/typography/fontpack/default.html. These are worth downloading and installing if you don't have them. More important, it's worth specifying these at the beginning of your font lists for Web pages. By the way, this page makes use of CSS, as does much of Microsoft's massive Web site.

STYLES AND STANDARDS

This second example (5.30) comes from the Web Standards Project, a group dedicated to the correct implementation of standards by browser makers in which both Lie and Fahmer are active. The home page is a beautifully simple design that looks as if it were one big, impossibly-slow-loading image, when, in fact, it is one streamlined table full of fast-acting text and a single wasp (http//webstandards.org). This page seems too beautiful to be an HTML document, too elegant and sparse, and too different looking. What are the differentiating features used here? What makes this so good looking?

5.30

© 1998 The Web Standards Project; Jeffrey Zeldman, site designer
(www.webstandards.org)

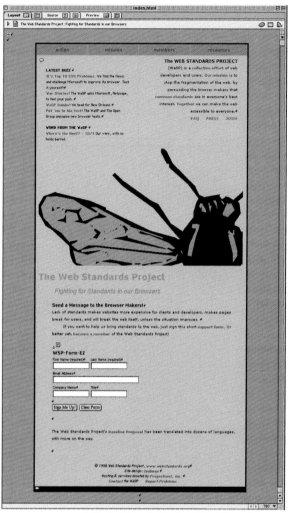

5.31
© 1998 The Web Standards Project; Jeffrey Zeldman, site designer
(www.webstandards.org)

5.32
© 1998 The Web Standards
Project; Jeffrey Zeldman, site designer (www.webstandards.org)

First take a look at the table, pictured here in Adobe GoLive to show the table boundaries (5.31). If you've designed or even looked at many tables, you know that they tend to get complex, full of narrow cells and changing spans used to achieve the desired graphic spacing. This table is clean. It has a geometrical purity that is refreshing. This is because the careful layout of all the text elements within table cells is achieved through the use of CSS positioning rather than spacer cells — it's part of the style definition. And if the text is changed, the style takes care of the proper positioning, so the table doesn't need to be completely rebalanced.

I should also point out that the cell padding for this table has been set to 4 pixels, which creates the black border, while padding has been turned off for all the individual cells of the table. As a result, the cell colors merge into a larger spread. This, as much as anything, gives this table the effect of being a single image. In fact, it is the kind of image that is often created in Photoshop and then sliced into a borderless table for Web viewing, as discussed in Chapter 3.

What you end up with is a more direct means to display information. Take a look at one of the text cells (5.32). First of all, the designer, Jeffrey Zeldman, the self-proclaimed Dr. Web, has specified Verdana as the first choice on his CSS font lists. For now, at least, Verdana has the advantage of looking special and un-Web-like. It also has a nice graphic quality that works well with this page.

Second, there are only two styles used for the text in this cell. Zeldman has created a body style he calls A and a bold style labeled B, which he has used for the first four words. The red text elements are all links, and Zeldman has defined linking text to match his body style, but in red. He sets off the three linking words at the bottom of the cell by using all caps.

Note that Communicator 4.5 doesn't right-justify this text correctly, leaving the last line sticking out too far, another CSS implementation error. And lest you think only Communicator is lagging in its CSS support, here's a page listing the 10 CSS problems with Internet Explorer (5.33). This page is not set up in

a table, but the text and headings are all formatted using styles.

It's important to remember that the Web is an international phenomenon, as is the Web Standards organization. Accordingly, Web Standards' mission statement has been translated into 11 languages (5.34). Now you can see one of the best features of CSS. All you have to do to create a new page is to

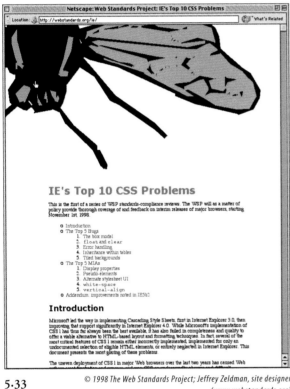

5.33   © 1998 The Web Standards Project; Jeffrey Zeldman, site designer
(www.webstandards.org)

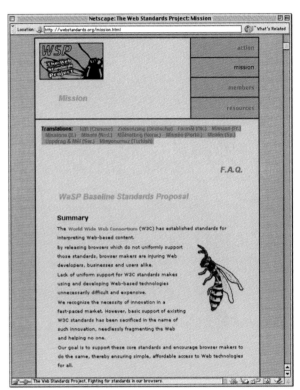

5.34   © 1998 The Web Standards Project; Jeffrey Zeldman, site designer
(www.webstandards.org)

replace the text. The style sheets take care of the rest (5.35). These pages look good in any language.

There's one more important point to make about this site regarding its use of CSS and its reliance on text. The navigational elements are kept to a bare minimum. This is a four-section site, and there are four global links at the top of most pages. All the other links are contained within the text. This reliance on contextual links is the way Web pages used to be designed, before there were tables and frames. Obviously, this wouldn't work for every site, but notice how the use of style sheets makes these links stand out in the text in a way that they wouldn't with older HTML tags without CSS. Also, the page composition is breathtakingly clean without the clutter of navigational elements we have become used to.

There's no question that CSS give us the structure and control we need to use text more graphically and creatively. However, many articles point out that designers will have to learn more complex constructs to take advantage of them, and that this will impede their acceptance. But all evidence shows that Web designers are eager to adopt any truly powerful new tool. And at the same time, there are already numerous tools that make CSS as easy to use as desktop publishing style sheets. The only question remaining for the acceptance of CSS is when Netscape and Microsoft will produce consistent, complete implementations of the standards.

EMBEDDING FONTS

For all their wonderful characteristics, CSS will never solve the problem of font distribution. You just can't count on any but a handful of typefaces being installed on a wide range of desktops. As modem speeds increase and other faster communication protocols become more common, it becomes practical to transmit more information. Why not send the font information along with the page? You only need to send it once for an entire site, and the information can be encoded and compressed to download more quickly.

Bitstream and Microsoft have already considered this solution, and while embedding font information in files is not new, it remains a relatively obscure technology. Bitstream's technology is known as TrueDoc, and Microsoft has dubbed theirs OpenType. TrueDoc technology has been incorporated into the most recent versions of Communicator, whereas OpenType is a joint standard with Adobe. Both standards are being put before a committee of the W3C, and we can only hope that a single standard will emerge. Sound familiar?

Both technologies encapsulate font information for transmission over the Web and rasterization on users' machines. The rasterizing software can be part of the browser or the operating system, or can be supplied as an extension, such as the Adobe Type Manager (ATM).

Many designers, especially type designers, are concerned that it's easy to steal the font information and use it without buying the typeface, and their fears are not unjustified. Microsoft (which is in the habit of giving software away when it suits their purposes), Adobe, and Bitstream are all conscious of the potential for abuse and claim to have technologies to solve

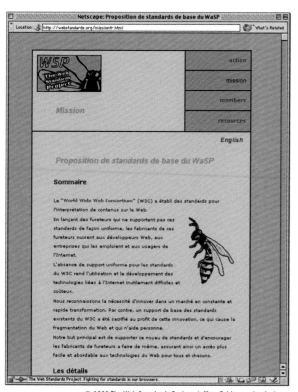

5.35

this problem. It's certainly one of the issues that the W3C will be addressing.

You can try out font embedding, if you're itching to do so. A product called HexWeb Typograph uses TrueDoc technology to allow the inclusion of a large library of fonts in your pages. Their Web page (www.net-investor.com) proves it (5.36). These are all embedded fonts, not GIF text. Like that Dymo font? You can even change the color of the tape, just as you would the color of any text.

To use this system, first specify the face and then reference the library, which happens to be one of HexWeb's servers. When the page is loaded, the browser default fonts are used, and then the page is refreshed when the font information has been retrieved from the remote server. Bitstream also has a TrueDoc font server that they've been testing for several months and intend to make commercially available before this book has been published. Here's a sample page from Bitstream comprised entirely of TrueDoc embedded fonts (5.37).

For their part, Microsoft recently released Web Embedding Font Tools (WEFT), which allow you to build pages in Windows for display using Internet Explorer. It is strictly a single-platform technology at this point, but the intention is to add other platform support eventually.

If a standard can be agreed upon and the security issues solved, font embedding promises to be one of our most dynamic tools. Suddenly, all the limitations of fonts will become as old-fashioned as those of lead type. Between CSS and embedded fonts, we designers will have what we've always wanted — control.

5.36

5.37

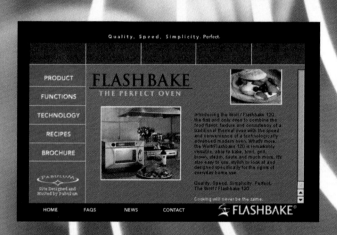

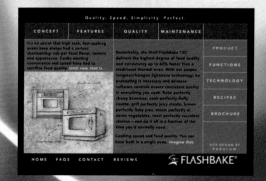

CHAPTER 6
INTEGRATING MULTIMEDIA
INTO THE STRUCTURE

Browsing the Web with a mouse includes what activity that channel surfing with a remote control doesn't? Interactivity. Even though I am no more active than the most sedentary couch potato, at least my mental synapses are kept well exercised as I navigate the daily complexities of the World Wide Web from my executive desk chair.

The ability to jump around at will, to choose one's destiny, was the original driving energy behind Web interaction. Not much was needed to make the Web interactive. The simple addition of links (hyperlinks) to the pre-Web Internet was all it took.

From an architectural point of view, links create the structure that holds sites together. To read more about this, see Chapter 2. But in the hyperkinetic world of the final years of this millennium, links aren't enough. The interactive monitorscape all browsers share is becoming downright seismic with interactivity — applets, scripts, and plug-ins are bringing all sorts of new active technologies to Web pages. In fact, the sights and sounds of the Web are getting more like television every day. Perhaps I should purchase a browsing couch to enjoy the Web of the future most fully.

We now have technologies that give us the full jolt of a cup of Java, that Quicken our pulse, that Flash and Shock. It's like a ride through the funhouse. But do these technologies change the basic linking

It's all cool and hip for the teenager, but we try to serve a higher purpose — the customer.

BRAD BROWN, PABULUM

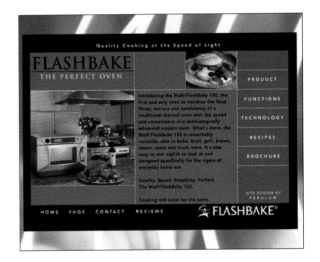

interactivity of the Web? Do they alter our ability to direct our browsing fate, traverse a site, follow a stream of consciousness, or navigate at will? Only if designed specifically for these purposes. Otherwise, these technologies expand the so-called multimedia capabilities of the Web—such as sound, video, and animation—but are neither interactive nor structural elements in and of themselves.

All the "add-on" Web-based multimedia technologies we'll examine in this chapter provide the means to both enhance the interactive experience and create more complex, less strictly hierarchical site structures. Also, as Internet throughput increases, multimedia technologies are becoming necessary elements of sophisticated site design. Is there anyone around who prefers black-and-white television?

USING "SAFE" PLUG-INS

We look at a number of plug-in technologies in this chapter, including Macromedia's Flash and Shockwave and Apple's QuickTime. These represent a very small sampling of plug-ins available, but they are completely cross-platform, widely supported technologies that you can feel very safe using to create general interest Web sites. Here's a very brief description of each. There are links to more information for each of these technologies included on the Web site that accompanies this book, located at www.idgbooks.com/extras/webarch.html.

Flash is a vector-based technology that has the advantage of extreme compactness and clarity. With Flash, you can design sophisticated typographic effects, blend text and images, and create animations that play very quickly. Because Flash is a streaming technology, movies start playing quickly before they've finished downloading. Flash movies can be created only in Macromedia's Flash program. So although the playback format is an open, widely supported standard, the creation tools are limited to one proprietary offering.

The same is true of **Shockwave**, another Macromedia technology. You must use Macromedia Director to create Shockwave movies. Unlike Flash, Shockwave is not a streaming technology and is not particularly compact. However, Shockwave is capable of much more sophisticated programming, so that whole games can be created in Director for playing on the Web.

QuickTime is a video standard that has been officially recognized by the W3C. There are many competing video standards, but QuickTime seems to be the most widely supported, and it also seems to be gaining momentum. Despite the fact that this is an Apple-developed technology, all current versions of Windows are supported, as is UNIX. QuickTime is another streaming technology, but you must set the options to match your connection speed in order to view movies while they download.

We don't discuss any sites that use **RealAudio** in this chapter; sound clips just don't show up well in screen shots. But this is another very commonly used plug-in technology. As with QuickTime video, there are many competing sound playback standards on the Web. But the RealAudio plug-in from RealNetworks seems to have the upper hand right now.

Java is not supported by a plug-in. Instead, it requires a run-time interpreter that is built into the browser. Despite lawsuits and injunctions on the subject, both Netscape and Microsoft have licensed Java and have included Java interpreters for several browser versions now. But Java is not a design technology, it is a programming language. Similarly, Java is not strictly intended for multimedia and animation as Shockwave and Flash are. Instead, all kinds of applications, including ones having nothing to do with the Web or even with the visual presentation of information, can be created using Java. This is one of the reasons why Java is important not only for the Web, but for software development in general.

For purposes of discussion, it's necessary to distinguish between *interactivity* and *multimedia*. Both terms are relatively new to the language, vague, and frequently used incorrectly and interchangeably. Interactivity requires some kind of action by the user; a single click is enough. But even a click requires decision making, and this simple engaging of the mind is enough to elevate the interactive Web above the enervating entertainment of television. (Sorry, pressing buttons on a remote control doesn't count.)

Because the Web is its own medium, it's redundant to speak of Web-based multimedia capabilities. But multimedia has gone beyond its name to include all computer-based activities that combine elements of print, audio, and video. It has even come to include the interactivity that characterizes the Web, so that hyperlinks have become a sort of media unto themselves.

We have looked at many Web sites that include animated GIFs and JavaScript rollovers to improve designs or otherwise attract attention. These provide the most basic ways to animate a page and, as we have seen, can even be used to animate the structure of a site, though only in a very limited way (see the GetSmart site discussion in Chapter 2 and the Getty site discussion in Chapter 3). We've also seen, with the G-Shock site discussion in Chapter 4, what a difference a technology like Shockwave can make to the entire design and structure of a site.

For this chapter, we'll concentrate on sites that go beyond what HTML can provide. We're not interested in single *cool* multimedia elements inserted into pages of otherwise *uncool* (but not hot, either) HTML. We want to see how these truly innovative technologies can be used architecturally rather than decoratively.

Confusion arises because these have become overlapping designations. So although links are not necessarily media elements, they can be, and although multimedia elements needn't be interactive, they often are. For the purposes of this chapter, we will not dwell on multimedia technologies, but on the use of multimedia elements to enhance site structure and interactivity.

SURVEYING MULTIMEDIA ELEMENTS

What does it take to add interactivity to a site? Or to put the question another way, how do we, as Web architects, take sites beyond the expected collection of well-designed pages bound by navigational links? Any site with an exceptional navigational scheme has achieved the first level of interactivity — no easy task. But we want to go beyond pure linking to engage those browsing the site as active, or at least more fully entertained, participants.

To answer this question, we need to look at the elements of interactivity. We'll start with a Web site that includes among its fashionable collection of shoes, clothes, and diatribes a laundry list of multimedia elements. On first entering the Kenneth Cole Web site (www.kennethcole.com), it seems that everything is black, except for a handful of text links — white, all caps, Helvetica — the height of fashion (6.1). Take your seats — the show is about to begin.

6.1

6.2

6.3

6.4

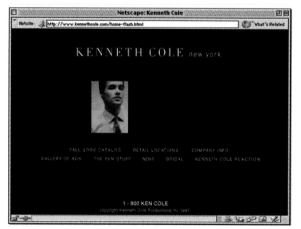

6.5

THE HEIGHT OF INTERACTIVE FASHION

First the credits roll (6.2). The letters K E N N E T H C O L E roll in from right to left, while more letters, N E W Y O R K, roll in from left to right (6.3). Just to give things a slightly edgy, somewhat obscure appearance, there are also strange interference lines in black. These turn out to be the five screen divisions that are used like video displays to give this show its visual rhythm. This animation has the feeling of a pair of Lexington Avenue subways passing under Bloomingdale's — very New York.

For those of us who have trouble making whole words out of large scrolling letters, the stage (the home page) now bears the Kenneth Cole logotype (6.4). The fashion show starts in the leftmost screen. A single image fades in and then out (6.5). Then a wider image filling three screens fades in, scrolls upward, and fades out before we really know what we're looking at (6.6). More fading, panning images, and finally, the five frames freeze for a few seconds while this year's ad campaign slogan fades in above them — "To be aware is more important than what you wear" (6.7). You may applaud now.

It's not quite the height of the New York fashion scene, but this little Flash animation sets the tone for a site that is as cleanly and cleverly designed as the product line it's presenting. It's just a single element, but it does what would be impossible with a typical static element. It introduces a sense of activity that makes this home page much more alive and engaging — a more compelling enticement to image-conscious browsers and buyers. The Kenneth Cole site, like Kenneth Cole Productions itself, is high fashion that makes a statement and takes a stand.

This site has everything the print campaigns have. In fact, it uses many of the same images and controversial tag lines. But right from the start, it also has motion. "We wanted to take what they had and extend it to the Web," said Matt Minkin, director of operations at Zentropy in Los Angeles, the site's designers. "They've taken care of their image and it's very consistent. We've given it interactivity."

TAKING A STAND WITH ANIMATED GIFS

Look at the Kenneth Cole *Reaction* section (6.8). In both design and marketing, Kenneth Cole is about eliciting reactions. This section is consistent with the rest of the site: white-on-black typography with imagery concentrating on products and models. There's a navigation bar across the bottom and a section title at the top. This title happens to be an animated GIF image.

6.6

6.7

6.8

R

6.9

R•E

6.10

R E•A

6.11

R E A•C

6.12

R E A C•T

6.13

R E A C T•I

6.14

R E A C T I•O

6.15

R E A C T I O•N™

6.16

R E A C T I O N•™

6.17

The single still image used on this page captures all the models in motion. Even though their motion is frozen, you can see that they are jumping, dancing, or just facing into the wind. The animated GIF heightens the sense of action simply by spelling out R E A C T I O N and leading your eye across the page with a moving red dot (6.9–6.17)—a simple effect unobtainable in print.

Let's move down the hierarchy to the *VIP Room*, a simple page that maintains the consistency of design elements for the site (6.18). Although almost all the color comes from the photograph, on this page, JavaScript rollovers highlight the links in red, the same color used for the animated dot on the section's title page.

QUICKTIMING MUSIC VIDEOS

Continue on to the *Video* link and wait while another multimedia element, a QuickTime video, loads (6.19). Or if you have a recent version of QuickTime with the plug-in set to match your connection speed, the video will start playing while it downloads, providing immediate gratification and more motion in the form of a singing, strolling Kenneth Cole suit.

This brings up the whole issue of pushing technology at the risk of losing browsers. QuickTime, for example, is an extremely widespread technology developed as a cross-platform delivery vehicle for video and audio. It has widespread support and has

6.18

6.19

been around long enough to have arrived on most desktops. On the other hand, Flash is relatively new. Macromedia developed it as a vector graphic standard for Web multimedia (see the sidebar, *"Using 'Safe' Plug-ins,"* earlier in this chapter), and has worked hard to gain support that is nearly as widespread as that for QuickTime. But it is not on nearly as many desktops.

By using Flash technology, Zentropy and Kenneth Cole are making the site experience richer for those who have the technology or are willing to download and install the plug-ins. It seems reasonable to assume that the sophisticated Kenneth Cole customer will appreciate and even demand the features that are only available by using these technologies.

6.20

GAMING WITH SHOCKWAVE

Let's look at the *Pleasure Zone* within the Reaction section (6.20). We can tell something is different, because the background is suddenly very orange. We'll try the game. It's a simple arrange-the-pieces puzzle, using a photograph of Kenneth Cole–clad models in action. Before we reach the game, we're warned that it requires Shockwave and are given the opportunity to download and install it if we haven't already (6.21).

The puzzle opens in a new pop-up window (6.22). This is another multimedia element requiring another plug-in. The Shockwave plug-in is becoming fairly ubiquitous among seasoned browsers, especially those who like games. My guess is that most people don't yet have it. This is just a simple game, not a crucial site element, and for those who find such things amusing, it's easy to add this feature.

6.21

FLASHING MESSAGES AND AMBIGUITY

Shockwave, QuickTime, Flash, animated GIFs—there's a lot going on within the Kenneth Cole site. It's also a Web commerce site; you can order products from the online catalog. Zentropy has used a lot of different element types to build a compelling Web environment. They've used the imagery and political puns so effective in Kenneth Cole's print ads and added playful movement to the mix.

6.22

6.23

Perhaps the best example of this on the site is the presentation of the current ad campaign (6.23–6.30). The ads are the same, but when presented as a Flash movie, one ad fading into the next, the effect is heightened. These aren't just clever puns used to sell merchandise, but statements of political attitude. There's a surprising ambiguity in these ads. We don't know whether to smile or blush. Whichever we choose, Kenneth Cole has succeeded in getting our attention and making us more aware.

6.24

6.26

6.25

6.27

6.28

6.29

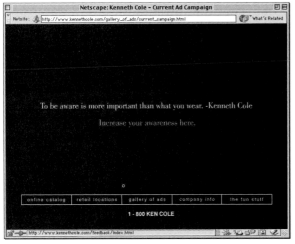

6.30

Rather than bludgeon us with multimedia until we scream "cool," this site incorporates multimedia elements to enhance an already successful brand image. These innovative elements serve the site without changing the basic construction techniques we've examined in previous chapters. The information architecture, navigation, consistent typography, and strong color scheme are all parts of well-designed sites, even without multimedia elements.

So what's the big fuss about multimedia? It appears to be a mere adjunct to HTML — a collection of plug-ins for creative designers to take advantage of, but not really a paradigm-shifting technology. As with all well-hyped innovations, the truth lies somewhere in between. Let's explore the possibilities.

IT'S ALL A GAME

The Shockwave puzzle used in the Kenneth Cole site is one of the most common programming examples in existence. The same game has shipped as a desk accessory with every Mac back to the original 128K model. It can also be found on the Web in at least one other incarnation, but in very different circumstances.

6.31

6.32

6.33

IKEA, the Swedish home furnishings giant, has attempted to recreate the shopping experience of their warehouse-like stores online. And just as the stores include a supervised play area for children, so does the Web site (www.ikea.com). The *Living with Kids* section of the site features a page of *Fun and Games* (6.31). And here is the same sliding puzzle. But instead of a scramble of high-fashion models (the young and restless), IKEA's friendly-looking green python, Djungelorm, is severed into the jumble for this puzzle.

SHOCKWAVE? JAVA? WHAT'S THE DIFFERENCE?

The interface for IKEA's version of the puzzle is a bit different, and the graphics are certainly brighter, but the puzzle is essentially the same (6.32, 6.33). And there's another interesting difference here that's not immediately noticeable. Instead of using Shockwave, IKEA's site designer, Deutsch, Inc. of New York, has programmed this version of the game in Java.

From the user perspective, it makes little difference if a Web game is developed in Shockwave or Java. However, the Java version is apt to be more compact and therefore to load faster. On the other hand, experienced Director users, capable of turning out Shockwave products, are more easily found in the design world than Java programmers capable of writing custom applets, an expensive commodity.

IKEA has incorporated Java applets in a number of places within its site. In addition to the three children's games, there is a pair of much more sophisticated interactive animations in the *Product Guide* section of the site (6.34). We'll start with the *Assembly Tips & Demo* link.

IKEA has made its mark as a purveyor of low-cost, high-quality furniture. One of the ways they keep costs down is by leaving much of the final assembly to the customer. This has led them to develop a number of streamlined assembly techniques and multilingual sets of clear instructions to go along with them. Here's a multimedia version that practically puts the furniture together for you.

Before we get to the actually assembly, there's a cautionary page that alerts us, "Java or Flash required" (6.35). There are two versions of this demo. If the Flash plug-in is detected, the Flash version is used; if not, the slightly larger Java version is loaded. If you don't have a Java-capable browser, it's easier to get one than it is to assemble your IKEA furniture. We have to click one more time to get to the actual demo.

Instead of opening a new pop-up window, this movie/applet loads in the same main frame used for all the content of the IKEA site. The color scheme, iconography, and typography are all familiar and consistent with the rest of the site. Despite this, Flash/Java takes over when the movie/applet is loaded.

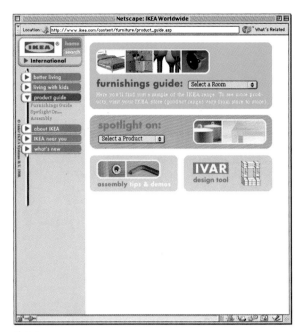

6.34

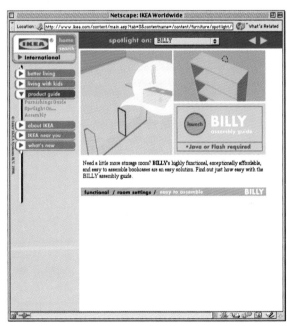

6.35

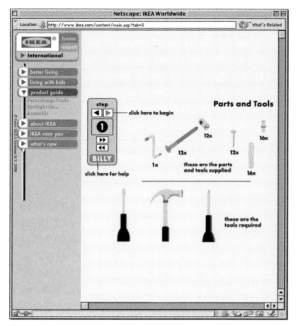

6.36

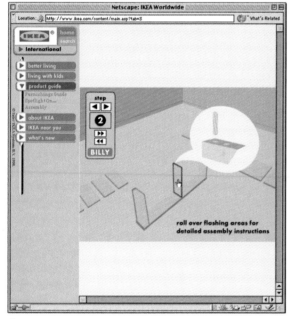

6.37

The only animated element in the first step is the flashing arrow pointing to step 2 (6.36). The rest is a simple parts list. The little controls panel is part of every step window. It not only tells us where we are, but also includes step forward and back, fast forward and back, and help buttons. Because this is a Flash/Java animation, clicking a button immediately loads the next step. We don't have to wait for a new page to be downloaded. Click onward.

Step 2 begins the animated assembly. The pieces are all laid out on the floor and begin to assemble themselves in order. Sound effects accompany the movement of each piece. When we're required to do something, the animation stops and the pieces in question flash to get our attention. At this point we're instructed to roll the cursor over the flashing areas for detailed instructions. The detail pops up and presumably we figure out what to do (6.37). Click onward.

Steps 3, 4, and 5 continue in much the same way, picking the pieces up off the floor, then pausing to let you view the assembly detail (6.38, 6.39, 6.40). If we were actually trying to assemble a bookshelf, this little animation would make it very easy, perhaps even pleasurable. Now the animation affixes the shelf to the wall and loads it up with books. The controls panel changes to let us preview the bookshelf in the three finishes available.

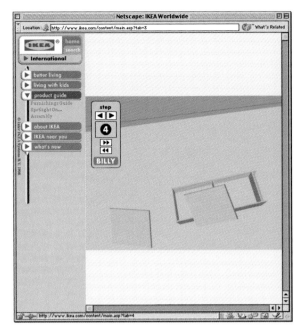

6.39

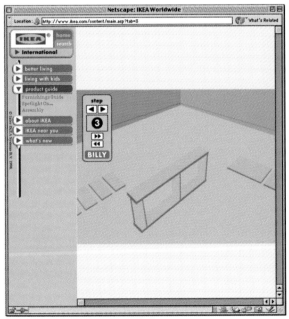

6.38

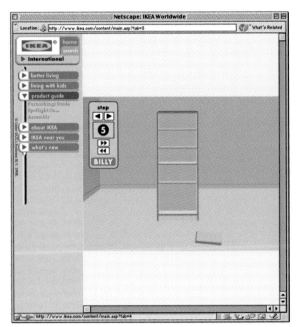

6.40

6.41

6.42

As a final step, we can click and link over to see photographs of the shelves (6.41). These so-called Billy shelves are simple enough, but IKEA provides a dozen different views of them so you'll really know what they look like. Just click one of the JavaScript rollover buttons to change the view (6.42). IKEA could have preloaded all the images and included them with the rollovers, but the cumulative size of so many images would make this impractical.

Even though the assembly demo is relatively crude, the equivalent of stick figure animation, it intensifies the feeling of reality of the site. We've all seen the very professional photographs of furniture pieces and room settings that fill the other catalog-like sections of this site, but somehow this animated schematic vision is more real. It gives us more of a feel of what it will be like when we get that flat box of parts home and try to fit it into our cluttered lives.

"COMPONENTIZED" APPLET

The same is true for IKEA's IVAR design tool. IVAR is the name of IKEA's component storage system used with this Java applet. This is neither a movie nor an animation. It is a design application, and as such, it comes with instructions (6.43). It's fairly simple, and

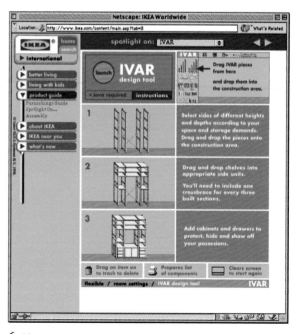

6.43

you could probably figure most of this out, but it's nice to be sure of your tools when you start building.

Essentially, this tool lets you drag pieces and put them together in an isometric model just the way a *real* designer would do with a T-square and triangle. It's a good way to simulate the assembly of these component shelving units. You can even print out a final list of components to take with you when you go to the IKEA store to make your purchase.

The IVAR builder launches into its own pop-up window (6.44). When you move the cursor over an element, it is selected and identified in the caption window across the bottom. Click and drag to place an element on the layout. If a piece doesn't fit, the applet won't let you put it into the model (6.45). It's easy to plan fairly intricate shelving combinations, and there's no pricing information to deflate your shelves in the air.

Although there is a user interface to be considered, the structure of applets is usually more of a programming than a design problem. Similarly, as far as the IKEA site is concerned, the various Flash and Java elements don't really affect the site structure. To the navigational scheme of the site, the multimedia elements are the same as any hierarchical element. Generally speaking, multimedia elements are incorporated into Web sites like any image element. We select multimedia elements as carefully as any image, but because they can add a unique quality to a page or site, the site structure is often used to highlight or emphasize these components.

In the IKEA site's case, the IVAR builder is highlighted on the table of contents page, the main page of the site (6.46). It's the first item in the *What's New* column and is further highlighted with an animated GIF. In the Kenneth Cole site's case, the whole site is suffused with multimedia elements, so that no single element receives special treatment.

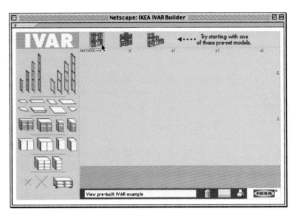

6.44

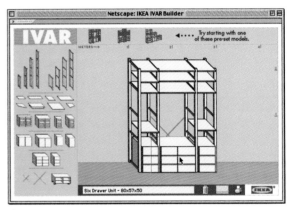

6.45

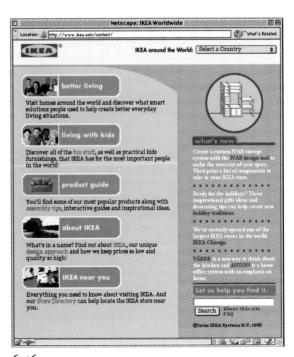

6.46

But what about sites that go further and turn the whole structure into a multimedia element? We've seen that it can been done. The G-Shock site discussed in Chapter 3 is entirely Shockwave-based, something most designers avoid because of the long load times that result. But with a technologically sophisticated Click Generation audience, movement and interaction were deemed more important than simplicity and attention to the lowest common denominator. Can we find a technology that gives us both broad appeal and a more active structure?

FLASH IN THE PAN

Surprisingly, our quest takes us to a truly uncool industry. It is a site for a product that is both mundane (there's one in every house) and innovative (you've never seen one like this before). The product is literally hot — the FlashBake/Wolf halogen-powered oven. It sounds intentional, but it's purely coincidental that the technology chosen to showcase this new product is also called Flash.

As already mentioned in this chapter, you need to download and install the Flash plug-in to view the FlashBake Web site (www.flashbake.com). This is what you'll see if your browser isn't Flash-enabled — a page telling you what I just did: Get Flash (6.47). At least you can link directly to the download from the site. This book is not so interactive.

If Flash has already been installed in your browser's plug-ins folder, then you're whisked right off to the Flash-enabled site of FlashBake. What's actually happening is that the home page uses a JavaScript to detect the presence of the Flash plug-in and opens a pop-up window if it's present. If not present, only the stagnant home page loads. (The HTML with this JavaScript for detecting the browser version and the presence of the Flash plug-in is included on the companion Web site, at www.idgbooks.com/extras/webarch.html.)

6.47

There's a momentary pause while the opening Flash sequence loads, and then images and words start fading in and out with the tag line for this product (6.48–6.51). All this happens fairly quickly, because we don't have to wait for the entire Flash file to download. When the little trailer is finished, the first page of the site appears (6.52). (There's a small, yellow arrow that you can click to skip the introduction and go straight to the first page.) I say *page*, but because this entire site is a single Flash file, the mention of pages is a bit misleading. Nonetheless, the sense of pages is still present, so I will continue to speak of them.

6.50

6.48

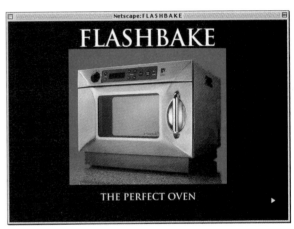

6.51

6.49

6.52

6.53

COMPARING STANDARD HTML AND FLASH

Pabulum, the designers of this site, built an HTML equivalent of the Flash site for those without the plug-in. There's no introductory animation, but the HTML first page looks fairly similar to the Flash version (6.53). The color scheme, layout, and typography are almost the same, and the navigation bar has simply been shifted from one side to the other. Pabulum's designers worked hard to achieve the same look in both versions.

Look a little closer. The typography in the Flash version has been carefully spaced with leading and kerning. The HTML typography looks unprofessional by comparison. The table and frames in the HTML version lack the precision and elegance of the Flash-generated grid with its clean, white hairlines. The images had to be made smaller in the HTML version to fit the table cells and to load faster.

Pabulum uses a classic navigational scheme. Links for the first-level hierarchy are contained in the column on the side, whereas tangential links are less important and appear almost as background elements across the bottom. Moving one level down in the hierarchy adds new section-specific links across the top of each page. Each of the navigational elements uses a different background color and rollovers to highlight active links.

ALTERNATIVE BAKING ON THE WEB

A conversation between Brad Brown and Tim Walter, senior designers at Pabulum, about the advantages of an entirely Flash-based site. (Brad Brown did the HTML, and Tim Walter created the Flash movie for the FlashBake site.)

TW: This isn't very conventional for a Flash site. We didn't want a lot of animation, but it's an effective way to show information. With a typical HTML site, there's a lot of down time while sites reload. But delivery is instantaneous with Flash, almost like a slide show. The client's response was very positive to this. From a design perspective, creation becomes very free-form with Flash. You don't have to worry about frames or tables.

BB: Another option that intrigued me is that you can do the majority of your work in Flash without going to four or five applications. And you can update easily without doing a lot of other changes.

TW: It's easy to work efficiently, but Flash isn't searchable, and you can't incorporate CGIs. The beauty of Flash is that files are relatively small and streamed, but that comes at a cost. I enjoy using Flash as an alternative to HTML, but only on projects that can accept the limitations.

BB: Flash is user-friendly for first-time users, because you have none of the

But as we move down in the hierarchy, we also become aware of the biggest advantages of Flash. Click the Product link in the Flash version, and the new elements scroll into place almost immediately (6.54). This is because the Flash site is a single file that loads while you're admiring the opening sequence. Once it is loaded, switching pages is nearly instantaneous.

LOAD ONCE, WAIT ONCE

Obviously, we have to wait for the Product page to load in the HTML version. We're accustomed to waiting for short load times, and this one is only about 10 seconds with a 56K modem. But once you experience a site that allows you to navigate without pauses, 10 seconds is an eternity. Pabulum has done all the things good Web architects must to create clean, clear navigation. Then they've turbo-charged it by creating the entire site in Flash. You can switch from page to page so quickly that you're tempted to click for the pure delight of seeing every page.

Now look at the second HTML page (6.55). This is still a good page, but in a side-by-side comparison it is easy to see that it doesn't hold up against the Flash equivalent. In addition to the problems mentioned before, look how the navigational elements start to

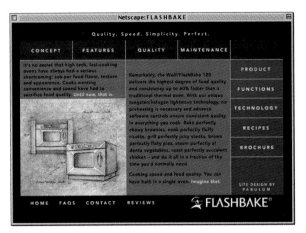

6.54

6.55

---

tricks of HTML to learn. It makes things really easy to do. I don't think you can mirror something that's vector-based in HTML. It's more vibrant, comes out at you more. The limitations of HTML don't exist in Flash. It comes across the Web really well.

TW: I started with a big folder full of information from the client. The company wanted the site navigation to be as intuitive as possible. They thought an icon-based system would be too confusing, so they wanted words. Industrial design firms like grids, and I thought that would

be a really good way to present stuff. We were able to play off the aesthetics established and address the client's concerns about a text-based interface at the same time.

BB: This is a single Flash file, but we could have used multiple movies and multiple HTML pages. It's simple in one aspect, because we have only one file. The HTML version is over 90 pages. It's a huge frame set.

TW: Animation is awesome, it's great, but with Flash we can do an entire site. It's an information delivery tool. Basically,

it allows us to just add stuff without getting obnoxious. Flash is being abused; there are already Flash clichés. Flash is really intended to be an animation program. This is totally different. It's the most efficient way to present information. And the control over text allowed us to use really cool things like kerning and leading. That was wonderful for me.

BB: We were getting really tired of our sites looking one way on a PC and another on a Mac. Flash looks the same no matter where you are. The Flash movie is

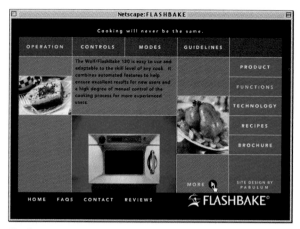

6.56

6.57

overwhelm the rest of the page. This HTML composition is seriously out of balance. It comes as no surprise that HTML has serious limitations, so rather than beat a dead horse, let's examine some of the other navigational tricks that Pabulum has created with Flash.

One of the features that makes the FlashBake site so visually compelling is the consistent size of all the pages. However, the limited size of the presentation makes it difficult to fit a lot of information on any single page. Instead of adding scrolling elements, Pabulum maintains the integrity of the grid and adds a "More" arrow to the bottom corner to indicate that there's more information on this subject (6.56). This might be annoying if you had to wait for the next page to load, but in this case, the animation of the next page sliding over the previous one is just fun. The navigational elements remain stationary during this animated sequence, and of course there's a "Back" button to bring you back again (6.57). There is also a *Recipes* section with two layers of forward and back buttons (6.58).

---

always going to look identical. It's the only truly cross-platform vehicle.

TW: The grid is 9 × 6, so all image placement is based on that. All the images fit perfectly into the grid, and it really helps the overall look of the site, because it's totally consistent.

BB: We tried to implement the grid in HTML, but there was too much code for the time we had, so we lost it. Pages were adding up to 70K each, because the graphics couldn't come down that much. But it's not the same quality of design. There's also the text issue.

TW: The client really wanted to push Flash. They kept saying how quickly everything was showing. Once the movie starts, it's all right there.

ACCELERATING THE NAVIGATION

The success of this navigational scheme doesn't depend on Flash. In either version of the site, you always know where you are, how you got there, and where you can go next. It's just that the elegance and ease of the Flash solution makes the navigation so much more compelling. It invites exploration. The Flash site feels small and friendly. There's a real sense of browsing; we have no idea how large this site really is. The HTML version includes over 90 pages.

As we've seen, there are other things you can do with Flash. For instance, on a particular page we can click a color swatch to see what this oven looks like in white, black, or professional chrome finishes (6.59). One wishes there were other colors to play with.

In addition to all its visual advantages, the Flash version was faster to create, and is more compact and easier to maintain. The file can be edited in the Flash program to add pages or make changes. And because all the information is in a single file, global changes are especially easy to make.

This is beginning to sound like company propaganda, but Flash does have its limitations. There's no database or CGI interface for programming, and Flash pages can't be indexed or searched. Although Flash is fully functional across platforms, it is not an open development standard. You're locked into Macromedia's solutions when you create Flash-enhanced sites. And even when you've loaded your site, not everyone has or wants to get the correct plug-in. Creating a second version in HTML is a big job. In fact, FlashBake has found that despite the obvious superiority of its Flash site and the ease with which one can link directly to Macromedia to download the Flash plug-in, the HTML site receives about the same number of visitors.

For FlashBake, Flash was the Web technology that best matched their innovative baking technology, and this turned out to be one of the more compelling arguments in its favor. But most important, once you've gone through FlashBake's Flash site, you end up really wanting to own one of their ovens. Only the price tag has kept me from calling. Maybe I'll buy a copy of Flash, first.

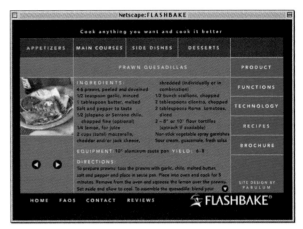

6.58

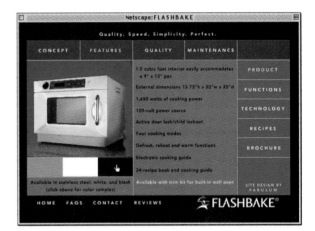

6.59

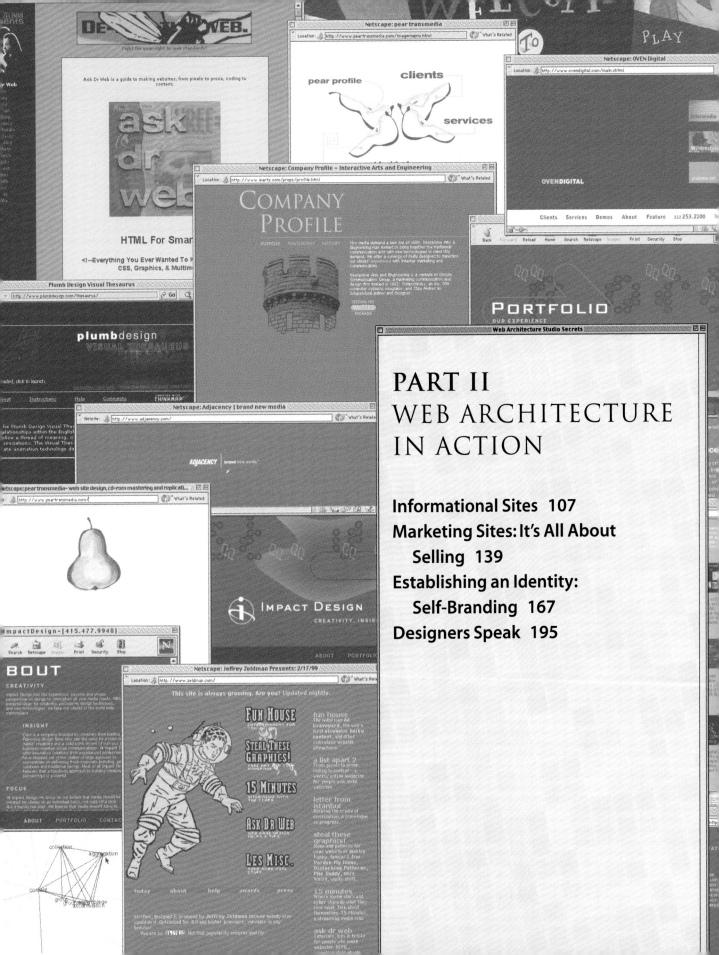

PART II
WEB ARCHITECTURE IN ACTION

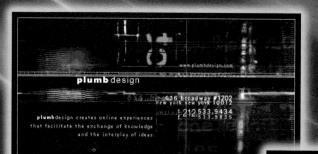

CHAPTER 7
INFORMATIONAL SITES

T he Web has become the great marketing melting pot, but it didn't start out this way. At first, information was everything and the notion of content as king was ascendant. But nowadays more attention and money are being spent on image, resulting in a discernable shift in emphasis. All the same, the Web remains the place to go for information. Just look at the ever-growing list of top-level categories on Yahoo!'s home page. And they're only one of many indices to a knowledge base that's expanding faster than our ability to keep track of it.

The fact that there is so much information and so many ways to search through it is the most exciting aspect of the Web. But as Web architects, our interest is in the presentation of information — how to make it readable, understandable, digestible, and even pleasing to look at. This is distinct from, but dependent upon, information architecture, which is concerned with the organization of information. You cannot present information well that is not well organized. However, for this book, we'll assume that your information is in order, and your main concern now is making that information accessible by building pages and sites around it.

We're all becoming librarians.

MICHAEL FREEDMAN, PLUMB DESIGN, INC.

WEB CIVICS

I am writing this section on December 20, 1998 — a day seemingly like any other, except for what happened the day before. As usual, *The New York Times,* sheathed in yellow plastic and wrapped with a rubber band, arrived on the front walk at about 7:00 this morning. But instead of the familiarly conservative six-column layout of the front page, there is an "end-of-the-world" headline, "Clinton Impeached," and for the first time in my memory, a two-column-width article filling the right side of the page. There's also an entire additional section devoted to the impeachment and the events — surprising, predictable, partisan, and sordid — surrounding yesterday's historic votes.

I shouldn't be surprised. *The Times* hasn't had many impeachments to cover in its history, and while it is not the end of the world, it is tumultuous and beyond our ability to predict what's going to happen. Even if, like Rip Van Winkle in the Catskills, we had been asleep for 20 years, we would know without even unfolding the newspaper that something important had happened.

Newspapers are designed to handle this kind of situation. For *The Times,* and other "serious" newspapers, the news doesn't get any bigger than a one-inch, 72-point, banner headline. You can imagine in the not-so-distant days of Linotype machines and hot lead that there was one machine in the corner of the pressroom that was used only on 72-point days, such as this one.

On the Web, there are no such well-defined rules for displaying information. One of the greatest assets of the Web is that all sites are created equal. One of its greatest detriments is that all information ends up being treated equal, as well.

ON THE WEB, ALL NEWS IS CREATED EQUAL

Despite the earthshaking news of the day, the morning was fairly typical for me. I ate my cereal and read some (though perhaps a bit more than usual) of the paper. Then I turned on the computer to read my e-mail and browse the Web. My default home page is set to Apple's Excite portal, which in some ways presented a larger surprise to me than the front page of *The Times.* The impeachment does not jump out at me off the page. In fact, I actually have to read the headlines to find the story (7.1).

On *My* (so-called) *Channel* there is no hierarchical ordering of information. All the news, reduced to a few headlines, is listed in chronological order by category. Later this afternoon, the impeachment will be old news, and it may not even warrant mention as a Top Story.

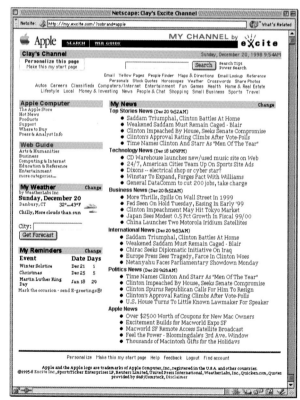

7.1   *Excite, and Excite Search, the Excite Logo are trademarks of Excite, Inc. and may be registered in various jurisdictions. Excite screen display copyright 1995-1999 Excite, Inc.*

My Netscape fares even worse (7.2), where the impeachment is already yesterday's news, and the horoscopes of the day seem to be the most prominent story. I suppose to some people they are. To be fair to the Netcenter news, I could customize this page to remove the horoscope as I have with my Excite Channel.

From an HTML point of view, the ability to customize pages and set cookies on the client machine is an important feature. It means that these "portal" pages can "know" what subjects I'm interested in, what local news, weather, and sports to deliver, and what stocks to track for me. Unfortunately, the Web portals I've seen do not have the ability (or smarts) to know what's "important." This is because they are really about data and not about information. Who's to say that the score of the football game isn't equal in weight to the vote from the House?

It's not difficult to turn data into useful information, but this is not part of the design of portal pages. I've assembled a collection of Web front pages for the day. *The Washington Post* (7.3), CNN (7.4), and

7.3

7.2

7.4

7·5

CBS (7.5), judging by their home pages, agree that the impeachment is the story of the day. All have a picture of our dishonored President, and all include a few summary words about the story. Clearly a human hand (and mind) is at work here.

WEB CITIZENSHIP 101

There are many places on the Web where you can find the complete text of the U.S. Constitution. This particular page of plain-vanilla HTML — no embellishments, just HTML headings — is maintained by the U.S. House of Representatives (7.6). There is no built-in search mechanism, but because the page is all HTML text, we can use the Find command in the browser to find references to "impeachment." This will bring us right to our favorite fragment of Article II, Section 4, "other high Crimes and Misdemeanors." (7.7) (I don't know why all the nouns are capitalized, but it does lend a certain air of gravity to the whole thing.)

This is a good example of pure source information. (It's also interesting to note how quickly this very long page of HTML text loads.) There's no bias here, just text. We can all read it, quote it, interpret it, and wonder at its ambiguities.

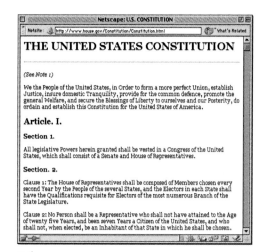

7.6

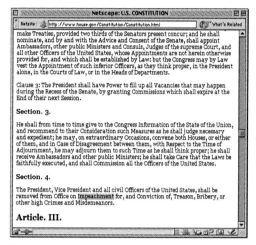

7·7

The online site for *The Post* has given us newspaper-like headlines translated into HTML. The broadcast news channels seem to favor text superimposed upon their images in a video-screen-like fashion. All these sites use a mix of image and text to convey the gravity of the situation. None of them does it as well as a one-inch banner across the printed page. And our eye isn't able to follow the headline to its story; our hand must do the work by clicking to it.

INFORMATION IS WHAT YOU MAKE OF IT

The newspaper sites give us a bit more to read on the front page, but you have to make the decision to read on by clicking. Once this decision is made, there's plenty to read. Without making a value judgement, it's pretty fair to say that finding information that we can read for factual detail on the Web is an exercise in clicking through, of following threads, links, hierarchies—whatever the Web architect has constructed to contain the information we seek.

I can find every nauseating detail of our public servants' sex lives on the Web if I spend enough time searching around. Or I can get a small daily dose in the paper or on the network news. Neither method has been shown to be more toxic than the other.

On the other hand, the Web allows us to look up the history of impeachment and the stories of Andrew Johnson and Richard Nixon, participate in forums on the subject, and even read the Constitution (see the sidebar, "Web Citizenship 101") and the entire transcript of the Starr Report and Congressional hearings online. Getting information from the daily paper is almost a passive activity by comparison to gathering information on the Web.

THINK GLOBALLY, CREATE WEB SITES LOCALLY

Just as we might choose a daily paper for the way it presents information, we will come to rely on Web sites that make information accessible in ways that are useful to us. These may be portals, Web-based versions of print media, or new reference sites that exist only on the Web. Of course, it doesn't hurt if the local paper also has a decent Web site.

We travel to central Georgia and *The Macon Telegraph*—not your national name-brand paper, but a middling-sized paper from a middling-sized community, a member of the Knight-Ridder chain of papers. Their historical take on the impeachment is both factually interesting, if brief, and somewhat lighthearted; without being impertinent, it's a pleasant change from the gravity we generally encounter. The High Crimes and Misdemeanors subsite resides within the larger context of the newspaper's site, but exists as an independent entity.

The home page (http://vh1337.infi.net/special/) relies on an animated GIF to catch the browser's interest. First the title appears (7.8), then images of the presidents who share the dubious distinction of congressional dishonor fade into view one at a time

7.8

(7.9–7.12). These are high-quality images drawn by a skilled caricaturist.

There is a pause after each image fades in to give us time to click for more details before the next image begins to appear. The animation has been carefully created to heighten the effect. When the montage is complete, there's a longer pause (nine seconds) before the sequence begins again. We can see all of this by examining the GIF file in a program such as Adobe ImageReady. This screenshot shows the sequence of 14 images (7.13). Under each frame is the specified delay time—shorter for the fading portions and longer for the pauses.

The animated GIF is a dynamic element, but there is nothing fancy or cutting-edge about this page. We can examine the page and see that the image has been cut up into an imagemap so that it's easy for browsers to find the links from this page. But there's nothing more complicated here than a couple of tables. That's all this page needs. It exists as a title page to a small historical pamphlet. It's like the large cartoon image that often accompanies the opinion articles on op-ed pages of newspapers. The image carries a lot of meaning all on its own.

7.9   *© 1998 The Macon Telegraph; cartoon © Tribune Media Services*

7.10   *© 1998 The Macon Telegraph; cartoon © Tribune Media Services*

7.11   *© 1998 The Macon Telegraph; cartoon © Tribune Media Services*

7.12   *© 1998 The Macon Telegraph; cartoon © Tribune Media Services*

7.13

MAKING FACTS LOOK INTERESTING

Clicking any of the four links takes us right to the information — snippets of presidential lore (7.14–7.18). The presentation of these pages is consistent and straightforward. The caricatures from the animated GIF reappear as slightly grayed-out background images. Emphasis is added to the text using straightforward HTML headings and red for highlights. A sidebar with graphs gives additional information and adds to the visual interest of each page.

These are not "high-content" pages. They contain summary information of a complex subject, and do it with grace and simplicity. The information is broken down into quickly digestible units, each unit of information nicely presented in a well-differentiated

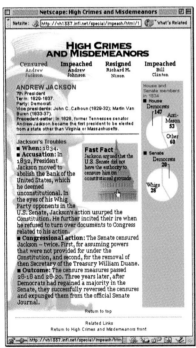

7.14

© 1998 The Macon Telegraph;
cartoon © Tribune Media Services

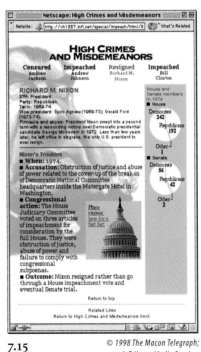

7.15

© 1998 The Macon Telegraph;
cartoon © Tribune Media Services

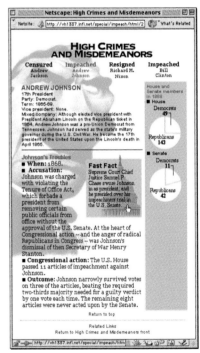

7.16

© 1998 The Macon Telegraph;
cartoon © Tribune Media Services

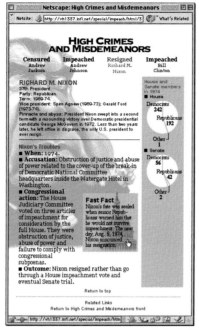

7.17

layout. Once again, it's just tables (7.19). When you examine these pages in a WYSIWYG-style HTML layout program, Adobe GoLive in this instance, you can see that an HTML table can be used to create a very strong graphic design.

This little site shows how important it is to pay as much attention to the hierarchy of information as to the hierarchy of pages. In a site this small, the navigation is trivial, so content really is king. This site's designers have made it much more interesting with the skillful use of first-rate drawings. They've layered the information through the traditional use of headlines and text positioning. They've added a sidebar of informational graphics with subtle shading to emphasize its separateness within the carefully constructed table grid.

There is an additional informational element included as a JavaScript rollover. On each of these informational pages is an image of the Capitol dome clearly labeled as a rollover (7.20). When the rollover is activated, a bit of trivia pops up.

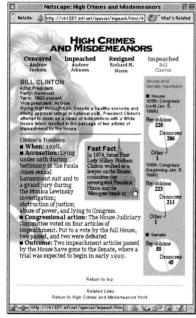

7.18

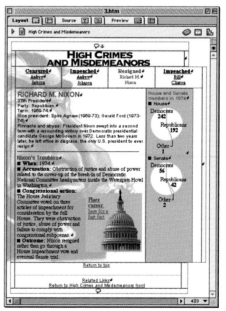

7.19

7.20

There's a couple more pages to this site: one of credits and another listing other Web sources for additional research (7.21). Notice how the simple navigation at the top and bottom is consistent with the rest of the site.

The information here is neither detailed nor comprehensive, but it is presented in an interesting and engaging way. If you compare this little corner of Americana to text books we have known, well, there's no comparison. In fact, take a look at Andrew Johnson's brief biography available from the official White House site (7.22).

There's more information here, but the presentation is as stale as day-old white bread. Notice, too, how the only navigation for this page is a pair of next and back buttons at the bottom. There's definitely a place for factual information presented in a completely straightforward manner, but when you're summarizing the life of a president in a single Web page, it helps to have something a little less dry.

It's easy to say that the political history of the United States is not dull, but it's another thing to digest and package it for a general audience. By treating their information with the respect due a front page story, *The Macon Telegraph* has succeeded in creating a small but valuable Web site. This is as much a lesson in the graphic presentation of information as in history.

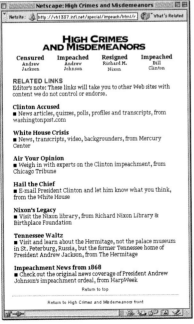

7.21   © 1998 The Macon Telegraph

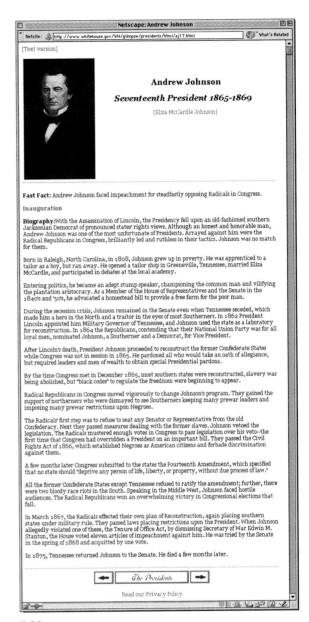

7.22

SELLING CONTENT

As the political soap opera of 1998 has made only too clear, we live in an age when we know too much. Yet, we want to know more. As Web architects, our job is to make as much information available as possible without overwhelming the viewer. Again, this is at least partially the job of information architects, a job that used to be a lot easier. For instance, given a collection of information to be printed as a reference, your only choice used to be to arrange it in alphabetical order. This is likely the world's most important organizing principle, something we all learned in grade school.

We all know how to look up a word in a dictionary or a name in a phone book. We've also learned through experience that browsing through alphabetical listings often leads to bits of knowledge we would otherwise never see. This aspect of browsing through pages or even browsing through the stacks of a library or book store is one of the benefits of research or shopping that is difficult to duplicate on the Web.

For instance, I was looking for information about the romantic composer Robert Schumann. Obviously, I could have searched through any number of search engines, but I decided it would be quicker and easier to use the old-fashioned method. I figuratively grabbed a handy encyclopedia, in this case Compton's Encyclopedia Online (CEO).

Compton's Encyclopedia existed long before there was a World Wide Web or even an Internet. This database of information has been collected and revised over decades. Its value is unquestioned. But it's not enough to translate printed text into HTML and expect it to be a compelling Web site, especially since the CEO is actually a commercial site requiring paid subscriptions for access.

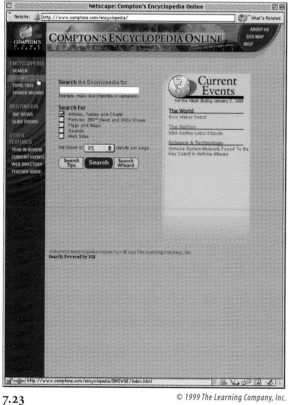

7.23

GOING BEYOND THE BOUNDS OF ENCYCLOPEDIC INFORMATION

The added value of CEO is in the different element types that the Web allows. The designers of this site have chosen to use a very basic graphic design to maintain clarity throughout. They've created a book-like template for the wide array of information stored in its databases. This makes it easier to navigate the site and find the information you're looking for, and it helps teachers to use the CEO as a pedagogical tool.

The CEO entry page (www.comptons.com) provides a number of ways to find information among the volumes of the encyclopedia (7.23). There's a search form similar to that of any search engine, and there are also links to alternate information-finding tools. These are presented in a persistent column of JavaScript rollovers down the left side of the page. An old-fashioned browse suited my purposes.

The browsing pages are arranged alphabetically with a list of head words indicating the range of each topic page (7.24). I clicked the *S* link at the top of the page to narrow the search and then the *Schoolmen to Scipio* head words (7.25). So far, I haven't done anything more than pull a volume of the encyclopedia off the shelf and begin thumbing through pages to get approximately to the right page. Using head words in the context of the Web at first seems like an anachronism, but it helps flatten what amounts to a hierarchical traverse down an alphabetical tree.

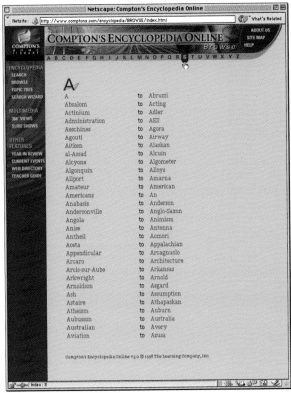

7.24   © 1999 The Learning Company, Inc.

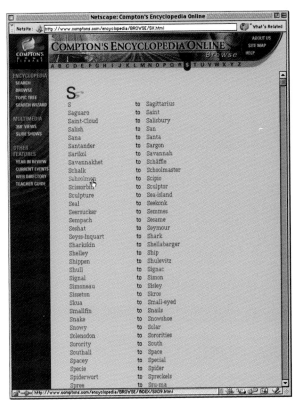

7.25   © 1999 The Learning Company, Inc.

At this point, the CEO shows a list of all entries within the head word range (7.26). Browsing down the list and clicking the first entry for Robert Schuman shows us immediately that Schuman with one "n" was a notable Frenchman. But before we click back to the famous two "n" Schumann, note the photograph on this page and its caption (7.27).

Obviously, someone at Compton's made the same error I did. This photo is of the composer and not the statesman.

Back at the browsing page, we can scroll down and see that there are many entries for Schumann with icons indicating shorter notes, longer articles, musical entries, and images. The main article is actually

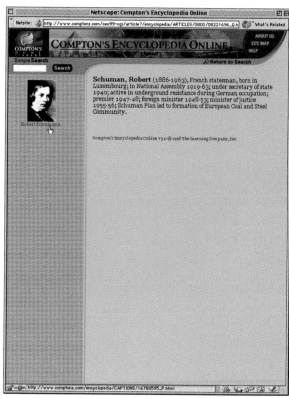

7.26   © 1999 The Learning Company, Inc.

7.27   © 1999 The Learning Company, Inc.

for both Robert and Clara Schumann, his wife, a famous performer and composer in her own right (7.28).

There's a brief article, a pair of thumbnails we can click to enlarge (7.29) (though the portrait of Robert is back with the Frenchman), and a list of musical excerpts. Clicking any of the links on the side, all of

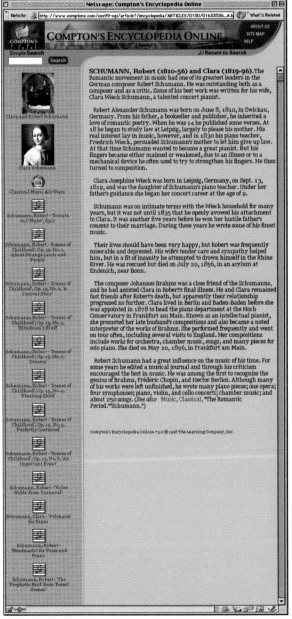

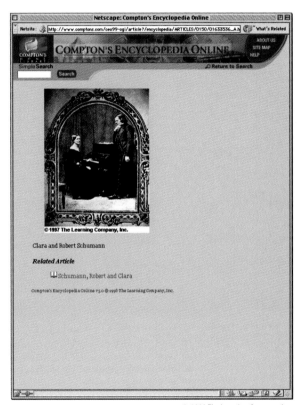

which have been cross-referenced to the article page, brings up a new page from the CEO database (7.30). Clicking a musical link starts the RealPlayer plug-in and downloads the clip (7.31).

The cross-referencing links appear to have been hand-coded by the creators of the database. It is a job that requires human decision making and is clearly prone to occasional error. But without it, a search might turn up the photo with no link to its associated article, so this is a valuable addition.

It took me six clicks to get to the information I was looking for. Was it faster than taking a volume down from the shelf to thumb through its pages? Given the load times for seven pages, probably not. But the Web version added some helpful audio clips, and there is also a potentially useful cross-reference to a CEO article on classical music. It is this ability to move quickly to related information that makes an online compendium of information more useful than the printed version. We are not limited to an alphabetical search; many other methods of finding information are available online.

CATEGORIES, CROSS-REFERENCES, AND SEARCH CRITERIA

Look at the CEO's site map (7.32). You can search, you can browse alphabetically, or you can browse through a so-called Topic Tree. This categorical search requires the information architect to assign categories to every item or article in the information database. The flip side of this activity is that there must be categories for every topic.

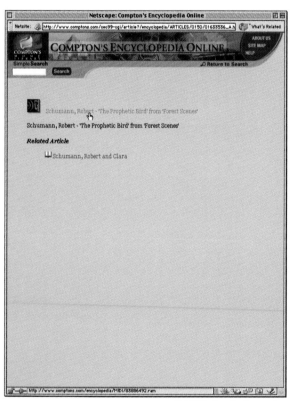

7.30   © 1999 The Learning Company, Inc.

7.31

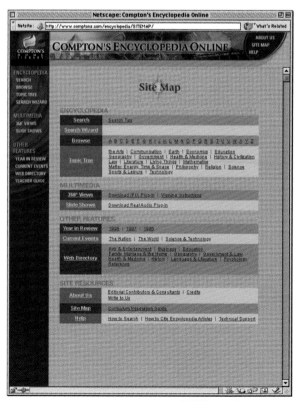

7.32   © 1999 The Learning Company, Inc.

The CEO has divided its encyclopedic realm into 19 categories, each of which is further divided into numerous subcategories (7.33). This form of topical categorization is becoming common on the Web. We see it at sites such as Yahoo! and Excite, where the categories have expanded over the years, along with an explosion of subcategories to cover the full scope of the Web's content. And, though not as thorough as others, the CEO includes its own Web directory of 11 categories (7.34).

There are also sections covering current events (7.35), the year in review, and a teacher's guide

7.34   *© 1999 The Learning Company, Inc.*

7.33   *© 1999 The Learning Company, Inc.*

7.35   *© 1999 The Learning Company, Inc.*

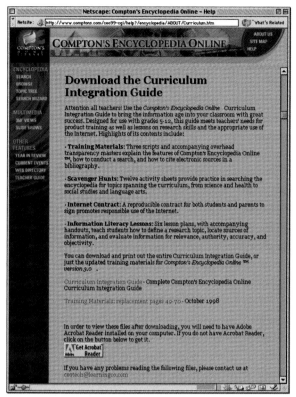

7.36   © *1999 The Learning Company, Inc.*

7.37   © *1999 The Learning Company, Inc.*

(7.36), all difficult and expensive features to add to a printed encyclopedia. This site is obviously meant to serve the traditional educational market. But by moving from traditional printed media to the Web, Compton's has been able to add multimedia items, more advanced search and browsing facilities, and up-to-date information, all of which strengthen the offerings of the encyclopedia considerably.

It's worth pointing out that through all the information presented on the CEO site, there is a single HTML layout of three frames. The left frame contains the first-level navigational links that are always available. The top frame image changes when you enter different sections of the site, but the three non-hierarchical links at the right, *About Us*, *Site Map*, and *Help*, remain the same (7.37). All the links in both frames use JavaScript rollover highlights as visual feedback to the user. All of this site's information is displayed in the main central frame.

One quickly becomes familiar with the way this site works — its look and feel, and this is important for a site that is intended to serve as a regular research tool. You don't want to have to spend a lot of time learning to find data. It should be as easy as, if not easier than, looking things up in a book. As Web searching becomes more standardized, the correct use of queries will become as important and commonplace as alphabetical order. By recognizing the differences in media, our designs can make traditional forms of information more broadly accessible.

FINDING A NEEDLE IN AN
ENCYCLOPEDIC HAYSTACK

Numerous reference sites are now available online, most of which are Web versions of printed reference books. If you want more detailed information than Compton's provides, subscriptions to the online version of the *Encyclopedia Britannica* (EB) are available. From an information architecture point of view, the EB, a much larger, more scholarly publication, was faced with more difficult challenges than Compton's. Here's how they dealt with them.

To get a handle on the scope of EB, take a look at the Encyclopedia Britannica site map (7.38). We can see from the JavaScript rollover pop-ups that there are tens of thousands of articles, all indexed, categorized, and cross-referenced, plus additional referenced materials from dictionaries, yearbooks, and other Britannica publications. Searches in EB turn up what seem to be as many references as we'd get from searches of the entire Web.

So where Compton's makes heavy use of multimedia elements, the EB has fewer of these, but a greater emphasis on cross-references. A search for "Robert AND Schumann" turns up 59 references listed in order of relevance (7.39). You can click a heading to open an article or click one of the *Related Resources* listed after each article summary. The EB does not use frames, so the sectional links at the top scroll up with the rest of the page. The left column is reserved for images, of which the EB has many fewer per article than Compton's. Notice how no hierarchical links appear on the search pages.

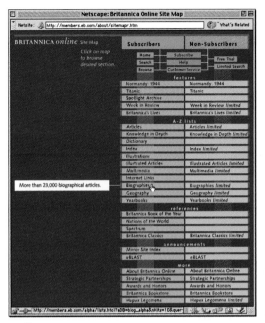

7.38

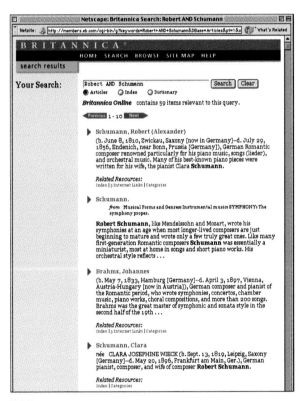

7.39

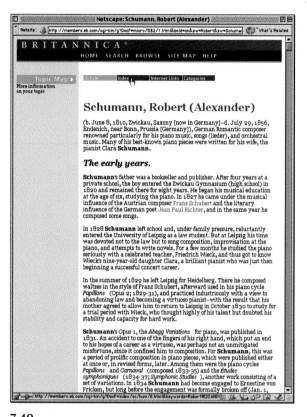

7.40

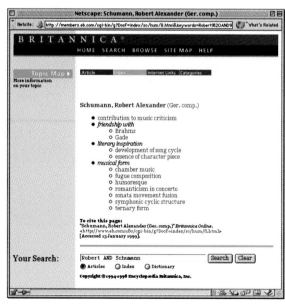

7.41

DESIGNING CONSISTENT TEMPLATES FOR INFORMATION PAGES

The article pages look much like the search pages, but with the addition of a *Topic Map* feature over the article heading (7.40). This provides a link to other links—the *Related Resources* of the search page. Clicking the Index link for any article builds an entire index for it (7.41). As far as information gathering goes, this is an extremely powerful research tool. It takes all the tedious legwork out of research; all that's left is to click the links and read the articles.

The *Internet* and *Category* links are included at the bottom of each article along with a bibliography (7.42). You can see that where CEO is built for a secondary school audience, the EB creates serious summaries that can lead to primary research. There is much more detail and, from an information architecture point of view, many more ways to get at it.

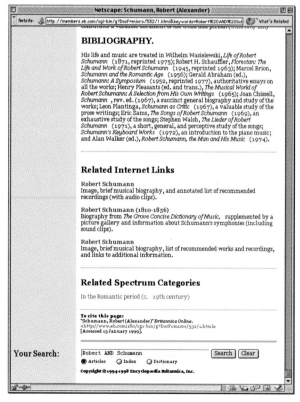

7.42

Even the design of the EB emphasizes its enormous database of information. The HTML is simple. There are relatively few multimedia elements, though this is likely to change over the years. Images are used for the top banner of each page and some of the special linking buttons. No special formatting is used on the text, so readability is a matter of browser defaults or user settings. Pages like this load quickly, with only slight delays for the backend database searches to bring up the information and build the pages on the fly. EB even maintains international mirror sites so that access won't be delayed by transatlantic travel to the home servers in England.

The *Encyclopedia Britannica* has always emphasized the weight of its volumes as a testament to the thoroughness of its research, and the EB Web site stresses the same values. To these, they have added easy access in the form of powerful search and cross-referencing tools, and it's these that make the site worth paying for.

DISSEMINATING INFORMATION BEYOND THE IVORY TOWER

Search engines and categorical browsing have become standard fare on the Web. These are the best ways to provide nonhierarchical access to information. For Web-wide searches and for sites with a broad range of information, these are the most efficient ways to guide the user. However, we're becoming so accustomed to these forms of goal-oriented information gathering that we may forget that associative browsing can still be a more direct and enjoyable way to locate information.

Within more closely focused sites, there's much more that can be done to present information in ways that are appealing and that encourage further exploration. Museums fall easily into this category, because even though they may hold an enormous range of things, their focus is always well defined. Even massive organizations, like the American Museum of Natural History (AMNH), are tiny when compared to the breadth of information contained in an encyclopedia.

MAKING GREAT HALLS FOR WEB INFORMATION

The Web site for the AMNH must serve several purposes. It must serve the public, as its exhibitions do, as well as provide information about the ongoing research of staff scientists. The Museum's magazine, *Natural History,* is one outlet for this mixed mission, and its Web site provides another way to disseminate information well beyond the walls of the museum itself.

The AMNH home page (www.amnh.org) is clearly intended to function as a great hall leading to the Museum's exhibitions. There is a column of six hierarchical links down the left that comprise the more permanent *displays* of the site and a matrix of changing images that link to the changing exhibits. These small square images are two-frame animated GIFs that blink between an image and a title (7.43,

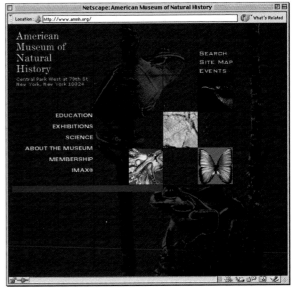

7.43   *Courtesy Museum of Natural History*

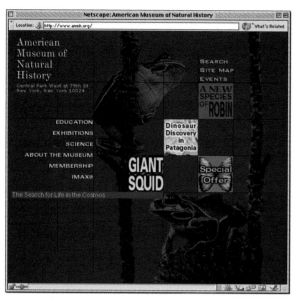

7.44   *Courtesy Museum of Natural History*

7.44). A Java applet is used for the rolling message in the blue rectangle under the hierarchical links, and there are three nonhierarchical links, *Search*, *Site Map*, and *Events*, that can be found in the upper-right corner on most of the section pages of the site.

We can see from the site map that the site is divided into five second-level sections, which are further divided into subject categories (7.45). The first section of this site is devoted to information about the museum and its programs, which is not the kind of information this chapter is concerned with. If this were a corporate site, I would categorize this as marketing information. However, most of the rest of the site is devoted to biology, paleontology, anthropology, astronomy, ecology, and exploration. Let's look at the facts.

ENSURING INFO DIVERSITY

The BioBulletin is a subsite within the AMNH domain that is updated quarterly (7.46). It is a function of the Museum's new Center for Biodiversity and Conservation, which serves to increase awareness of

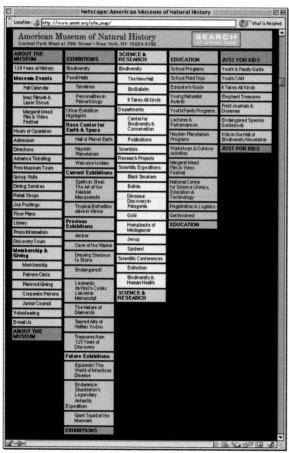

7.45   *Courtesy Museum of Natural History*

7.46   *Courtesy Museum of Natural History*

the world's dwindling species and our efforts to reverse this trend. There are four feature stories each quarter, presented on a map of the world to emphasize the global scope of the problem. There is also a Java applet with a rolling bulletin of messages at the top of the page. All the links on this page (and most in the site) are JavaScript rollovers, with the rollovers for the feature stories changing the map heading.

The home page for the BioBulletin contains two frames. The main frame is the BioBulletin subsite, and the thin frame across the bottom contains links back to the main Museum site. This effectively creates an autonomous site within the AMNH domain, which is how this subsite is maintained. The Science Bulletins Group creates the content separately from the rest of the AMNH site, and it's possible to view the BioBulletin pages without the AMNH frame at the bottom (see Note).

Everything in the design layout of this page emphasizes the horizontal. Within the feature frame is a strip of hierarchical links, *Success Stories* (7.47), *What You Can Do* (7.48), and a link back to *The Hall of*

NOTE

The frame constructs of HTML work by creating pages that are divided into sections that refer to other HTML pages. Any link that loads within one frame has no effect on the content of the other frames on that page. So it's possible to build a complete site and load the home page into a single frame of another site. This creates a site within a site, which is the way we're viewing the BioBulletin pages.

The BioBulletin site is maintained in its own directories and can be viewed as an independent site. But when you visit the site from within the AMNH site, the AMNH navigational frame remains at the bottom, making BioBulletin effectively a subsite. It functions exactly the same, but includes the capability to link back directly to other AMNH pages.

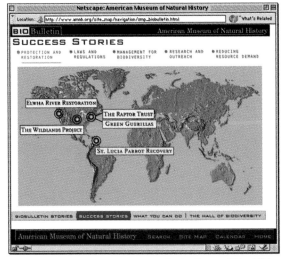

7.47   *Courtesy Museum of Natural History*

7.48   *Courtesy Museum of Natural History*

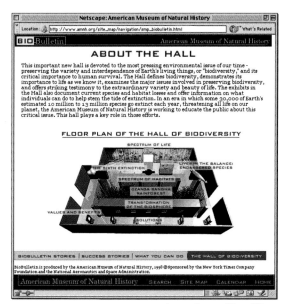

7.49   *Courtesy Museum of Natural History*

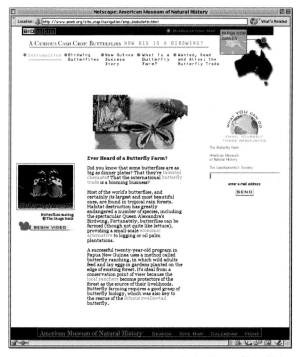

7.50   *Courtesy Museum of Natural History*

Biodiversity (7.49). There's much to read about here and more activities will be added to the site over time. All of the content for this site matches the exhibits in the Museum's Hall of Biodiversity. In fact, the feature stories are first created for kiosks in the hall and then put up on the Web site.

"We considered using Director for the kiosks, but that would have required a port to the Web version," said Alissa White, copartner and creative director of MediaFarm, the New York design firm hired to create the kiosk displays for the Museum. "So we decided early on to create everything in HTML. The main difference is that the resolution of the kiosk displays is 1024 × 768, while we took it down to 800 × 600 on the Web."

Let's take a look at the feature story on butterflies, "A Curious Cash Crop: Butterflies, How Big Is a Birdwing?" The bullet on the map shows that this story is primarily about butterflies in Papua New Guinea, and this ties over to the first page of the feature, which includes a small inset map of the island nation (7.50). This introductory page includes the familiar BioBulletin banner across the top and the AMNH navigation frame across the bottom. Both use light-colored type on dark backgrounds, which clearly differentiates them from the main features.

This is a cleanly designed page with a lot going on. All the page elements are arranged in two centered tables (pictured here in Adobe GoLive to show the cell and table borders) (7.51). There are three columns topped by the headline and a number of links leading to the chapters of the story. The story segments can be viewed in any order, which makes these links hierarchical rather than sequential.

The left-hand column contains a small image and a link to an introductory video in RealPlayer format. The right column is used for additional links to related sites or for pull quotes from the feature story. The wider center column has a collage on top and the text of the story. There are many informational links used within the text to explain terms or connect to related items within the other story sections.

Each section of the story is up to a dozen pages long, and there are tangential links to information outside of the story. There are next and back buttons to lead you sequentially through the story (7.52). Material in the columns changes to reflect the content, whereas the hierarchical links across the top remain the same.

Although the information is presented in small pagefuls to make it more easily digestible, the articles are not as short as we've come to expect on design-oriented Web sites. This is because the AMNH site is an information-oriented site that also happens to be well designed. In *The Hall of Biodiversity*, there are seats at the kiosk displays so that museum goers can read the stories. The experience is the same for Web browsers. You can read straight through articles as if they were in a magazine, or jump about freely to the next interesting chunk of information, which is the way we've grown used to using the Web.

7.51

Courtesy Museum of Natural History

7.52

Courtesy Museum of Natural History

PUBLISHING SITE CONTENT

If you think about these articles, they are not so different from those that appear in *Natural History* magazine, with its lush photography and generous spreads. We can see both the advantages and disadvantages of publishing this kind of information on the Web. The information can be broken down much more clearly on the Web and organized to take advantage of other resources, like a glossary or links to other sites. But the photographs in the magazine are much more beautiful, larger, more detailed, and generally more engrossing.

And like the magazine, the BioBulletin site is a publishing venue. It is built out of templates that are filled from a database containing the story text and images for the articles. Danny Scheman, White's co-partner at MediaFarm, refers to the BioBulletin site as a "publishing system." MediaFarm has built an editor's interface to the database so that the Museum's Science Bulletins Group can update the site with new stories without getting involved in HTML coding or issues of file loading and serving. Updating the database updates the site.

In fact, while I was viewing the site with my botanist brother, we came across a small identification error in the caption of one of the images. We informed the site maintainers at the Museum, and the correction was made within the hour. This system of creating an editorial interface with templates that are filled from a database is similar to that used by many of the most popular sites on the Web. Any site where the information is updated regularly must be designed so that the HTML doesn't need to be re-created every time. In the case of the BioBulletin site, the updates are quarterly, but for newspaper sites, Web portals, weather sites, or even catalogues (see Chapter 8), information is always changing.

SHAPING INFORMATION

The Web gives us the ability to update and exchange information instantaneously. This is as important in the advance of human knowledge as the invention of movable type and the printing press. For Web architects, the rate of change of information doesn't necessarily change the way we design and build a site. A stock price doesn't look any different for having changed one second earlier. The urgency of information doesn't necessarily affect its relative importance to other data on an informational page. There are many other factors besides timeliness that affect the ranking and display of information.

Take, for example, a dictionary. We think of this kind of information as being fairly static. My 30-year-old American Heritage should be as accurate as my new Random House, and they are in fact both fine references. But even the rate of change in the English language is increasing, and neither of these is really up to date.

It's obvious that putting these resources online will enable them to include the latest usage, but will the same standard encyclopedic listing format provide the most usable organizing system for the Web? I think it's just as obvious that it does not. As standard references go online, the familiar two-column layout with headwords is being replaced by direct word searches.

As we discussed earlier in this chapter, it's also possible to add browsing capability to aid searches through an alphabetically ordered list. But words don't categorize as easily as entries in an encyclopedia. In order to make online dictionaries and their ilk truly more useful than their bound equivalents, a new way to visualize data and associate data elements is needed—and I just happen to know of one.

LOOKING DIFFERENT, THINKING DIFFERENT

Right from the first page we are told that "The Plumb Designs Visual Thesaurus is an exploration of sense relationships within the English language. By clicking on words, you follow a thread of meaning, creating a spatial map of linguistic associations." (7.53) This doesn't sound like an alphabetical list. Welcome to the brave new world of Thinkmap, a Java-based data animator.

Thinkmap is also a proprietary development tool created and used by the Plumb Design group to give their clients uniquely interactive sites where the data becomes the animated images. (Thinkmap will likely be a commercially available product in the future, but is not in distribution currently.) But I don't want to turn this discussion into a promotional piece for Thinkmap. Instead, let's see what happens to information and the way we interact with it when it's presented using a technology like Thinkmap.

The Thinkmap applet loads while we are reading the short explanation of the Visual Thesaurus. Then we must click the page to open the Thesaurus window (7.54). Immediately we know that this isn't your typical thesaurus. Words float across the window, arranging themselves in some sort of logical order, a "sense relationship" in Thinkmap terms (7.55).

Before we actually do anything with this application, it helps to know a little of what's going on behind the scenes, as described by Plumb Design itself: "The Visual Thesaurus accesses data from the WordNet database, a publicly available resource developed by the Cognitive Science Laboratory at Princeton University. This database, first created in 1985 as a dictionary based on psycholinguistic theories, contains over 50,000 words and 40,000 phrases collected into more than 70,000 sense meanings."

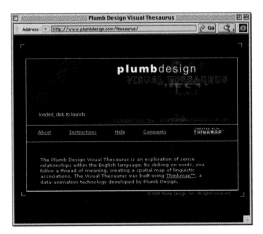

7.53

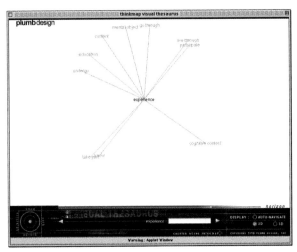

7.54

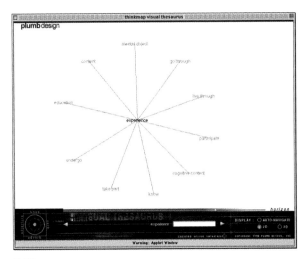

7.55

7.56

When you compare the WordNet experience to the Visual Thesaurus, you can see that the presentation of data makes a huge difference. WordNet uses a standard search form and displays results as a text list (7.56). It's hard to believe that the information in these two displays comes from the same database. We don't even need to make a value judgement here. The two interfaces are different and serve different purposes. From our perspective, the one is traditional, providing nothing that a printed version doesn't already offer except speed, whereas the other lets us make word associations in a way that only linguists might have been able to before.

From a design perspective, the WordNet page is usable, but unremarkable. The emphasis is on information straight out of the database. It's up to us to read through and make sense out of it. Speaking lexicographically, the information on this page is clear, concise, and insightful. But it does not lead the browser to further investigation. The next step is completely up to the browser's initiative.

DATA BECOMES INTERFACE

Interview with Michael Freedman, director of new business development, Plumb Design, Inc., New York

Q: How did you come up with the idea for Thinkmap?

MF: Thinkmap was invented by my partner, Marc Tinkler, as a way to understand Web traffic — real-time analysis of data that is constantly changing. We view it as a powerful tool that enables people to navigate through and better understand complex interconnected information.

Q: And what about the Visual Thesaurus?

MF: To test our software, we look for publicly accessible databases and develop unique interfaces to them. The database in which the thesaurus is based is an incredible resource for understanding the English language, but we're just scratching the surface of it. When we first launched the VT, we thought of it as merely a demonstration

The Visual Thesaurus applet presents information in a way we're not used to seeing it. This may take a moment to digest, but it is also such an interesting display that it invites investigation. Without knowing what will happen, we immediately want to start dragging the words around or clicking to bring links to the front and create new links — word associations. Clicking on the word "content" sends Thinkmap back to the database for more information. The new root word becomes highlighted, and a new group of word associations floats into view (7.57). If we let the display continue floating, it eventually reaches a stable, but still floating, state (7.58).

Although this page is dominated by the display window, there are also a number of controls across the bottom. Because there are many synonyms for content, we can narrow the scope of the display by bringing more pertinent information forward. The control in the lower left-hand corner of the display lets us highlight synonyms according to what part of speech they are. The default position gives equal weight to all

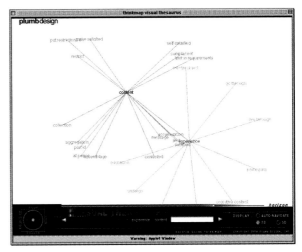

7.57

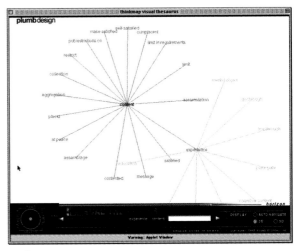

7.58

of Thinkmap, but we're getting a lot of notes from people using the VT as part of their everyday lives. They might be looking for names or the right word, and they pop words into the Thesaurus, set it to autonavigate, and just wait. People are being very creative.

Q: Why put a new interface on an old list?
MF: If you just want one word, the text-based interface is probably better. But most people use a thesaurus to find the right-sounding word with only a vague idea of what they are looking for. A standard thesaurus is great, because lists are great. But you can't navigate lists. With Thinkmap, you can get close to the word you are looking for and then navigate until you find the perfect word.

Q: How do you make information from a database more accessible to Web browsers?

MF: There's a lot you can do with really well-designed database-driven sites. But it's not just a matter of how information should be stored — the information architecture. We're trying to fuse information architecture and site architecture. With the Thesaurus, the information architecture becomes the actual architecture for the site. Our interest is in interface design — next-generation design where the data itself becomes the interface.

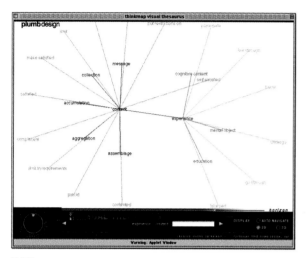

7.59

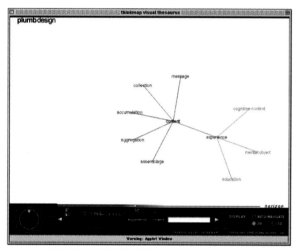

7.60

word associations. When we click "noun," the nouns move closer to the root word and the other words move away (7.59).

At this point, the display is getting a bit crowded, but by adjusting the horizon slider the amount of information—the depth of the search—can be decreased or increased (7.60). Usually the search engine controls the display, but in this case, the user is in control. I like the association between content and experience that the Visual Encyclopedia has drawn for us here. We wouldn't see this if we'd used the conventional WordNet interface.

You navigate through the information by clicking words to create new associations (7.61) or by using the navigator bar to click previous associations or to type in a completely new word to look up (7.62). You can also scroll through the history list of root words, using the back and forth arrows. It is an interface rich with possibilities for examining the data.

The Visual Thesaurus display can get pretty cluttered, but this is an accurate reflection of the data, which is itself complex. We can control the complexity of the display and thereby hone in on what we're looking for. It may be that for a simple one-word search, it's easier to use a conventional thesaurus. But for associative searches, those where we know approximately what we want but aren't quite sure of the right word, the Visual Thesaurus provides a kind of access to information that we've never had before. Here's a Web-based interface that makes possible the kind of serendipitous discoveries you have thumbing through reference books or browsing through volumes in a library.

The beauty of Thinkmap is that it is a generalized data animator; it will work with any number of standard databases. It's written entirely in Java, so it's completely platform-independent. This means that any organization with information already stored in a database will be able to use this method to browse through their data. The site developers must create the rules for building associations, but it is the browser that orders and categorizes the information simply by navigating through the data. Information never looked so good.

INFORMATION AUTOMATONS

The Thinkmap technology organizes existing information and then presents it in such a way that we see it differently than we otherwise might have. A couple of sophisticated products are also available that concentrate on the automated organization of existing knowledge bases, but with more conventional presentation engines. These are perhaps more important for information architects than for Web architects, but they provide a structure for information that directly affects the design of sites.

Semio calls itself "a pioneer of text mining software that enables medium-to-large sized organizations to increase the value of undiscovered knowledge buried within large volumes of unstructured, text-based data." By *text mining*, they mean text indexing and extraction, the building of "lexical networks," which they call "concept clustering," and the graphical display of information, including navigational elements.

In other words, text mining does for unstructured collections of text-based documents what data mining does for numerical information. Sounds like the basis for an informational Web site, but we shouldn't leap forward too quickly. Semio intends its product primarily for use on intranets, so there aren't a lot of publicly accessible Web sites using this technology. It's just too bandwidth-intensive for the mass of modem-bound Web users right now. But it is clearly a portent of things to come.

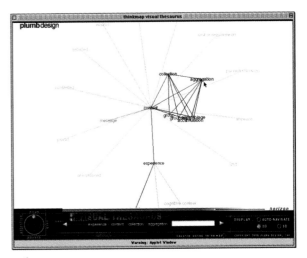

7.61

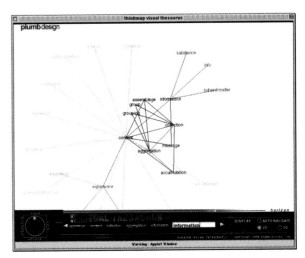

7.62

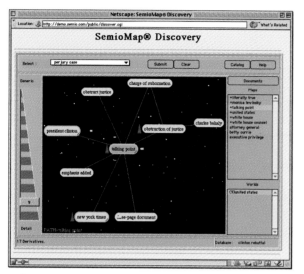

7.63

SemioMap's Discovery display bears a striking resemblance to Thinkmap's interface (7.63). But this is due more to outward appearances, the use of nodes and links, than to similarities in their functionality. SemioMap's associations are fixed in their spatial field rather than floating as they are in Thinkmap. But the associations take on extra dimensions with links to other maps and worlds. The nodes themselves refer to articles that have been associated with the subject through the text mining process.

On the other hand, Inxight sells its Hyperbolic Tree for Java specifically for Web use. Here's how they describe their product: "Inxight Software is the premier supplier of knowledge extraction and visual navigation components for information-intensive applications in the Business Intelligence, Knowledge Management, and Electronic Publishing industries." But what does it all mean?

Given a collection of information — call it a knowledge base — Inxight provides a means to organize and display this information on the Web. So instead of painstakingly designing a navigation system, Inxight creates the hierarchical navigation scheme for you. Numerous demonstrations of this technology are provided at the Inxight site, including one for the American Museum of Natural History (discussed earlier in this chapter).

Here's what the AMNH site looks like presented as a hyperbolic tree (7.64). You can see that one of the nodes on this tree links to the Center for Biodiversity, and we could click this node to go to its page. The entire structure of this site is on display, and it's evident where there is more and less content. Clicking a node brings it to the center of the display along with its subnodes, which become available for linking.

You can see that large collections of existing data can easily be presented on the Web this way. Inxight does not "mine" associations the way SemioMap does, nor does it create free-flowing associations of ideas as Thinkmap does. But it is able to present linked associations that are easily navigable for a user browsing the information.

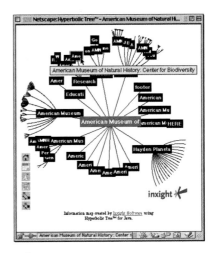

7.64

CHAPTER 8
MARKETING SITES:
IT'S ALL ABOUT SELLING

T oday we are going shopping. If I had written this book a year earlier, this chapter would be much less interesting, or at least there would be less to write about. But in the time warp that has become known as "Web time," commerce is consuming the Web. There's nothing that can be sold that can't be sold on the Web. Happily for me, the hottest items seem to be books, with the inexplicably successful amazon.com leading the way. Computer hardware and software, electronics and cameras of all kinds, clothes, gifts, music, and even stocks and bonds are finding buyers eager to place orders over the Web.

Not even fears of insufficient Internet security have stemmed the rush to sell on the Web. The percentage of retail transactions occurring electronically may still be small, but all reports from the last holiday shopping season and the months that passed since indicate that the rate of increase in Internet commerce is huge.

This isn't surprising. Most obviously, Internet shopping is fast and convenient, and it doesn't require finding a parking place. Less obvious to all but Web architects and designers is the fact that Internet shopping can be a positive experience. Although most Web commerce sites are little more than catalog lists, a few well-designed sites bring much more to the display. The elements may be different, but the same sophisticated design that goes into a successful store is necessary for a compelling Web e-commerce site —

Most e-commerce sites quickly corral the user into a very mechanical, software-driven ordering process. It's often like entering a beautiful showroom entrance, only to be suddenly whisked away to a giant warehouse to select your product, then pay a teller in the corner making change out of a shoebox.

ANDREW SATHER, ADJACENCY

a site worth visiting because it has interesting features, or just to see what's new.

The common metaphor for Web commerce is the electronic shopping cart. There are a number of server-based applications that allow us to create a catalog of items for sale — the database. You can then build an HTML front end to select items from the list, put them into the metaphorical shopping cart, and finally process the order. Because such transactional software is changing and becoming more sophisticated faster than it can be documented, we'll concentrate on the front-end design issues.

THE STRUCTURE OF SELLING

To find a successful Web shopping experience, let's turn to an expert in retail selling — Starbucks. Starbucks isn't so much a purveyor of coffee as the definition of the late-twentieth-century American essence of coffee. You can buy a cup of coffee at any of what seem like dozens of neighborhood Starbucks coffeehouses, but that's not why this brand has become synonymous with coffee. It's about packaging, and in this case, every Starbucks store is the package — the furnishings, the décor, the products, and even the people that work there. Is it possible to duplicate this kind of experience on the Web, and more important, will people buy it?

BUYING AN EXPERIENCE

Here we are at the Starbucks home page (www.starbucks.com), empty coffee mug in hand (8.1). It's early February, and in case I'd forgotten, Starbucks is reminding me that it's time to make my Valentine's Day purchases. The site loads with a start-up image of figures drawn in a style that has served Starbucks well over the years. The colors are retro, as is the cartoony style. It's supposed to make us think romantic thoughts of Paris bistros (the French poodle), of Roman holidays (the word "Amore"), and maybe even of coffee. It's humorous, hip, and aimed directly at Starbucks' loyal customer-base. This isn't my favorite drawing style (or color scheme), but it serves its purpose well and sets a mood effectively.

This introductory page is made more welcoming through the use of a simple animated GIF. You can click to link to the next page, or the page will automatically refresh to the Starbucks home page after 20 seconds. The Refresh variable of the `<META HTTP-EQUIV>` tag is used to achieve this effect. The effectiveness of this page depends on regular updates. Anything that stays around too long will quickly grow stale. The same is true for the home page.

Starbucks' seasonal home page features the pink color scheme and the same couple sitting down to a single cup of what one presumes is coffee at the Caffé Amore (8.2). We know that it is sunny on the streets

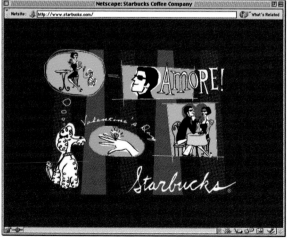

8.1

8.2

of this romantic European city, because both figures are wearing dark glasses. This is just a single background image over which lies a complex table of images. As you can see in this screen shot taken in Adobe GoLive, most of the images are text images, several are sliced and divided across multiple table cells, and only two contain HTML text (8.3).

The home page includes the familiar Starbucks logo, links to the main hierarchical sections of the site (store, company, coffee, and business services), and a featured item from the store that you can link to directly. There are at least a dozen links from this atmospheric home page, but for this chapter, we're most interested in *The Store.*

The top-level page for Starbucks online store continues the Valentine's Day theme with a bouncy "Ciao Amore!" Prominently displayed under this is a gift suggestion that we can click to directly, without searching (8.4). These elements change as often as the holidays and the weather. The more permanent residents of this page include the steamy blue swirls of the background image and the navigational elements across the top (8.5) and down the left side (8.6). The main display area is divided into two columns over a white background. The featured item is on the left, and the right column includes links to special sections, the *Gift Matcher,* the *Doonesbury & Starbucks* collection, and the *Coffee Taste Matcher* (8.7).

8.4

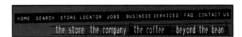

8.5

8.6

8.7

8.3

When you look at the image of the entire page, you might assume that this was a frames-based layout (8.8). It is not. Instead, everything is arranged in tables, including an embedded table for the featured item's price listing. How does all this work as a store?

MAKING CHOICE THE PRIME SELLER

The top navigational elements provide links that cross the site hierarchy. Because they are all slightly askew, an imagemap is used for the links instead of table cells. The Dymo label–style links are mainly nonhierarchical and provide direct access to various specific features of the Starbucks site outside the store. The four jaunty links under the Dymo strip represent the main hierarchical sections of the site. Sections are differentiated by title and background color. But none of this pertains to the store, only to the store's site within the site.

The left-side navigation is store-specific. Each of these headings links to hierarchical sections within the store. There is also a count of items currently in

your shopping cart, a product search field, and two nonhierarchical links at the bottom indicated with green, instead of the section-specific blue backgrounds.

As you can see, there are four ways to reach the store's catalog: direct access for a couple of featured items, hierarchical categories that enable us to peruse what's available, product search, and the two "matcher" links. For starters, we'll go straight to the specialty of the house, *Coffee by the Pound.*

Even without frames, the layout remains basically the same—the same site-wide top-level navigation, the same section-specific left-side navigation with the addition of coffee categories, and the same main display area (8.9). Starbucks has systematically broken down their wide range of coffees into five categories, thereby deepening the hierarchy of this site.

8.8

8.9

All of Starbucks' coffees are listed on this page. This page (like most in the online store) includes one item we can order directly, Caffè Verona, "the perfect romantic dessert coffee." This item changes seasonally. If this is not the item we want, we can proceed down the ordering hierarchy, either by choosing a category from the left-side navigation bar or by clicking one of the coffee names. The most direct route to the coffee of choice is the Coffee Quick Pick menu (8.10). Simply select from the drop-down menu and click the Add to Cart button.

And as if these weren't enough ways to select coffee, Starbucks also has the *Coffee Taste Matcher* link: "Let our Coffee Taste Matcher help you find the perfect coffee to suit your taste." I suspect that for many buyers, the selection of coffees is a bit overwhelming, even intimidating. Everything about this site in general, and this section specifically, is geared toward a friendly, casual ordering experience. Like a waiter who always compliments the diner on her order: "An excellent choice, signora."

8.10

MAKING TASTE VIRTUAL

The Taste Matcher is a simple form with radio buttons for the choices (8.11). This coffee drinkers' profile consists of seven multiple-choice questions, for which there are no wrong answers. They've worked hard to make this questionnaire nonthreatening, with the result that some of the answers seem whimsically ambiguous; but we're not taking the SATs here, so a little fun is okay. Who knows? Filling out the Starbucks Taste Matcher may prove to be the first great Internet party game.

This is not a fancy game requiring a plug-in technology, but a straightforward form based on standard HTML. (The HTML for this form is included on the Web site that accompanies this book, located at http://www.idgbooks.com/extras/webarch.html.) It's not even a particularly sophisticated questionnaire. Clicking the Send button submits the answers to a look-up table that matches coffees to your profile of answers.

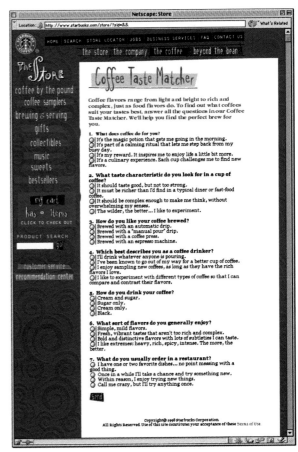

8.11

8.12

8.13

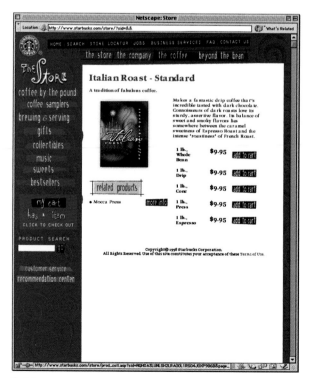

8.14

The results list provides me with a choice of ten taste-appropriate coffees, each linked to its description and ranked as a Sure Thing, Adventurous, or Daring choice (8.12). I'll take the sure thing, Italian Roast. It reminds me of my romantic trip to Venice many years ago. See how evocative a name can be. Despite my naturally skeptical nature, this site seems to be having its way with me.

Which brings us to the actual ordering page (8.13). So far, this site has been all about experience with little about shopping. It's all soft-sell. Even the coffee labels are heavy with taste-appropriate imagery. This is Starbucks' stock-in-trade; we know it's good coffee, because we feel good about it. But now we have to make a decision. Click one of the Add to Cart buttons, and the item is added to our shopping cart. We're still on the same page, but a Related Products item has been added, and in the left-side navigation bar, our shopping cart has been updated so that it now contains one item (8.14).

We haven't actually bought anything yet. In fact, we're encouraged to browse further and add more items to our cart. But a pound of coffee is all we needed. (If I lived in the civilized world instead of the hills of Connecticut, I'd just head down to my very local Starbucks outlet, but that's a different experience.) The standard Web shopping metaphor includes a cashier, where we must now proceed to check out.

CASHING OUT

The Starbucks online store is designed to make product selection pleasant and easy. We lingered over our decision, but we could have expedited matters by going straight to our coffee of choice. And choice is what coffee buying is all about. There's something for every palate. Now it's time to put the trappings of finely designed marketing behind us and let technology take over.

We click the Click to Check Out button. The shopping cart software that has been tracking my purchases displays the order, a pretty simple matter since there's only one item (8.15). I can edit the order, choose to keep shopping, or check out. And lest we forget, I could simply leave the Starbucks Web site at any time without completing a transaction. But it's coffee we came to buy, and it's coffee we'll get.

But we can't check out without giving Starbucks some information. All of the processing of shipping and billing forms is handled by the shopping cart software. For repeat customers, Starbucks will keep this information in a cookie on your computer for you. Then you can sign in with your name and password and avoid some of the tedium of filling out forms (8.16).

Even though the shopping cart software is doing most of the work at this point, the designers of this site have embedded all the transaction details in the familiar blue store layout, and they're using the same friendly buttons to help make the process feel a bit more intimate and less cold.

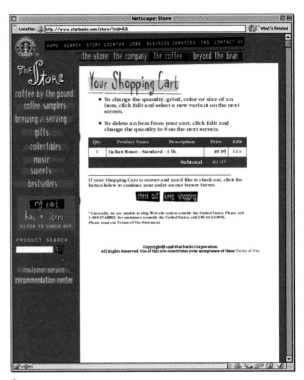

8.15

8.16

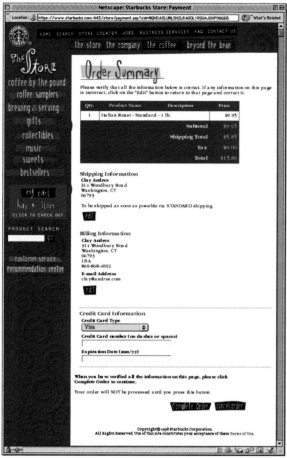

8.17

The site has been successful in every way. The navigation helped us make our selection, and the design and choice of elements made us feel good about our selection. But if we were to decide that this system isn't the most efficient way to buy a single pound of coffee, we could exit gracefully by clicking the Cancel Order button (8.17).

Structurally, Starbucks has done everything right in order to gain loyal Web customers. The site is now familiar to me, I've signed up with an online account, and I know that if I want to send a gift in the future, the Starbucks online store is a convenient and pleasant place to go.

SUBSTANCE OVER STYLE

Welcome to the vertiginous online world of Patagonia, where substance is style and the beauty is in the details. Here is an understated home page (www.patagonia.com), relying on one of those patented Patagonia photographs where yet another Patagoniac is seen challenging the wilderness, showing a glimpse

E-COMMERCE IS SERIOUS BUSINESS

Interview with Andrew Sather, creative director and CEO of Adjacency, San Francisco, CA

Q: When did you build your first e-commerce site?
AS: We did our first e-commerce implementation from scratch back in 1995, before there were any e-commerce packages. We always bet that the Internet was about empowering and engaging and giving users tools and information. All the others thought the Web was going to be like TV, all about advertising. We saw that one right.

This was the first big e-commerce Christmas. 1998 was the year of e-commerce. By the end of 1999, 95 percent of our clients will be doing e-

commerce. We have ongoing relationships with a lot of our clients, and two or three years ago they wouldn't have considered e-commerce. Now they're all doing it.

Q: What difference does the e-commerce package make to the site design?
AS: We have used many packages based on our clients' IT preferences, but have found that most of them can't handle the traffic and seriously limit functionality. Functionality should not be dictated by the limitations of the software but by the user experience.

of Patagonia gear, just barely identifiable as such (8.18). This kind of photo is the signature of Patagonia's picture-book-quality catalogs. For the cognescenti, these photos bespeak the Patagonia style and define its image, which is, oxymoronically, the antithesis of "image" and the absence of "style."

At the same time that Patagonia follows the road not taken, its market is decidedly familiar and Web-savvy. (Excuse me while I pull a Patagonia parka over my Gap khakis before heading out to Starbucks.) The difference is that Patagonia does not celebrate style or fashion per se, but is instead focused on its mission of making lives better. It does this with evangelical fervor, supporting environmental causes and at the same time making the world a better place for Synchilla.

These values are reflected in the Web site and the online store, which are economical in their use of space and pages, yet full of detailed information about the Patagonia line and Patagonia causes. This site is a celebration of Patagonia people as much as Patagonia products.

8.18   © Copyright Adjacency, Inc.

Functionality should be dictated by the brand promise. A brand's personality can be used throughout as a touchstone for the way the site should interact. Brand and user experience should dictate how an e-commerce site functions. That's why we prefer Open Systems technologies: Oracle databases on Sun servers running Apache.

Q: How difficult is it to design e-commerce sites, and how much does the design really matter?
AS: Too many people design e-commerce sites to a lower visual stan-dard than other sites, because they're just stores. It has to be beautiful to be useful. On the other hand, it's easy for a designer to design a great-looking car. But it's a lot harder to make a car that goes and looks great. It's more important for designers of e-commerce to under-stand the technology.

Q: How do you take a brand and create an e-commerce site for it? Do you have to start with a marketing site and add retail functionality? Are the two things different?
AS: Strategy drives everything we do.

We use good design to realize our stra-tegic vision, and technology supports and enables the design. That's the logical flow. For instance, the idea that you have a shopping cart disgusts us. Plenty of stores in the real world don't have shopping carts, but it's part of every e-commerce package. It's brand-inappropriate.

We see a logical flow from a marketing site to e-commerce. The only difference is in the proportional relationship be-tween functionality and design. You're no longer designing a publication. It becomes an application. We've always

8.19

8.20

8.21   © Copyright Adjacency, Inc.

FINDING ADVENTURE IN SHOPPING

Hierarchically, the site is divided into two sections, the online store and the corporate site. The home page provides equal access using JavaScript rollovers to guide the intrepid Web browser (8.19, 8.20). Today we'll be traveling the trade routes.

Patagonia has been on the Web for nearly four years, during which time the San Francisco–based Web design firm, Adjacency, has inimitably defined their Web presence. The site started small and has gradually expanded, adding the online store over a year ago and redesigning it a few months ago. You could almost say that the site has grown organically as the Web and Web technology have grown. What we see are the fruits of a long-term relationship, a refined site honed through time and experience.

The Store's home page also features a photograph of a woman defying both nature and gravity (8.21). It's almost as if Superwoman purchases her tights from Patagonia, and it is these that gave her the ability to perform superhuman feats. There are also two iconic images under the heading "How would you like to browse?" The choices are "By Activity" or "By Product Type."

---

viewed it as an application. It's interface design, it's not like reading a book. It's more process design.

Take the Patagonia brand. It's always been an R&D-driven company. It's full of enthusiasts. They're driving everything from the functionality of their products. Everything they make accomplishes a task. Look at their Web site. It's beautiful in its simplicity. It's not garish. The rich image is the image of the product. The image quality within the store is very good. That's important because people need to know what they're getting. There's a huge amount of information about their products and their environmental soundness. That's driven from the philosophy. It's driven by products, not fashion statements.

What we've always done is see the Web as a way to present vast amounts of information that people can take or leave. All Web sites need to tell you how a product fits your specific needs.

In this case, there are two category fields: activities, which includes snowboarding, biking, paddling, climbing, and so on, and product type, which includes jackets, pants, shirts, hats, surfboards, and so on. These are not hierarchical site divisions, though they may appear to be. All the product information is kept in a single database, and we are given a choice as to how we would like the data sorted for presentation. If we analyze this online catalog as a collection of data instead of products, we see that by adding categorical fields to the data, we increase the number of ways the data can be sorted and organized.

There is also a navigation bar, or a combination of navigation bars, across the bottom of the page. The first gray bar has a search form that can find products by five-digit catalog number, the quickest way to view a specific item. The second light-blue bar includes a drop-down menu listing ten best-sellers and three nonhierarchical store links for general information, queries, and comments. Both these strips use HTML text for the linking buttons. The bottommost beige strip provides hierarchical navigation across the site, with the *Online Store* link highlighted as the current browsing location. These are GIF images.

FOLLOWING THE TRAIL

Here's what we get when we browse by activity. In technical terms, the first sort criterion is activity (8.22). From a design perspective, notice that there are no fussy backgrounds. There are page titles and links in horizontal bands of color, but very little to distract from the information on the page. Let's start at the top of this page and work our way down.

8.22   © Copyright Adjacency, Inc.

Across the top of the page is a gray strip with a drop-down menu that lets us change the primary browsing field at any time (8.23). We are never stuck with a single sort method and can switch our browsing method as it suits us. But even though this element heads the page, it is not what our eye sees first. In fact, it is so understated that it's possible to ignore this primary navigational element completely. But by putting it at the top where we're used to finding navigational links, Adjacency has made it appropriately accessible. And as we'll see, it also provides primary hierarchical navigation for the online store.

Next down the page is a blue horizontal strip providing a contrasting backdrop for the page title, "Browse by Activity," which overlaps (engaging) the photograph (8.24). And under this is a detached gray strip with three small anchor links, *Men's, Women's, Kids'*. This is actually a line of HTML text in a table cell with a gray background. Since the page is too long to fit into a browser window, clicking one of these scrolls the page down to the linked anchor points dividing the contents into these three groups.

The three page divisions follow. *Men's* and *Women's* are divided into ten identical activities, but some of the product types within the activities differ. The *Kids'* products have not been categorized by activity, so the product type categories are listed on this page. To choose the appropriate garment for a given activity, you select from a drop-down menu. So if I were looking for a pair of trousers to wear while cross-country skiing, I would use the appropriate activity menu and select Technical Jackets and Pants (8.25).

Before we leave this station to follow the trail to the products pages, let's finish our overview of this major site terminus. Across the bottom of the page are some additional navigational elements. This is the same strip of elements we saw on the store's home page,

but without the product search by catalog number. It's assumed that you wouldn't have come to this page if you were looking for a specific item from the catalog.

EXAMINING THE DETAILS

Now we're ready to look at products. Choosing a product type from one of the activities sends a request to the database to build a page of thumbnail images. Because the entries in the database change seasonally, and most items can be found in multiple categories, these pages must be built on the fly. In our case, there are seven items that fit the activity and product type we've selected, Men's Running/Biking/Etc., Technical Jackets and Pants (8.26).

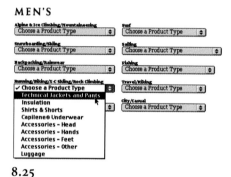

8.25

8.23

8.24

Even though the information on this page is very different, the layout is the same as it was for the Browse by Activity page. Notice how the top navigation bar has been extended to reflect the depth of our travel within the Online Store. Because we're still browsing by activity, the pop-up menu gives us immediate access to the other product types within the currently chosen activity (8.27). There's a new photograph (and new credit at the bottom of the page), a new page title to reflect the activity, and an additional subtitle to indicate the product type within the activity. The bottom navigational element remains unchanged.

Sandwiched between the colored bars of the top and bottom navigational elements are thumbnails of the products we've selected and links to related information. A single GIF file, retrieved from the database, comprises the image of the item and the item name. The price information is not stored with the GIF, but in a separate numeric field. It is retrieved at the same time and added as HTML text to the same table cell.

The sidebar of Related Info fills a gray box to the right of the thumbnails. For this page, there are links to articles about layering, shell performance, and shell features. These come from the catalog, where they are used at the beginnings of sections or as sidebars. On the Web site, links to them can be added wherever they apply. But there's a problem with linking to articles that take the Web shopper away from the product pages. How do you get back to where you left off?

Adjacency recognized this problem and used a little of what Andrew Sather, Adjacency's founder, calls "special sauce" to solve it. When you link to a page of related information, it, too, is built on the fly, just like the product pages (8.28). This allows the page to be aware of what came before it so that it can include a link back. In both the top navigation bar and at the end of the article are Back to Thumbnails buttons. When you're done with the article, you can go right back to the same products page you came from.

This is not standard HTML nor any of the latest HTML extensions, plug-in technologies, or client-side scripting tricks we've touched on elsewhere in

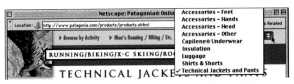

8.27　　　　　　　© *Copyright Adjacency, Inc.*

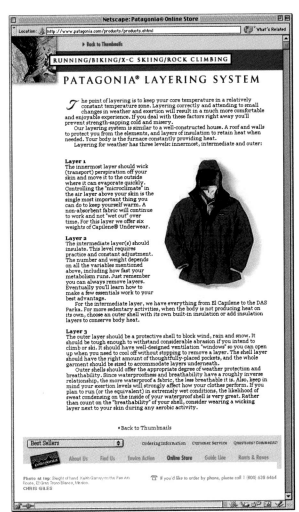

8.28　　　　　　　© *Copyright Adjacency, Inc.*

CLIENT OR SERVER, WHICH SIDE ARE YOU ON?

The terms *client side* and *server side* refer to the relationship of computers in a network and the location of any processing that's going on. Specifically, the Internet is often referred to as a peer-to-peer network, because processes, most often in the form of messages, pass from one computer to another, and all nodes on the network are more or less created equal.

But for some Internet processes, this equality changes to a client/server relationship. An obvious example is with databases, where you would never download an entire database of information to be processed on the local machine. Instead, the database resides on a server machine where the actual queries are processed, and then the requested data is transmitted to the client machine. The process of displaying and analyzing the data can take place on the client machine.

Java applets are transmitted from the server machine to the client machine, and it is the software on the client machine, the Java run time module, that interprets and executes the applet. This is a client-side technology.

Perl is a programming language that runs on servers. It can be used to generate database queries, build HTML pages from the results, and then transmit the answers to client queries in the form of finished pages. This is a server-side process. It does not share the platform-independent qualities of HTML or Java, but can generate platform-independent results for transmission over the Internet.

this book. It requires server-side programming in a language like Perl (ModPerl and ePerl in this case) to intercept the client-side information, get the requested information from the database, and build pages to send back to the client (see the sidebar, "Client or Server, Which Side Are You On?"). In most cases, especially with a well-designed site like Patagonia's, we're not really aware that this is happening. Things just seem to work smoothly.

Now that we know Patagonia's philosophy of layering, we can return to the thumbnails page and click the Storm Cycle Pants to find out what they're made of. The product pages are also built on the fly from information in the database. The layout is similar to the pages we've already examined, except that there's no Patagoniac-in-action photo to compete with the high-quality product photo. "You have to know what the product looks like," says Sather. Also, there are previous and next arrows and a Back to Thumbnails button in the blue title bar (8.29).

8.29   *© Copyright Adjacency, Inc.*

What's happened is that an entire sequence of product pages has been built, and we can browse back and forth between products on the thumbnails page. If we had been looking at a different product category, the thumbnails page would have been different, as would the sequence of product pages. There's a lot of attention being paid to the way browsers use an online catalog, and it shows in subtle touches like these.

The product information sandwiched between the familiar navigational elements includes a photo of the product, color swatches, a succinct description, and order form buttons. There are also many more details available. Click the image to see it enlarged. There is a gray strip of product-specific links for sizing (8.30), details (8.31), and to view a companion piece (8.32). All these pages are assembled with links built specifically for the current browsing session.

Every product page that is built includes size and color selection drop-down menus. The item name, number, and price as listed in the current catalogs are

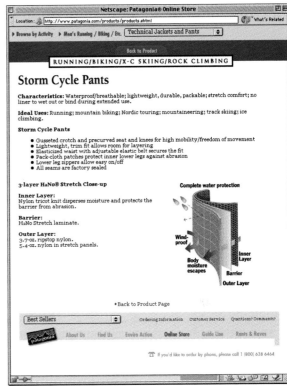

8.31   © Copyright Adjacency, Inc.

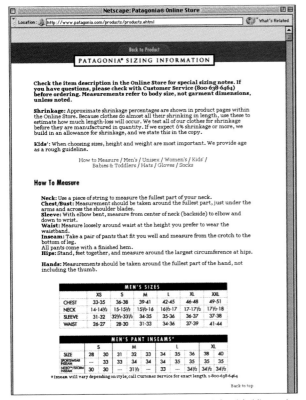

8.30   © Copyright Adjacency, Inc.

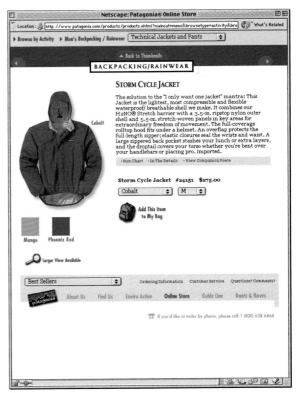

8.32   © Copyright Adjacency, Inc.

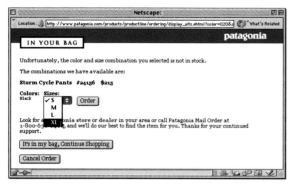

8.33   © Copyright Adjacency, Inc.

8.34   © Copyright Adjacency, Inc.

added after the description. And, of course, each product page includes an "Add This Item to My Bag" button. Appropriately, Patagonia uses the backpack metaphor instead of the shopping cart or shopping bag.

There's more user-friendly intelligence in the ordering process. When an item is not in stock, instead of a simple message (or worse, in some e-commerce sites the item is backordered before we can change our selection), we are given alternatives. In this case, black trousers instead of blue appear, and we can change the order or cancel it on the spot (8.33). It's easy to keep this level of detail in a database, and in fact, it's necessary for a well-run online store. The trick is to design and program the Web-based user interface to use this information.

Our activity-based product search helped us to make a selection quickly and provided us with a level of detailed information that I don't think can be found at any other Web commerce site. It's the Patagonia way. Let's also examine the Browse by Type shopping experience.

There are no drop-down menus from which to make further choices on this page, but an additional category for *Other Stuff We Make* (8.34) is included. Instead, all the appropriate subtypes are listed, and we can click them to go directly to thumbnail pages. This time we'll click on *Men's Insulated Pants.*

The resulting page of thumbnails has a new list of products, but it has been built in exactly the same way the previous thumbnail page we examined was (8.35). The query is sent to the database, and the template page is filled with the data that's returned. Note that the link and title information is different to reflect the new route we've taken to the products.

Speaking generally, the procedures for Web commerce are already pretty well established. Once an order is entered, we can continue shopping to add items to our "bag," or we can "check out." The Patagonia site makes the order form available for instant viewing while you continue to shop. An additional navigation bar is added to the bottom of all the store pages. It uses the same blue fill as the title bar at the top of the page, and includes a drop-down menu with a list of all items in "My Bag" and a "Go to Order Form" button (8.36).

This additional bit of order-specific navigation is implemented as a frame so that it persists across the bottom of the page as you continue shopping. In fact, this frame is a part of every page, but it remains empty — in other words, there is no file referenced by this frame — until an item is added to "My Bag."

The checkout page is a straightforward HTML form, which, like everything in this site, seems to be

8.35   *© Copyright Adjacency, Inc.*

8.36   *© Copyright Adjacency, Inc.*

8.37   © Copyright Adjacency, Inc.

8.38

designed with an eye toward detail (8.37). It's not a big thing, but the layout of this page makes it pleasant to look at, easy to follow, and just a little bit nicer than other order forms. It's a small part of the positive Web shopping experience.

There's something very lush about the Patagonia catalogs, and the online store has the same feel. Yet it is not fussy or (in Sather's words) fluffy. There are no animated elements, no eye-catching images, just high-quality photos of products and Patagoniacs. It's a lushness born of simplicity, if such a thing is possible.

Founder Yvon Chouinard sums up the philosophy of Patagonia with a quotation from Antoine De Saint Exupéry, a philosophy closely adhered to by the Adjacency design team: "In anything at all, perfection is finally attained not when there is no longer anything to add, but when there is no longer anything to take away, when a body has been stripped down to its nakedness."

MAKING SHOPPING INSANELY GREAT

Do you think Steve Jobs, the most Zen of computer executives, would agree with Chouinard and Saint Exupéry? Would a fruit-flavored iMac meet Patagonia's standards of perfection? It's certainly the perfect accessory for one of Patagonia's brilliantly designed outer garments. The comparison of Apple to Patagonia is not as far-fetched as it may first appear. For starters, both companies boast cult-like customer followings and both have Web stores designed by Adjacency.

But before we rush headlong toward a lime green iMac, let's see what a typical PC vendor's store looks like as a point of reference.

From the navigation bars alone, it's evident that Dell's online store (www.dell.com/store) is an integrated section of Dell's larger corporate site (8.38). The top and bottom navigation bars that sandwich the content of every page of this site are nearly identical except that the top bar uses icons for the link buttons, whereas the bottom bar does not. These icons, along with the Dell logo, are the only graphic images on this page.

This is an orderly layout with attractive icons and appealing colors, but what is Dell selling? The emphasis seems to be on categories of buyers, but buyers of what? Except for the understated subhead, "Buy a computer direct from Dell online right now," you would barely know that this site was selling computers. Where's the focus? To be fair, it's unlikely we'd be here at all if we weren't looking for computers.

"Dell's online store is nothing more than a visual articulation of their channel model," said Adjacency's Andrew Sather. "It doesn't address the end user. It's saying: 'This is how we're structured as a business.' It's not addressing the user need, but the company's need to categorize people."

So it's categories they want, but I want to know what computers they sell. There seem to be lots of choices. The trouble with these categories is that they don't define distinct segments of the market. Instead of guiding us to the right computer, Dell forces us to make a decision about ourselves that may have little or nothing to do with our computing needs. This may seem like a fine point, but what happens if our business has exactly 400 employees? Then, according to the Dell online store, we are neither large nor small. Should this really affect what computers we buy? And if I only have 399 computers, will I get less attention than a company with 401 computers?

But because I mentioned iMacs, let's see what Dell puts into the Home/Home Office category. The layout of this page is consistent with its predecessor, but this page actually has pictures of computers on it. We can choose a desktop (Dell Dimension), laptop (Dell Inspiron), or follow the Software & Peripherals link (8.39). The only information provided about these systems is in an animated GIF that is really just a banner ad for the new 366 MHz Dell Inspiron.

We can go from this page to one of the three product lines chosen for us, or we can use the drop-down menu to select one of four specific models. A bunch of other links also appear on this page. On the left are links to store information, and on the right are links for *Dell Deals* and *Dell Extras*. With tangential links on each side, hierarchical links top and bottom, and an intentionally limited screen size, there's very little display space left for information about the computers.

I don't want to dwell on the shortcomings (from a design and usability perspective) of Dell's online store for too long. The Dimension page lists two models with numerous configurations available for each (8.40). All of this is squeezed within the four-sided

8.39

8.40

8.41

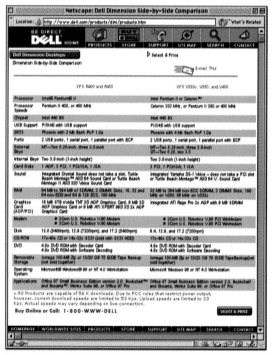

8.42

navigational fencing mentioned before. Do I want an XPS R or a V Minitower? The descriptions aren't much help.

Clicking the little Learn More button brings up a list of features. This has the best picture so far of what the Dimension really looks like and a long list of links for more information about this model's subsystems (8.41). We can go to a side-by-side comparison of the two models (the buttons in the left-side navigation bar), but this looks like the ingredients list from a box of cereal (8.42). Go ahead, read the fine print. I assure you no Dell computer is made with cottonseed oil. More important, you can see that those persistent hierarchical links aren't helping us much here.

We can go back to the information page that got us here or back to the selection and price page we saw before that. This is good, but we can't really go forward to get additional information from this page, which is a dead end.

To be fair, it's easy for Web architects to criticize a site that follows the status quo without fully considering issues of usability, aesthetics, and design. A quick survey of computer manufacturers and online computer retailers shows a pretty similar approach. Pick a category, select a computer model, then configure. If you want to know more, we'll add plenty of links around the edges. Once we all agree that this is the working model, who's to complain? It's obviously usable, because lots of people are using it to order computers.

Cut to the Apple Store (www.apple.com) (8.43). Any questions? We know it's about computers, we know what they look like, we know how much they cost, and we know that there's other stuff. We even know that the iMac comes in five colors, because its image is an animated GIF that cycles through the fruit flavors.

This page is as clean as they come. The images and text are listed hierarchically from top to bottom, largest to smallest, most important to least, all centered into a perfect pyramid of information. There are no hierarchical navigation bars, just a black strip of store-specific informational links across the bottom, with the Apple logo used as a link back to the corporate site.

Want to know how fast the new iMac is? First you'll have to choose a color (8.44). Some might say that this color selection page is too whimsical and simply gets in the way of the ordering process. But really it is a way to make the most of the difference between the Apple brand and other computer companies. And after all, the most talked-about new feature *is* the color case, not the 33MHz bump in processor speed. The only link added to this page is a simple Back button in the upper left-hand corner. Let's go on.

It doesn't matter which of the new colors we select; the product specification page is the same. But it's

8.43

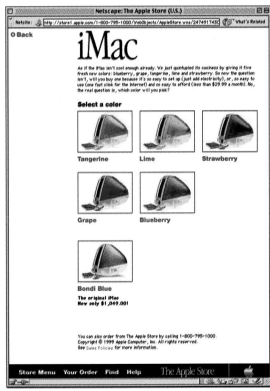

8.44

built to match the color we've chosen (8.45) The information is the same, only the images, supplied from the product database, change. Actually, the text, too, comes from the database. This makes it easy to update the database for price or configuration changes without changing the page templates.

We've got a neatly lined up side-by-side comparison here that tells us at a glance the difference between Good, Better, and Best. The *Learn More* link gives a

nicely laid out list of specifications (still displaying the lime color we selected) (8.46). There's also a link to a spec sheet in PDF format that's easy to print out. (Purchasing departments like to have these things printed.) We can read all there is to know about the guts of an iMac (including a 266MHz PowerPC G3 processor and 512K backside level 2 cache running at 133MHz) and then click a Back button to put us right where we were before.

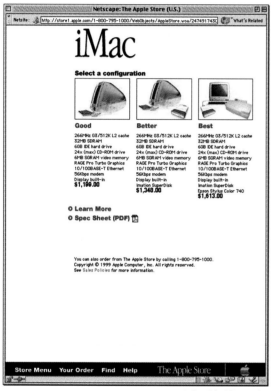

8.45

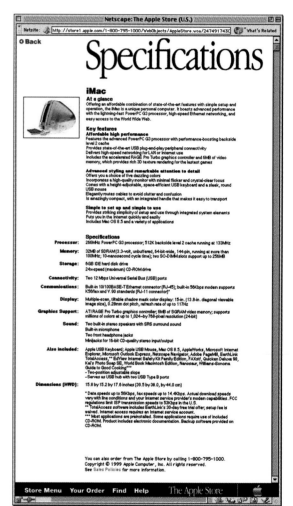

8.46

Clicking Good, Better, or Best takes us to the Info & Options page (8.47). The iMac image heads the column (in our chosen color of lime), and there's a summary of the base configuration. Below this we can choose from several add-on items, each of which is listed with a price and a Learn More button that gives the item's vital statistics. At the bottom of the list is the order total, which can be recalculated by clicking the button.

The iMac does not have many options available from the Apple Store, but let's take a look at the PowerMac G3 page (8.48) and its associated Build to

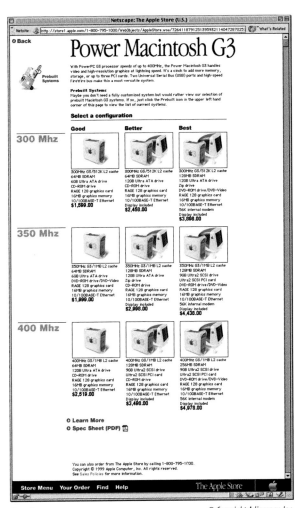

8.47

© Copyright Adjacency, Inc.

8.48

© Copyright Adjacency, Inc.

Order page (8.49). These pages are built on the same templates used for the iMac, but they're supplied with different information from the database. The product page shows a 3 × 3 matrix of 9 systems, each with an image, configuration specification, and price. It's so simple, yet it's really a masterpiece of side-by-side-by-side comparison.

On the Build to Order page (notice how each page is clearly titled so you always know where you are), there's an image of the new ice and blue G3 and summary information next to it. The Options list stretches down the page so that you have to scroll to look at all the items, but each is identified with a high-quality image next to it and explained in a *Learn More* link that's clearly marked. At the bottom is the subtotal and recalculate feature.

Options are chosen from drop-down menus that include the item name and the price differential from the current configuration (8.50). This feature is actually very similar to the Dell site. The difference here is

8.49   *© Copyright Adjacency, Inc.*

8.50   *© Copyright Adjacency, Inc.*

that there's a visual clue for every option, and the layout is more generous, not confined to a randomly narrow column width. Sometimes information just can't be squeezed into the space that's chosen for it. This often happens when a design parameter is established for reasons that have nothing to do with the information to be displayed. You often see this with printed material, as well.

This is a humanistic approach to computer ordering. Take a box and fill it with your choice of options from whatever happens to be on the shelf. Or choose one of the preconfigured systems and don't bother to think about it. What makes this so humane is that all the choices are there. The site, and the corporation behind it, are not making any assumptions about the customer, and the ordering experience is what the user makes of it.

Click the Continue button at the bottom of the page to move on to the Info & Options page, which again is built on the same template as the iMac version of this page (8.51). There's a longer list of add-on options to choose from and an additional Modify button next to the summary information in case you want to return to the Build to Order page to change the configuration. The three-page checkout sequence

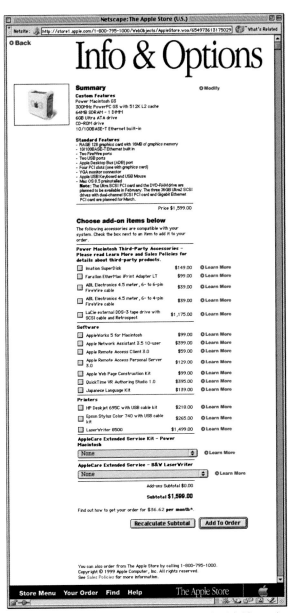

8.51

is similarly user friendly, a model of forms design (8.52, 8.53, 8.54).

The layout here is unfettered, expansive. There's no clutter to distract or encroach on the matter at hand. The information is presented in a way that's clear and readable. Also, even though we have to scroll to see the details, we can digest the whole page at once. We know what to do without needing to link to a page of ordering instructions.

A modular page design like this is necessary for any e-commerce site. Things will change, and change must be accommodated without calling for a designer every time. If Apple came out with its rumored

eMac line of personal information managers tomorrow, these would fit right into the forms, templates, and order processing protocols of today's Apple Store.

Although Adjacency prefers to build its e-commerce sites using Open Systems, they are able to work with client preferences when requested. When NeXT was purchased by Apple, the WebObjects database system came with the company. This object-oriented applications builder was used to define all the diverse elements that make up The Apple Store—the systems, pages, and orders that a complex Web shop consists of.

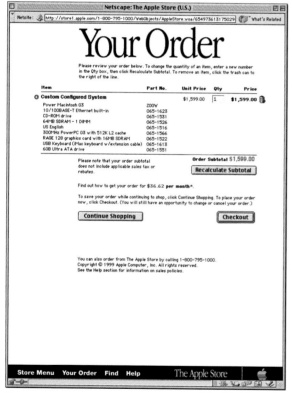

8.52   © Copyright Adjacency, Inc.

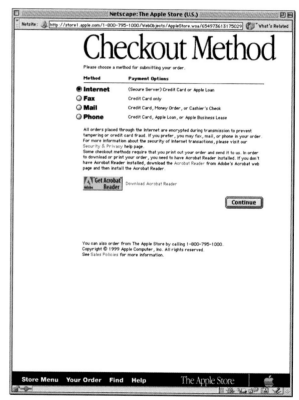

8.53   © Copyright Adjacency, Inc.

Object-oriented technology is by its very nature modular. It's especially useful for modeling real-world events and interactions. This emphasis on modularity also allows scalability, so that a small application with relatively few transactions can be built efficiently and then expanded and scaled up to enormous size just as efficiently.

In comparing a development system like WebObjects to the various e-commerce packages available, Sather does not mince words. "WebObjects is a cool, robust product that allows you to hook up to different database systems really, really easily. It's not a package, it's more of a tool, like Java. It doesn't tell you what the end product should be like. Anything that's powerful that doesn't try to predetermine what the end product is like is good. Packages are great for Bob's Bake Shop. But big brands that have too much to lose by not getting it right can't go with the packages. They'll get better, more modular, but they aren't there yet."

Adjacency, which views all Web sites as applications, has used the object metaphor and object-oriented tools to create an e-commerce site that is successful both functionally and aesthetically. As Web architects, we can't help but be insanely impressed.

8.54

© Copyright Adjacency, Inc.

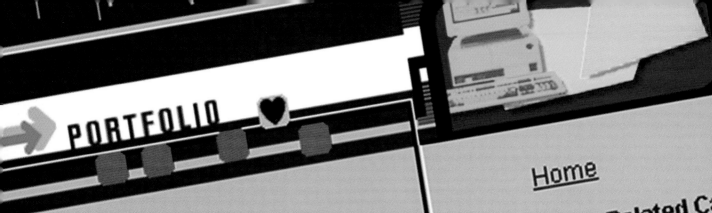

PORTFOLIO ♥

Home

Other Related Ca

IBM RS/6000

Webspy

mom razorfish web

o school

ber 1996

zorfish

pany. Like a
nesses, a
of us are still
he ears.

wn up and having fun now in the naked city,
big you think you are, you're never too big for

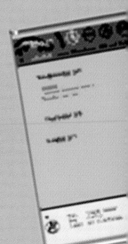

calendar

CHAPTER 9
ESTABLISHING AN IDENTITY: SELF-BRANDING

I t's fascinating to look at the houses architects design for themselves. Given the opportunity to express themselves without worrying about the petty concerns of clients (Who cares if the bathroom has no doors?), what does the unfettered imagination of the master bring forth? Philip Johnson's Glass House, Frank Lloyd Wright's Taliesin, and Mies van der Rohe's Barcelona Pavilion are all fascinating studies of whimsical design turned into reality. Similarly, it is often the sites of Web architects themselves that attract the most attention and admiration from their colleagues.

DEEDS SPEAK LOUDER THAN WORDS

We'll begin this chapter where we left off the last one, with Adjacency. How does this group that's so successful at defining the essence of brand identity and then translating it to the Web handle their own Web persona?

The first thing you see on the Adjacency home page (www.adjacency.com) is color: bright red. Right in the middle it says "Adjacency, **brand** new media," with an emphasis on brand (9.1). It's bright and bold, but at the same time understated and elegant. Most of all, it's succinct, it loads quickly, and in four seconds it refreshes to Adjacency's menu page. This page also employs a hidden design trick. A JavaScript is used to open this window to a width of 670 pixels, which is the design width for the entire site. (This JavaScript can be found at the Web site that accompanies this book at www.idgbooks.com/extras/webarch.html.)

Effects are easy. For simple elegance, you really have to sweat.

ONE WHO'S BEEN THERE

9.1

©1997 Adjacency, Inc. (www.adjacency.com)

WHOSE BRAND IS IT ANYWAY?

Adjacency's menu page is divided down the middle: menu and Adjacency-specific information displayed on a red background to the left, client logos and awards displayed in a white background on the right (9.2). The left is all about the Adjacency brand and the right is about the brands that have made Adjacency successful. Adjacency would like us to believe that they have made these well-known brands a success on the Web, too.

This divided page looks like other standard two-frame arrangements we've examined in this book, with navigational elements in one frame and content in the other. This makes it easy to update the content — for instance, the What's New information on the logo side of this page — without changing the menus.

Oh, but it's not really a simple two-frame construction; it just looks like one. That vertical stripe down the middle is actually two more frames, each containing nothing more than a background color and a 6-pixel width specification. (The page layout of four vertical frames is shown here in Adobe GoLive (9.3).) Nothing is left to chance or the vagaries of browser versions and platform differences. Doing it this way ensures perfect alignment every time.

The left navigational frame uses animated JavaScript rollovers that are especially nice (9.4). Instead of being either "up" or "down," the buttons appear to depress as you roll over them, as if there were a movie attached to the action. Even the shadow depth changes. It's not exactly ultra-realism, but there's a hint of life in the animation.

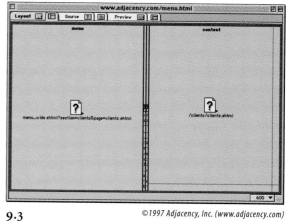

9.3   *©1997 Adjacency, Inc. (www.adjacency.com)*

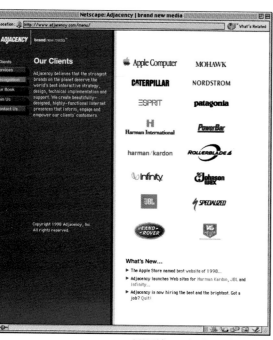

9.2   *©1997 Adjacency, Inc. (www.adjacency.com)*

9.4   *©1997 Adjacency, Inc. (www.adjacency.com)*

More important, Adjacency has chosen to empha-size its clients rather than itself. It's easy to make a strong statement with a red background. But the real identity of a design firm is the work they've done and for whom, and Adjacency has made this evident through the design of their top-level page and site division, *Clients.*

And what a client list, all with national or international brand recognition. Unlike many other self-promotional sites, Adjacency links each corporate logo directly to the Adjacency-designed site for that business. (Notice in this screen shot how, as we pass the cursor over the link, the URL for JBL is shown in the links field at the bottom of the browser window (9.5).) There are no intermediate explanatory or self-congratulatory pages, no sites within frames, and not even a new browser window. The sites speak for themselves.

Promotional sites tend to be hierarchically simple, and Adjacency's is no exception. The navigation buttons indicate the scope of the site's hierarchy, and very little depth is needed beyond this single level. Each section link changes the navigation bar color and loads new information into the information frame. The background color changes to match the section link button, which has the effect of hiding the button and leaving only the button text showing. So without the buttons' changing, you can see at a glance which is the active section and which buttons link to other sections — a neat trick (9.6).

In fact, this frame isn't really reloading each time it changes color. The entire frame is a sophisticated JavaScript rollover. This is why the animations run so smoothly and the colors change so quickly. The entire animation loads the first time we come to this menu. Rolling over a button triggers the button animation. Clicking a button changes the background color of the frame and loads a new file into the target frames to the right. Changes occur not only to the information, but also to the colors of the two vertical stripe frames.

9.5

©1997 Adjacency, Inc. (www.adjacency.com)

9.6   *©1997 Adjacency, Inc. (www.adjacency.com)*

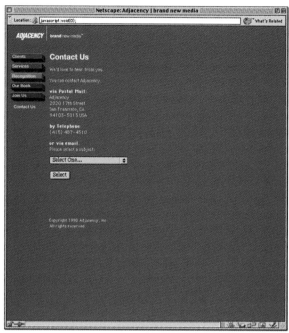

9.7

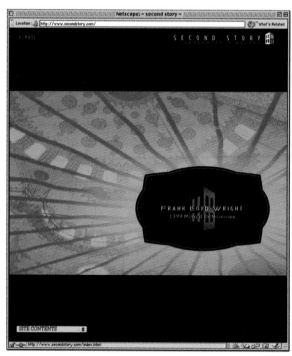

9.8   *Second Story®*

Additional links within sections are listed under the summary text on the left and affect the informational frame on the right only. In the case of the Contact Us button, where there is no associated information to display, the right-hand frame is filled with the same background color as the button, making the page appear to be a single frame (9.7).

In founder and CEO Andrew Sather's words, site design "is about empowering users." This site is really a one-trick pony, but it serves its purpose elegantly and allows changes and additions to be made relatively easily. It also allows visitors to the site, including potential customers, to get a good idea of what Adjacency is about.

FINDING A SENSE OF SELF

If there's any fault to be found with Adjacency's site, it is that they are too self-effacing, something they're able to get away with because their clients are so well-known. But most agencies need to identify themselves. Clients like to know where agencies come from and what they've done.

Second Story Interactive Design doesn't always work on the Web and, along with site designs, needs to include other multimedia projects in their self-promotional site. Yet their emphasis is as strongly client-oriented as Adjacency's. The Second Story home page (www.secondstory.com) features a vivid Flash animation in a frame sandwiched between contrasting black navigation bars (9.8).

The Flash movie loads quickly and plays smoothly. Over a background of an ornate dome (Why a dome? It's hard to say, but it makes a stunning backdrop) is superimposed a plaque that highlights the most recent awards given to Second Story's projects. As the awards scroll by, the background color fades in and out, first gray, then yellow, back to gray, and then blue, and so on. It's a dramatic effect that works well with the scrolling typography and the Second Story logo. (There are no links from the Flash movie to other pages of the site.)

The ornately decorated dome makes a striking contrast to the stark black navigation bars. The top bar includes a mailto link and the Second Story logo, which doubles as a home button on all other pages (9.9). The bottom navigation bar contains a single linking element in the form of a drop-down menu (9.10). At first it's difficult to accept the fact that this one menu provides all the hierarchical and structural linking for the site. But for a site so compact, it works very well. You simply select from the menu, and you're transported to the correct page. There's no Go button or a need for any extra steps. (The HTML for this drop-down menu, its links and dividers, is included on the Web site that accompanies this book at www.idgbooks.com/extras/webarch.html.)

9.9   *Second Story®*

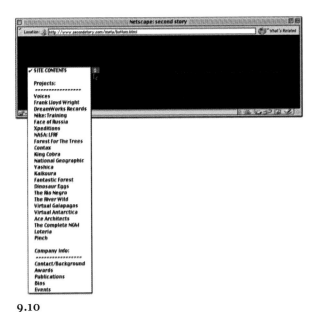

9.10

LOOK MA, NO BUTTONS

The menu shows that only two divisions exist in the first level of the hierarchy, *Projects* and *Company Info*. But neither of these needs a separate introductory page. Instead, the menu provides all the navigation needed to proceed to the pages on the next (and last) hierarchical level down. We're left with a two-level hierarchy with a level missing, a pretty neat trick.

All the content pages of the site fill the space between the two hierarchical bars. The Project pages are divided into two columns, with the narrower column on the left devoted to atmospheric elements, usually a heavily pixelated image from the work. The rest of the frame contains the actual content. This includes titles, a site link, descriptive text, reviews, project details, and an animated GIF showing screens from the actual project. One page is enough to show each project (9.11).

9.11   *Second Story®*

9.12   *Second Story®*

Although the project pages share a format, color and typography are used to make each description distinctive (9.12, 9.13). Only the text, images, and colors change. There are no next and back buttons and no JavaScript rollover navigation. None are needed, because the persistent menu at the bottom takes care of all navigation.

The *Company Info* pages are similarly laid out. More pixelated images fill the left column, and photos and HTML text in tables provide the content (9.14). We even get to find out a little about the people behind the portfolio (9.15). The work is clean, easy to use, and sophisticated.

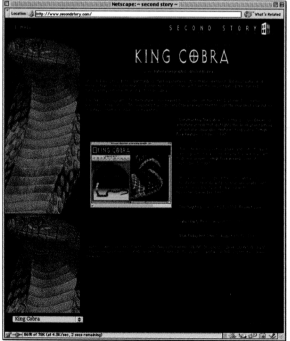

9.13   *Second Story®*

9.14   *Second Story®*

THE USER INTERFACE IS THE SITE

At the opposite end of the agency spectrum from Adjacency and Second Story is Studio Archetype, the Skidmore, Owings, and Merrill of Web architects. We're not talking about a boutique site here. This site is a full-fledged corporate presence with a lot of content organized into a deep hierarchy. There's even a slick navigational scheme to match.

Studio Archetype was founded by design guru Clement Mok, whose early work included the design of icons for Apple and much study of software user interfaces. In many ways, this Web site feels like a finely crafted software application in which the user interface is so clean and intuitive that you never need to crack the manual.

All the navigational elements are established on Studio Archetype's home page (www.studioarchetype.com) as is the case with the other two sites discussed so far in this chapter. You might think upon first seeing it that this site was similar in size and scope. But what's remarkable about the Studio Archetype site is how much information it includes in a site that feels small (9.16).

LAYING OUT A SITE INTERFACE

In Web design, we often speak of pages as if we were designing books or magazines, but this site is designed along the lines of a video screen. Perhaps it is just the rounded corners of the navigational elements

9.16

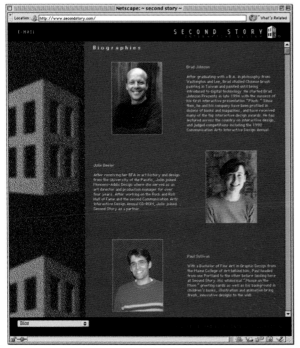

9.15

Second Story®

that frame the content that make me think this, but the feeling here is distinctly different. Even though it is the navigational scheme that is most important in establishing the "user interface" for this site, it's the layout of these elements that makes the navigation work. The layout of this first video screen, though it appears straightforward enough, has been constructed with the utmost care.

The framing elements we see on the home page are the same for every page of this complex site. There's a title bar across the top (9.17), with the main navigation bar under it (9.18). The site is divided into six major divisions as indicated by the six classic Mokian icons in the navigation bar. Each icon is a separate GIF file, and not even a table is used to align these. The images are just abutted against each other and the title bar above.

Across the bottom are three nonhierarchical links in a gray bar (9.19). The *Client Extranet* link, where clients can review their works in progress, changes to a *Home* link on all other pages. And for those clients who might be interested, but are stuck with an old browser, there's an extra line of HTML across the bottom with the studio's name and phone number.

These two horizontal gray bars of abutted GIF images make up the navigation scheme for the entire site, and all content is sandwiched between them. The vertical space between the two bars can easily grow to accommodate more or less content on any given screen. But even as pages change in size, we always know what we will find on the top and bottom. You don't need HTML frames to accomplish this consistent arrangement of framing elements.

In the middle of this home page sandwich, the meat of the construction, is an arrangement of images from featured stories from the Headlines section of the site. These supply the visual interest for the page and provide non-hierarchical links to the new and noteworthy at Studio Archetype. These are laid out in a table, but not with one cell for each image, as you might expect. In this screen shot of the table, taken in Adobe CyberStudio with the cell borders expanded so that they're more visible, what looked like five images of different sizes turns out to be six images in six identical table cells (9.20). Why?

For simplicity's sake, Studio Archetype seems to be keeping tables and cells as simple as possible, preferring to slice images into even sizes than to complicate the table. As long as Borders and Cell Padding are set to zero in the HTML, you can slice an image anywhere and put it together in a table without the seams showing. This turns out to have a practical explanation. The fewer the number of HTML tags and constructs on a given page, the faster it loads. This page has been streamlined without sacrificing artistic control.

Also notice how one abutted image casts drop shadows over the next. In defiance of physical reality, these shadows are actually drawn onto the shadowed image rather than the image creating the shadow. It's a way to make a series of images look like one coherent screen. Yet this clearly wasn't constructed as a single image in Photoshop and sliced into pieces (although there may have been a prototype created in Photoshop at some point). It's a carefully realized assembly of distinct pieces.

9.17

9.18

9.19

9.20

This home page uses no frames. It is straight-forward HTML with a table used to display the content. JavaScript rollovers are employed for all the button links, and there is one additional JavaScript, though its presence is not immediately apparent.

ENHANCING THE USER EXPERIENCE

Strict hierarchical navigation combined with a few "what's new" links doesn't provide the total user experience that Studio Archetype is famous for designing. By clicking the "See Our Web Work" image, an additional navigational element is opened: an external window with external links to the Web sites Studio Archetype has designed for its clients (9.21). This is implemented as a JavaScript that calls the OpenWindow procedure to open a window of speci-fied size and characteristics. (The screen shot has been expanded to show the complete list of sites.)

Now we have a browsing window of links existing separately from the main site. We can browse through the site using the navigation bars or switch at any time to the actual projects. Do we want information about Studio Archetype, or do we just want to see their work? This dual access allows the portfolio section to be arranged as multiple categories, adding layers to the hierarchy. But the extra layers don't make information any less accessible, because the direct links are always available.

The first page of the *Portfolio* section presents the additional hierarchy in the form of three tabs: Clients, Services, and Industries (9.22). What was entirely reserved for content is now divided in two, with navigational elements on the left and content on the

9.21

9.22

9.23

9.24

right. The navigational HTML text is all white on a deep blue background, and a light-colored background is used on the content side for contrast.

Notice how the blue background is also used over the content side and for the active button in the sectional navigation bar across the top. This button is rendered with a reversed shadow so that it now appears to be depressed — part of the background rather than of the navigation bar. The lettering of this button is rendered in relief to highlight it as the active section. All this work on a single button ensures that we always know where we are and where we can go.

The use of the blue background color also works as a unifying element to tie the frames of this screen together. With the new layer of navigation, there are now four frames: top, left, and bottom navigation, plus the content frame, which at this point is essentially empty. We must select a service or another tab to get at some information.

CATEGORIZING INFORMATION

The default tab is for Services, of which there are eight categories. Tabs are implemented as an image-map linked to a JavaScript. Clicking a tab map area builds a list of categorical links, and each category is further subdivided. For instance, clicking the Industries tab rebuilds the categories list and changes the content frame at the same time (9.23).

Clicking the Consumer button expands the category list to include links to consumer sites (9.24). The content frame also changes to reflect the currently active level. These links are a subset of those in the Projects window, but represent the specified industry only. Rather than a long alphabetical list, we now have a few related sites to choose from, presumably the ones we're more interested in seeing.

The reason for this emphasis on organization is that solutions for each Studio Archetype client present themselves differently. For instance, for Revo (9.25), the sunglasses manufacturer, case studies for both the Web site (9.26) and for the branding (9.27) are shown. Notice that a link to Revo's Web site is included. The Sites Window discussed previously contains the same link.

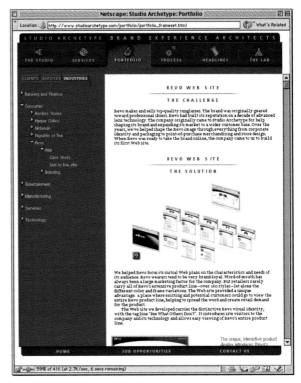

9.26

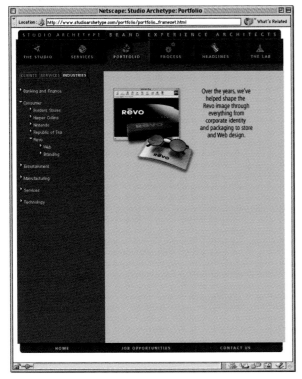

9.25

9.27

9.28

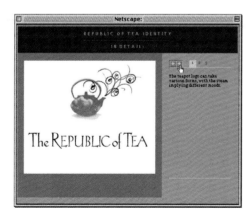

9.29

For Republic of Tea, there is only an identity case study and no Web site (9.28). But within this case study is an image that can be enlarged (the magnifying glass icon) and several links to additional images that show the variations created for this identity system (the See Details icon).

These links are implemented as JavaScripts that open additional browsing windows. The Identity Details window includes additional JavaScript buttons that can either move through the sequence of images or go directly to a specific image (9.29). This may seem like overkill when there are only three images in the display, but you can see that this same window template could be used for other case studies with more images to view.

If you click back on the Services tab and then the Identity category, you can see that both Revo and

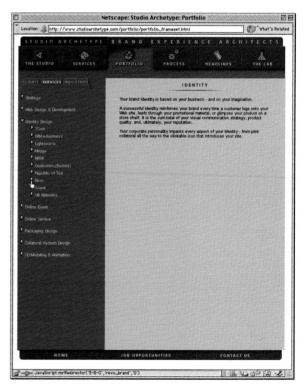

9.30

Republic of Tea are listed (9.30). (Branding and identity turn out to be used interchangeably.) Or if we'd just like to be impressed by the seemingly endless client list, we can click this tab and choose case studies alphabetically (9.31).

It's nice to have a lot of clients, but serving a larger market adds complexity to a Web site. In this case, it means organizing information so that it can be found in different ways depending on the goals of the browser. There are numerous navigational routes to the same content pages.

At the top level, the *Studio* (9.32) and *Strategy* (9.33) sections are organized the same way as the *Portfolio* section, but without the extra level of tab-differentiated hierarchy. The *Process* section contains only two pages, an introduction and an explanation

9.32

9.31

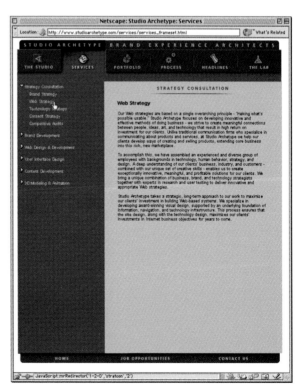

9.33

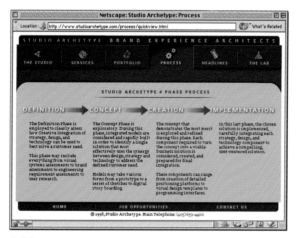

9.34

9.35

of the four-phase process (9.34). It's small, but important enough to warrant its own section. The *Headlines* section is a single page, but it contains many links in two categories, *Lead Stories* and *Press Releases*, that are updated regularly (9.35). All the image links on the home page are taken from this section. The same frames layout is used for each section, but each employs a different background color.

SOMETHING DIFFERENT

The final top-level section, *The Lab*, is organized a bit differently (9.36). The content is split horizontally rather than vertically, and there are no frames. In a column headed UI Nuggets, there's a single link to DHTML Experiment. (One presumes this page has been designed to accommodate future experiments.) Clicking this button executes a JavaScript to open a

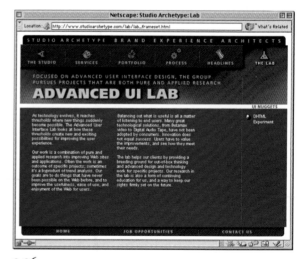

9.36

new browser window containing the experiments (9.37). There are two simple DHTML demonstrations, but compared to some of the other sites described in this book, they're not particularly experimental.

This is a reflection of Studio Archetype's broad client base. Their work is aimed at mainstream businesses — businesses that appreciate the excellence in graphic and user interface design they bring to their work. Being in the mainstream does, however, limit forays into newer technologies like those included in Dynamic HTML or plug-in technologies like Flash. But this does not preclude working for technology leaders, like IBM, or creating sophisticated e-commerce sites for clients like UPS. In fact, it shows that there are probably very few clients that actually need sites that use the most-advanced design technologies. Studio Archetype attains sophistication through attention to detail rather than by including new technology for its own sake.

GAINING AN EDGE WITH THE TECHNO-AESTHETIC

In contrast to Studio Archetype, Razorfish (www. razorfish.com) is always pushing for the new and different. It gives their work an edge that you'd think

suited only less mainstream, more image-conscious clients. You can see this edginess in their work for Casio G-Shock watches, discussed in Chapter 3, but there's nothing edgy about the Carnegie Hall site discussed in Chapter 2.

While Razorfish's reputation rests on its savviness and ability to use cutting-edge technology to solve real-world problems, its clientele is no less diverse than Studio Archetype's. Not what you'd expect from a group that exists in what might be called the Web avant garde. Just look at their client list (9.38). Wow!

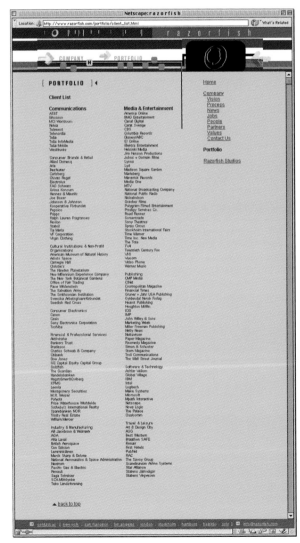

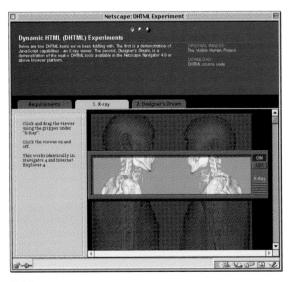

9.37

9.38

9.39

9.40

9.41

9.42

Razorfish has spent the last year acquiring offices around the world, and now it's really big. You could almost say that the sun never sets on the Razorfish empire. Just look at the Razorfish map of the world (9.39), complete with JavaScript rollovers, time zones, and drop-down menu—yikes! Can the Far East be far behind?

CREATING AN ORDERLY RANDOMNESS

It should already be quite evident from the first two screenshots that the Razorfish aesthetic is quite different from Studio Archetype's. Yet, superficially, the Web sites of the two companies have numerous similarities. This is because they share the same market and are solving the same kinds of problems. But it's interesting to see how different the solutions look. It's all a matter of presentation.

There are no "cute" icons on the Razorfish site. The typography, use of imagery, and unusual color combinations make these superfluous. On the other hand, Razorfish's site features three horizontal color bars, just as the Studio Archetype site does (title bar, hierarchical navigation bar, and nonhierarchical navigation bar across the bottom), that sandwiches content in the middle. All of this is established on the Razorfish home page, as it is on Studio Archetype's (9.40).

And, as on the Studio Archetype site, the featured content of the home page is culled from news of what's new. But Razorfish has given us catchy phrases for links: "Racking up 1143 satisfied pub-going gamers in only three days." The imagery is contained in a video screen to the upper-right of the page. This video feature remains present on all the site's pages and changes to reflect current content. It's filled with animations of partial pages, fading logos, and jumping imagery. It's like being in a room where the TV is on, and although you're not really watching it, every now and then an image catches your eye.

Almost subliminally, other things are flashing, too. In the title strip, the strange digitalesque logo is comprised of randomly flashing bars (9.41). In the navigation strip, which includes the video screen, three arrows pointing to the three main hierarchical links pulsate when rolled over (9.42). As the page loads, the button text fades in, the arrows come zipping in from the sides, and the little brown TV screens shoot into place from beneath. Note the *H* in one of the miniature video screens to indicate that this is the Home page. It's all accomplished with animated GIFs and JavaScripts.

And there's more going on in the background. The success stories that make up the main content of this home page and the typographic image that heads the list are all supplied from an Oracle database accessed through Allaire's ColdFusion (9.43). This content is built on the fly, complete with JavaScript rollover buttons that link to the story pages. It's automatically updated as new success stories become available. The content is also randomized, so that the featured stories reshuffle with each visit to this page.

Even the bold stripes of color set up a vibrating visual effect. In fact, the top elements are referred to as the "vibes" bar. Only the column of navigational HTML text on the right (9.44) and the strip of Razorfish offices across the bottom are seemingly static. But even this strip uses JavaScript rollovers for the button links (9.45).

STRUCTURING BEYOND HIERARCHIES

This page uses frames to separate its various elements, so that clicking one of the success stories loads new content only into the one frame while other elements remain unchanged. The site hierarchy is a model of simplicity. There are only two first-level divisions, *Company* and *Portfolio*. The Razorfish Studios button links to a related, but separate, site dedicated to Razorfish products and projects, including a third site for the Razorfish SubNetwork, a collection of experimental or "interesting" sites.

The hierarchical simplicity is deceiving, intended more as an organizing tool for the Web architect than as a navigational aid for the browser. File systems may demand hierarchy, but the user experience does not, and the Razorfish designers are very aware of this distinction.

When we click one of the featured stories, we jump through the site hierarchy directly to the case study. As browsers, we don't need to know this. We just see

9.43

9.44

9.45

new content in the frame, as well as an updated right navigational frame (9.46).

But this isn't all that changes. The images in the video screen are section-specific and reflect the list of related case studies now contained in the right-hand navigation column. The miniature video screens, one of which formerly contained the home page *H*, have changed; note that the screen next to the Portfolio link now displays the Warner Communications styl-

ized *W* logo. But we're not done yet. The other small videos also contain logos as animated GIFs activated by JavaScript rollovers. These are filled at random from the back-end database of portfolio information. In this screenshot, the video we're rolling over contains an animated logo of a pumping heart (9.47).

When you click the heart, a little animation plays out. The miniature screen slides up and over and replaces the active video that previously held Warner Communications's *W* logo. The content and content-specific navigation frames change, and we see that the heart is the logo of the Razorfish intranet "affectionately called Mom" (9.48).

9.47

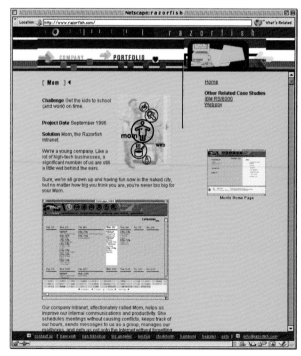

9.48

9.46

In the *Company* section of the site, an identical system is used. Although the content-sensitive navigation column doesn't change, the letters in the miniature video screens around the *Company* link in the top navigation bar change at random. In this screen shot, the active video screen displays a *V* for the current *Values* section. The rollover screen shows a *J* (9.49). Clicking this button starts the animation of little screens and changes the content frame.

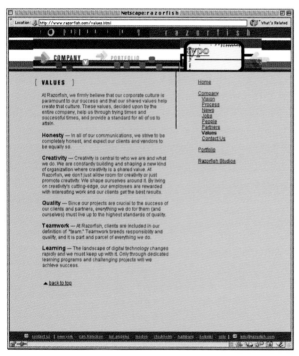

9.49

EXPANDING THE POSSIBILITIES

Obviously, this navigational scheme is more "fun" than useful. A *P* can lead to the *People* or *Partners* section, you never know which. It's just random linking, but it gives the Razorfish site a feeling of informality, of "anything can happen here," that reflects the attitude of the company—an air of fun and excitement in site exploration.

Other pages in the site include search forms that connect to the back-end database to supply information about company news, jobs available, and the people who work at Razorfish. The database will allow the international Razorfish offices to supply custom content to suit their local offices without changing the HTML or structure of the site. So although the "look" remains distinctly Razorfish, the features can highlight successes in Helsinki, Hamburg, or wherever else Razorfish sets up shop.

There's one more very nice touch that caught me totally off guard when I discovered it. When you leave the Razorfish site to view other sites in your browser, a cookie is set for the current browsing session. If you happen to return to the Razorfish domain during the same session, you're returned exactly to the page where you left off. It seemed like a mistake at first, because I'd never seen this used before. But it's easy to imagine many larger sites where this capability would prove very useful. For now, it's another example of the Razorfish mind at work; always exploring the technology for new ways to make the Web browsing experience more fluid.

Are there many corporations that would feel safe with the red/brown and lime green aesthetic of the Razorfish site? Are random linking games going to be the navigational rage of the new millenium? These aren't the right questions to be asking. Does the site convey a strength of design and a knowledge of technology that attracts new customers? It does, and it's difficult to argue with Razorfish's success.

9.50

FROG JUMPING

Some designers just seem to have an innate sense for what we like or even find irresistible. Frog Design has shown this gift for twenty years in its innovative industrial designs. Now they're doing it with Web sites.

Here again, Frog's home page (www.frogdesign.com) uses two horizontal navigation bars to frame the content, which in this case includes a compelling case study of one of its latest success stories (9.50). Interestingly, this page does not establish the look for the rest of the site. It is intentionally used for the introduction only.

PUTTING THE BACK PAGE UP FRONT

This home page (which Frog refers to as a back page) is divided into three horizontal frames. The top Feature bar contains direct links to Frog's *Internet Development* section, including *Client*, *Profiles*, and *Capabilities* subsections. The print is small and easy to miss, which is perhaps intentional, because you also miss all the Shockwave animations if you go this route. But it does provide a quick route to some of the basic information potential clients are looking for.

Instead of a title bar, Frog puts its name right in the content section of the page. The logo is carefully positioned over the darker portions of the back-

SEEKING FLUIDITY, ESCHEWING THE STATIC

Interview with Thomas Mueller, creative director of the Razorfish New York office

Q: What's going on here? None of the pages of the Razorfish site seem to contain much HTML beyond a bunch of JavaScripts.
TM: (chuckling) It's all magic. There are a lot of subtle tricks, and we're interested in seeing if people really use them. We use it as our exploratory ground. Basically, the whole site is using Java-Scripts with a publishing tool in the background. We had to scale back a few things so that they'd work more reliably.

Q: There's a very simple hierarchy here, but one is almost unaware of it when

browsing through the site. Was this intentional?
TM: Yes, it is to some extent hierarchical, but a hierarchy is really something for us as Web architects to use to structure an organization and put information in buckets. But the user, the site visitor, doesn't really care to make a mental map of how the site works. What matters is finding the things in the site useful wherever they are. We're moving away from hierarchical trees and static hierarchical structures to a more fluid organizational model for sites. Fluidity stems from the fact that the hierarchy is much

ground image. It was created with a dark anti-aliased fringe and then saved as a transparent GIF so that it would blend in properly.

The main content frame includes the four-color Frog logo and four images over a somewhat blurry background of what must be a Frog design. The four rectangles are JavaScript rollovers that spell out "Fly with," "Frog," "Go," and "Lufthansa," and they all link to a JavaScript OpenWindow procedure (9.51).

The case study window that pops up is an unusual shape for a browsing window, long and narrow, but it provides a unique layout for the images and text. There are four pages to the study that can be viewed by clicking the four links on the home page or by clicking the miniaturized links in the upper-right corner of the case study window (9.52, 9.53, 9.54, 9.55). This case study is so beautifully presented that there's really no need for others — at least not from the home page.

9.52

9.53

9.54

9.51

9.55

more unique to the individual visitor. It's based on individual needs, which the site structure can assemble itself around. To implement those kinds of ideas, to create a more liquid site architecture, requires a lot more technology investment.

Q: What will that technology be?

TM: The technology is available, we have it at hand. It's finding clients, organizations that are open and willing enough to use these technologies. With them, we can affect how organizations function as businesses. We can go beyond promotional activities, marketing and communications — in business you can't just build static tools. By using these technologies to build sites that allow for either customization or personalization, whatever makes the most sense for the client, that's what we work with. The creativity of the solution to solve business requirements — that's what drives technology solutions.

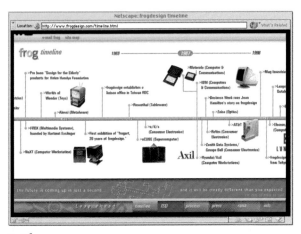

9.56

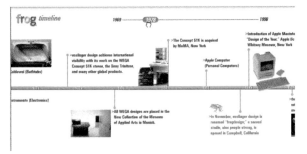

9.57

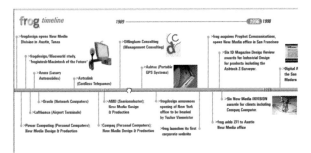

9.58

9.59

This home page experience exists as though it were outside the site. The green navigational frame across the bottom serves as the real entry to the site. You can choose Shockwave or No Shockwave — the content is the same in both. This is a good site without Shockwave, but we want to see all the action, so put on your plug-in and let's go in.

SITE AS VIDEO EXPERIENCE

Frog uses a fixed-sized screen, which gives it a video-like display feel. The effect is intentional, and the screen is framed with a subtly notched border of photographic film. Everything happens within this frame.

After the first Shockwave movie is downloaded, we find ourselves in the middle of the Frog timeline, in 1987 to be precise (9.56). We know this is a Shockwave screen, but nothing is happening. It's waiting for us. We can either slide the year lozenge between 1969 and 1998 (9.57) or simply click anywhere within the frame and drag the timeline itself. As we drag one way, the years go the other way (9.58). But the neat part is that if you heave the timeline over with some force, it continues to scroll a little, as if it actually had weight and carried momentum with it as it scrolled. The effect may be pointless, but I moved the timeline back and forth for a while anyway.

Under the Shockwave screen is a bright-red horizontal element in the form of a rolling JavaScript message, "The future is coming up in just a second and it will be mostly different than you expected." (9.59) This message (internally referred to as the

Rana strip) changes daily, as you'll see from the screen shots of this site taken over a three-day period. Under this are the hierarchical navigation controls. There is one JavaScript rollover for each of the six top-level sections of the site: *timeline* (the current section), *ISD* (Integrated Strategic Design), *process*, *press*, *rana* (Latin for frog), and *info* (9.60). Each is color coded and lights up when rolled over. The button for the current section is always rendered above the others and in gray to match the separator bar.

You can see in this screen shot of the elements in Adobe GoLive that this timeline page was constructed without frames or even tables (9.61). The top bar is assembled from three abutted GIF images: the *email frog* button on the left, the *site map* button in the middle, and an empty gray and white bar finishing out the right. The big puzzle piece in the middle of this screen shot is the Shockwave-animated timeline, followed by the Java bean representing the scrolling JavaScript message. At the bottom are more abutted images (with JavaScript rollovers for the button links).

Even though there's a lot going on here, the page has been stripped of all unnecessary HTML. Constructing a cohesive page out of abutted images only works when the exact size — the height and width parameters of each element — is specified as part of the `<IMG>` tags.

The frame size, along with the top and bottom navigational elements, remains constant across the rest of the site. The changing content exists within the fixed elements (see sidebar, "To Frame or Not to Frame?"). There's an additional navigational element in the

9.60

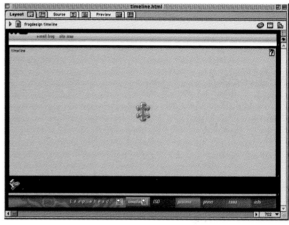

9.61

TO FRAME OR NOT TO FRAME?

When faced with building a site with top and bottom navigation bars sandwiching changing content, many designers would choose to use a frames-based HTML construct. With this method, the persistent elements do not need to be redrawn each time, only the middle content portion of the window. However, because all browsers cache pages and elements, redrawing a navigation bar that's already been cached is not necessarily a time-consuming proposition. The cached images will not be downloaded for subsequent pages. Because the navigation does not depend on frames, Frog chose the implementation of greatest simplicity — no frames.

9.62

9.63

9.64

form of a site map. The Site Map button opens an external window of site links arranged hierarchically by section (9.62).

The Site Map window duplicates the hierarchical buttons of the main window's bottom navigation bar, but provides direct second-level links as well. It also provides a slightly different user experience by opening links in a new window instead of using the same display window for all pages.

Within major sections, additional navigational elements become part of the content window. For instance, the ISD section has its own introductory page and four subsections, which are listed across the top in italic text. This navigation bar within the content section is constructed of six abutted GIF images with JavaScript rollovers used for the button links. The construction technique is the same as it is for the other navigation bars. But varying the style makes these elements appear to be a part of the content rather than existing as a third navigation bar, which is what they are.

The actual content is a single larger image containing the introductory message and a colorful frog sitting at the intersection of innovation, imagination, interaction, and implementation (9.63). These four *I* words are matched to the four subdivisions of this section.

CONCENTRATING ON NEW MEDIA

Clicking the *new media* link updates the subdivision navigation bar and changes the content image. The navigation bars for pages at this level of the site hierarchy not only provide links (Where can we go?), but also identify the current location (Where are we?). On the bottom bar, the ISD button is highlighted in gray. On the sectional navigation bar, where all the other buttons are gray, the New Media button is highlighted in green. There's also a down-pointing triangle to indicate that "You are here."

We're at *interaction* now—the identifying quality of New Media. Although it isn't immediately evident, this is probably the deepest section of the site. All of the text on the Interaction image (this page's content) is an imagemap with a single link into the hierarchy of the New Media (Interaction) subdivision.

Among the gray text headings, Interactive Marketing, Software Prototyping, Graphic User Interface, and so on, is one heading in red with a right-pointing triangle, Internet Development. It's the "Let's look deeper" button.

What becomes immediately apparent when we enter this third level of the site hierarchy, the *internet development* subdivision, is that Frog has done a lot of work in this area (9.64). There's an overview page and five categories of information: *projects/clients, capabilities, profiles, process,* and *awards/press.* These links are presented in the same bar that previously showed the *ISD* subdivision links, so that even though we are moving deeper into the site, it doesn't feel very deep. The theme for this subdivision, "Nature abhors nothing," appears in a strip across the bottom of the content section and remains for all the pages of the *internet development* section.

The *projects/clients* page fills the content section with a list of client names and their corresponding projects in a scrolling list (9.65). There are many projects, plus a few clients listed without linkable sites. Each of the green links opens a window within the Frog-designed site. There are also red links that connect to the *profiles* section of the *internet development* subsection.

The *profiles* section includes a pair of success stories and links to the customers' sites (9.66). An additional navigational element is added directly under the *profiles* link listing the stories. It fits nicely under the down-pointing triangle. Because there are only two stories at this point, the one currently displayed is black. To go to the other story, click the green link.

IT ALL RESULTS FROM GOOD DESIGN

I've been concentrating on the frameless construction of these pages and the site's consistent navigation, but have barely touched on the imagery and typography used here, areas where Frog has clearly differentiated itself. But look at the divisional link labeled *rana.* This turns out to be Frog's design magazine, or more specifically, the *integrated strategic design magazine* (9.67). The rana logo, constructed of familiar letter forms used in a very original way, is colorful and distinctive.

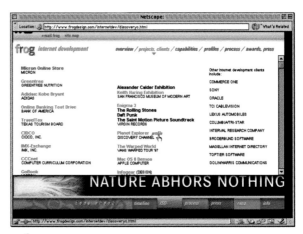

9.65

9.66

9.67

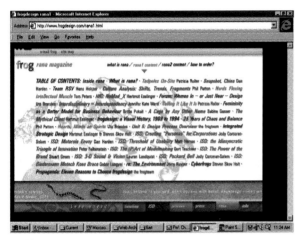

9.68

There's no attempt to include content from the magazine on the Web site. But the table of contents page, with its spare typography, very basic layout, and use of color to distinguish items, gives us a good idea of what to expect from the magazine (9.68). They've given us a lot of information in a concise format.

But this is the beauty of Frog Design's work. It's simple, elegant, and understated, but it's full of visual clues that tell us exactly what's going on. We've seen this time and again in the examples used in this book. Given a set of problems, how do you reduce them to an elegant solution? The good Web architects are able to do it every time. The design and construction of

Web sites always starts with a data set full of contradictions, but there is always a unifying theme, a way of pulling the disparate elements together.

We have looked at Web construction techniques from an architect's perspective. We've seen that the elements of good design and good communication can only be brought together to build a compelling Web site when they are inextricably linked — when they serve a single, well-defined purpose. With all of these self-promotional sites, the purpose is to convey the company image and philosophy. It's not enough simply to be a good designer. Great sites require an understanding of the company. If it's your own company, your design must do the double duty of expressing your philosophy, as well.

Web architecture, like any discipline that combines art and technology, is a matter of making compromises. Technology is changing rapidly, but the basic reasons for creating sites don't change. We aren't creating habitable spaces, but we are concerned with day-to-day human interaction. Today's Web architects are designing and building the great communication revolution of the 21st century, and it's hard to believe that the designs we've looked at in this book, sophisticated as they are artistically and technologically, are still just the first experiments.

CHAPTER 10
DESIGNERS SPEAK

During the course of writing this book, I sent a survey to a number of Web architects to see how they faced the various issues of dealing with clients and how this affected their work. It's immediately evident reading over the survey answers that there is no *right* way to design, build, and maintain a Web site. The philosophy of the architect, the personality of the client, and the nature of the work are never the same for any two projects. It's a collaborative business that requires Web architects to listen carefully and then translate ideas into a living, breathing site.

Once a site leaves the studio and joins the World Wide Web, it takes on its own life. The patterns of use, the frequency of visitors, the inclusion in Web indices, the changes over time—all contribute to the life and evolution of sites. As Web architects, how do we deal with so many variables?

RAYMOND GARGAN, COFOUNDER, INTERACTIVE ARTS & ENGINEERING

1. How does the typical client/designer relationship differ with Web work than with other design work, or does it differ at all?

A few important distinctions come to mind. There is always more education involved with a Web project than a print project. This causes us to be more careful to explain our design decisions fully and to document the decisions made with the client. Another important difference when working with large clients is the need for an interdepartmental team at the client's organization. Sometimes we begin working with the

10.1

IS people. Sometimes we begin working with the Marketing people. We really need to work with both.

2. How do you define a client's Web needs and set goals for the Web site?

We try to develop a clear set of objectives during the proposal stage of a project. It's also important to agree upon ways to measure the degree of success in obtaining these objectives. These definitions come from both client interviews and independent research into the client's markets and competition. Normally, we will draft a statement of goals and run it by our immediate client contacts for their input before formalizing it.

3. Once you understand a client's needs and wishes, how do you translate this into a coherent Web site?

This can only be achieved through the use of the proper chants, dances, robes, and special herbs and mushrooms. But more practically, it's an iterative development process like architectural design. We propose solutions that are reviewed and refined based on client input and testing until all are satisfied that the objectives have been achieved.

4. How do you set checkpoints for Web work and keep to a schedule?

Clients will often have a launch date in mind, but rarely will demand any specific intermediate milestones. Although every project is different, there are some basic milestones in design and development where we will require client input and approval. We use these milestones to keep the project moving ahead. Typically, these include:

- Statement of objectives
- Site map finalization
- Overall design of top levels in the hierarchy (including color palette, navigation scheme, and so on)
- Copy review
- Detailed design, usually by major sections
- Staging and testing

5. Administratively, how do you keep track of Web projects, and what mechanisms do you use for keeping the client up to date on work in progress?

Each site has a project manager who is responsible for meeting deadlines and budgets, as well as keeping the client informed of progress. Normally, we use the site map as a visual tool for tracking progress. Each "page" on the map is either color-coded or gets a symbol to indicate its progress. Staging of prototypes and regular meetings, both internally and with the client, are important. Naturally, scheduling and resource conflicts can arise when there are several projects in the works simultaneously or when unrealistic promises are made to the client.

6. When is a site ready for launch?

A site doesn't have to be completely finished before launch (no site is ever really finished). But we feel that all the major sections of the approved site map should have been staged, tested, proofread, and reviewed by the client—sometimes even market tested. We try our very best to avoid using the ubiquitous "Under Construction" page. If a piece of a site is not finished, it's better not to have a link to it than to link to a dead end.

7. When do you start planning for the maintenance of a site?

Maintenance should be planned and scheduled from the very beginning of the project. We include a plan for this in our proposals. Maintenance should include a regular schedule of tests to evaluate the site's position in keyword searches at the major search engines.

8. How active are clients in site maintenance, and do clients require training to play a more active role?

Clients that have the staff and talent resources should be very active in maintenance. We have from time to time provided training, consulting, and telephone support to help our clients update their sites. In addition, it's desirable to set up customized sys-

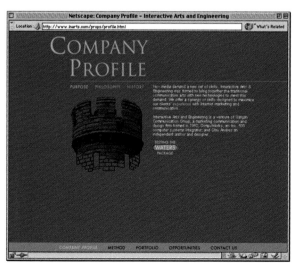

10.2

tems that allow clients to do specific, limited updates, such as replacing text files in an existing template.

9. When and how do you start plans for site marketing?

Site marketing is fundamental to the design of the site and should be considered at the start and at virtually every step of the process. This is especially true for sites that don't have an established brand identity or the advertising budget to develop one. They will rely primarily on search engines and reciprocal links to provide traffic. An understanding of how keywords are used by search engines is essential. Not only will it affect the choice of words used in the copy, but it will affect the layout as well.

10. How has site marketing changed, and is it possible to predict future Web marketing directions?

It's no longer sufficient to rely on search engines. The competition is immense, and some search engines take far too long to index a site. Customer awareness of the organization and its Web site must be supported by online and traditional media advertising and public relations.

MILES MCMANUS, OVEN DIGITAL

1. How does the typical client/designer relationship differ with Web work than with other design work, or does it differ at all?

Our work is mostly produced for digital delivery, although for larger clients we develop print collateral and identity work as well. With us, the process is practically identical. I think the important thing for the process has not been the fact that we're working *for* the Web so much as working *on* the Web. That is to say, the digital environment has become so integrated with everything we do that I can't imagine working without it anymore.

For example, once we've had a chance to develop a relationship with the client — they've gotten to know us and vice versa — we're able to turn over projects for them in a very efficient manner. By creating a secure area online for each of our clients to review our work and keep track of deliverables, project schedules, and other information, we've made the process much more interactive and convenient for everyone concerned.

Our clients often have more than one layer of review, often taking place in more than one location — with our extranet, it doesn't matter — as long as an

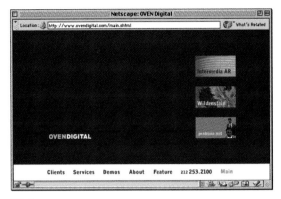

10.3

intranet connection is there, so is our work. We find that this results in much better, more complete, and faster feedback, which helps us keep up with our clients' changing needs and priorities.

2. How do you define a client's Web needs and set goals for the Web site?

Our best bet is to try to understand our client's business. At the outset of every new relationship, we do our best to get as much information as possible about the client's goals, business imperatives, revenue streams, customers, competitors, and internal structures. That way we can see how the goals for each project fit into the bigger picture of the business as a whole, and this invariably leads to better products.

3. Once you understand a client's needs and wishes, how do you translate this into a coherent Web site?

Again, it's a question of relationship. We strive to earn our client's trust though listening, careful analysis, and education. When this trust is achieved, we are truly able to fulfill our role as consultancy. The first step is to identify the information relevant to the creation of the product, and the ongoing process is one of using our experience and expertise to maximize the effectiveness of that information in the given medium. This has a lot do with context-sensitivity: Content is content, but it needs to be treated differently for different delivery platforms, different audiences, etc. As a full-service agency, our approach is holistic: It goes beyond look and feel to the structure of information, to the identification and implementation of technical solutions, and to development of the proper editorial voice.

4. How do you set checkpoints for Web work and keep to a schedule?

10.4

Our entire office is run from a tightly integrated, highly automated Intranet/extranet system, which we developed in-house. It provides functions for time tracking, providing estimates for future work, and the creation and publishing of schedules and budgets.

5. When do you start planning for the maintenance of a site?

During the proposal phase. Most of our work is delivered to our clients as a set of templates for use with an updating or content management system. As such, flexibility, modularity, and extensibility are among our highest design priorities. Because of our experience, we're usually thinking along these lines before the client even mentions maintenance.

6. How active are clients in site maintenance, and do clients require training to play a more active role?

It varies with the client. Some of our larger clients have had a Web presence for years. They have well-established infrastructures, and they come to us to help make the effort as a whole more coherent. It's important to remember that a Web presence is in many cases an enormous, unwieldy undertaking, involving thousands or millions of pieces of information, people in offices around the world, and the unique "self-publishing" reality of the deadline-less environment. In these cases, our role goes beyond setting up a management system for the client and into the realm of consulting on the overall approach — how a system fits into an institution, and how the digital side of a business is an organizational force in its own right.

7. When and how do you start plans for site marketing?

We begin to discuss marketing options at the outset of our process, during the discovery phase. Our view is that it's essential to guide the client in coordinating its online presence with its other public manifestations. We want to make sure that the site itself — and any marketing strategies that promote it — are tightly integrated with the company's brand, advertising and marketing strategies, and overall positioning.

8. How has site marketing changed, and is it possible to predict future Web marketing directions?

One of the major ways that site marketing has changed is that the cross-fertilization between print, outdoor, merchandise-related, and online advertising and marketing is taking off. Site marketing used to consist of displaying a few banners, applying for awards, and perhaps doing some guerrilla marketing to newsgroups. Today, site marketing is about getting URLs everywhere that the company's name appears.

As to the future — we look towards further convergence of the online and offline worlds. In addition,

10.5

we hope that new technologies will make easier the leap from reading a URL on paper to then sitting down and typing it into a computer — direct mail or other free distribution of business-card sized CD-ROMs, for example. But the possibilities are really wide open.

ROYA ZAMANZADEH, CEO, PEAR TRANSMEDIA

1. How does the typical client/designer relationship differ with Web work than with other design work, or does it differ at all?

The biggest difference is that our clients (95 percent have access to the Web) can view our process online. This eliminates misunderstandings and long timelines. Even in the sketch phase, everything is fairly low-res and has limited colors. It's all in the computer, so being on the Internet allows us just to post or mail over a screenshot and get instant feedback. It doesn't matter if the client is in the same city or in another country.

Here at Pear, we spend a lot of time online and on the phone simultaneously with our clients to get their needs met and produce instant results that they find satisfying. This way the relationship feels more personal than the old fashioned "going to a meeting all well dressed with fancy portfolio and elaborate sketches" kind of meetings.

2. How do you define a client's Web needs and set goals for the Web site?

If they need us to do strategic planning and marketing for them, then we have experts who take care of nailing down client branding and identity needs by doing qualitative and quantitative research, as well as extensive market research.

If they think they have all that taken care of, then we listen to them carefully, and ask them for examples of either actual work or methods they like or don't like. We get a feel for their company philosophy and their target market. This is usually followed by internally researching the client's specific industry, target market, and competitors. The goals for the Web site, if not already defined by the client before contacting us, are also defined in the initial kick-off meetings. We ask a lot of questions, make suggestions, and repeat the things we understand to avoid miscommunication.

3. Once you understand a client's needs and wishes, how do you translate this into a coherent Web site?

We approach the Web project from several sides at once. One aspect is the look and feel, where the actual visual design plays the biggest role. Representing a client's identity and brand is very important also. Creating an image for a new product with the same representation as their other marketing material is one of our other specialties.

The more invisible part of the design work is the site architecture and navigation. Pear puts a lot of thought into practicality and guiding the user to a pleasurable experience without forgetting the representation or marketing needs of the client.

Important issues are making sure the important information is easily accessible, obvious orientation exists within the site, and the user gets to see the things the client wants them to see.

Hand in hand with the architecture goes the information design: what type of navigation buttons/icons/images to include, how to create not just a look and feel but also an intuitveness that goes hand in hand with the client's image and philosophy.

4. How do you set checkpoints for Web work and keep to a schedule?

This is our project managers' responsibility. The more experienced they are, the easier the ride. We have never experienced delays that were caused by our

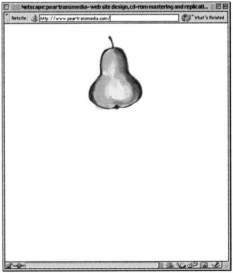

10.6   *Squeezing magic out of technology*™

internal team. Luckily, delays have always been due to the clients.

5. Administratively, how do you keep track of Web projects, and what mechanisms do you use for keeping the client up to date on work in progress?

This falls to our account managers. They update the schedule online for clients as changes occur. They follow up with clients on deliverables and with internal project managers for our deliverables. We use tracking sheets with check boxes, hold twice-a-week project meetings internally, frequently update the client project site, and provide weekly written updates for the client.

6. When is a site ready for launch?

When all quality assurance and browser testing has been completed and OK'd, and we post it on the server.

7. When do you start planning for the maintenance of a site?

It's either before or after launch, when we sit down with the client and go over their maintenance needs. It depends on how much updating and maintenance they need and how soon.

8. How active are clients in site maintenance, and do clients require training to play a more active role?

There are all kinds of clients. We usually provide clients with a written document on how to maintain

the site if they require it. This way, if they have assigned a person internally, it will be easy for them. We also make sure that our design standard is not changed by anyone except us. This way we can guarantee consistency and quality.

9. When and how do you start plans for site marketing?

Again, it depends on the client. If they require it, we start as soon as the contract is signed. This is a very important part of strategizing for the best solution. If they have had that done already internally, then we meet with their marketing team and go over their research and findings in order to make sure the site matches their criteria.

10. How has site marketing changed, and is it possible to predict future Web marketing directions?

Clients are much more aware of its necessity in Web design and development. Without one their brand and identity can be affected. Two to three years ago most clients didn't realize that Web sites needed the same attention as other marketing mediums. They were testing the waters. But now it has become a crucial part of their campaign. In the near future, we will see much more emphasis on it and more tools for it.

10.7   *Squeezing magic out of technology.*™

10.8   *Squeezing magic out of technology.*™

TIM CLEMENTS, PROJECT MANAGER, ARANEUM.DK

1. How does the typical client/designer relationship differ with Web work than with other design work, or does it differ at all?

I believe the relationship can be enhanced through thoughtful use of the medium. At Araneum, we always establish a project Web site where we can interact with the client. We establish a discussion forum and a document archive, among other things, that we can use to follow the project's progress chronologically. The forum enables us to discuss issues with their entire organization. This all saves a lot of time by not having to hold five-hour meetings with meaningless discussion. Of course, we do hold regular client meetings, but not as many as we would have to without our project sites.

2. How do you define a client's Web needs and set goals for the Web site?

We use a very similar profiler to the one here: http://www.secretsites.com/profiler/content_profiler.shtml.

3. Once you understand a client's needs and wishes, how do you translate this into a coherent Web site?

Through a process of producing a series of drafts, each time fine-tuning to client feedback and our own experience.

4. How do you set checkpoints for Web work and keep to a schedule?

By drawing up a project time plan indicating milestones, and so on.

5. Administratively, how do you keep track of Web projects, and what mechanisms do you use for keeping the client up to date on work in progress?

There do not seem to be any really good project management software available that is either cross-platform or browser-based so that all our staff can work together. We are therefore well into developing our own bespoke browser-based project management solution.

6. When is a site ready for launch?

As soon as we and the client are satisfied that the goals and spec have been met and after it has been thoroughly user-tested and tested for errors, etc.

7. When do you start planning for the maintenance of a site?

This is normally established quite early in the process. We would normally build the site according to who will be updating and maintaining the site, us or the client. We have developed a number of content

10.9

management tools that enable our clients to update, add pages, sections, etc., all through a very simple interface, without having to even see a line of code.

8. How active are clients in site maintenance, and do clients require training to play a more active role?

It really depends upon the size of their own organization. Many large corporate clients have their own Web departments whose staff would be typically trained in Microsoft FrontPage. In these instances, they can normally handle simple updating themselves. If our design is quite advanced, we would prefer to implement changes ourselves. There's nothing worse than seeing our designs broken by the client.

9. When and how do you start plans for site marketing?

This tends to be undertaken by the clients themselves. However, we are able to offer our clients advice on the most up-to-date ideas and, if necessary, carry out this work on their behalf.

10. How has site marketing changed, and is it possible to predict future Web marketing directions?

There appears to be a lot of collaboration going on between noncompeting sites where products complement each other. If I search for something in a search engine, I'm more often than not asked if I should search for books containing that name at some online bookstore!

From my own consumer experience, I am often taken in by the methods used by some of the large

10.10

online players such as Amazon. My consumer profile is obviously being built and modified every time I purchase something or express an interest in a product, and this is a very subtle form of marketing. It's just the same in any supermarket where tempting products are placed right by the checkouts.

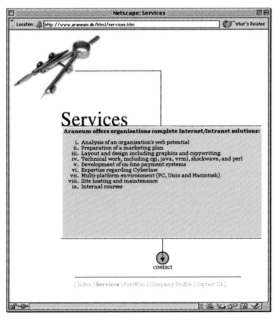

10.11

NINA DIETZEL, CREATIVE DIRECTOR, IMPACT DESIGN

1. How does the typical client/designer relationship differ with Web work than with other design work, or does it differ at all?

The Web design process contains more need for cognitive thinking compared to traditional design. The Web design process is challenged on a more complex level. For example, we have to take into account that the viewer can move in all kinds of directions and that the experience is interactive. The downside of Web design, on the other hand, is that it can be so limiting because of its technical issues, bandwidth, etc. And of course, you don't get to smell the ink when it is "printed."

I think the solution to the above-mentioned challenges/restrictions is to treat them the same way as any other traditional marketing challenges. After all, it is solving a visual communications problem, it's just that the parameters change from situation to situation, whether it is print or Web design. I think what Impact Design does best is to solve our clients visual challenges, regardless of the medium.

2. How do you define a client's Web needs and set goals for the Web site?

Typically, when we kick off a project with our clients, we have an in-depth discussion about what they hope to achieve with their Web site and what their particular marketing objectives are. We ask them questions such as are they selling a product or service, are they selling wholesale (business to business) or retail, who's their main audience, who are the main competitors, what are the expectations, where do they want to be — conservative or far out, visionary, fun — what are their brand attributes, and many more. (Naturally, those discussions very often trigger many more questions, depending on specific client circumstances.) The results of our kick-off discussions then serve as the base to our creative brief.

3. Once you understand a client's needs and wishes, how do you translate this into a coherent Web site?

It's magic! We take the creative brief and translate the messages into visual concepts, usually starting out with the home page to set the look and feel for the rest of the site. This is where the real work begins behind the scenes, and the process is really not so different from any other traditional design project.

We try to provide solutions from a very conservative approach to one that is very far out. (What the client wanted is somewhere in the middle field of our design explorations.) Through various internal work sessions and critiques, we establish which one of the design concepts are the most appropriate in their approach. We then prepare the best solutions for presentation in our next joint work session with the client.

This process repeats itself a couple of times with refinements that the client or our team may want to make. When the home page and "look and feel" of the rest of the site is graphically and technically established, a freeze is set on the site, and we ask the client to sign off on the creative part of the project. After that, pure production begins.

4. How do you set checkpoints for Web work and keep to a schedule?

We lay out checkpoints and a schedule in our proposals. This becomes our guideline throughout the project. When we hand over a proposal to our client, it spells out everything that happens along the way, when and what the clients can expect (how many concepts will be presented and discussed in our joint work sessions, etc.). We also keep close track of all the project developments in our password-protected project management Web site (see answer to #5).

5. Administratively, how do you keep track of Web projects, and what mechanisms do you use for keeping the client up to date on work in progress?

We emphasize daily project management throughout the duration of the project. By relying on frequent face-to-face meetings during the many development stages, a password-protected project management Web site on our server to monitor progress, and through joint work sessions to review project goals and milestones, we establish multiple lines of open communication for everyone involved in the project. The project management site serves as a bulletin board for meeting minutes and in-house production notes, and also includes PDFs of recent graphic developments.

6. When is a site ready for launch?

A site is ready for launch when we have met all of the project objectives and thoroughly tested the site on all OS platforms. There should always be champagne at this point (yum).

10.12

7. When do you start planning for the maintenance of a site?

Right away—changes can come up from our client's side very quickly, and much of it is simply keeping the site fresh with updates of information. Some clients even request a change of "window dressing" from time to time, so that people don't get bored visiting the site.

8. How active are clients in site maintenance, and do clients require training to play a more active role?

I think it is fair to say that most of our clients do want to play an active role, but hardly ever really get around to really doing it themselves. They seem to be way too busy with their own daily schedules and workloads. We have offered training in the past, and we're using a set of "admin tools" in a current project.

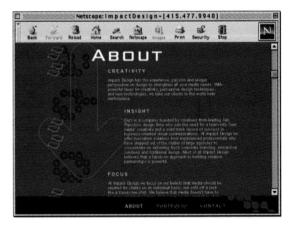

10.13

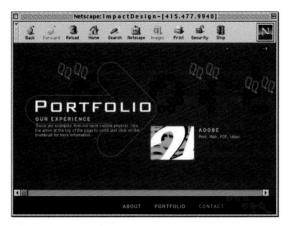

10.14

These tools are Web-based prompt windows that enable the user to easily update templates and upload them to the FTP site. We're making the maintenance/updating process very accessible from our end. What happens next is in the client's hands, and often they come back to us to help them, because they're simply too overwhelmed with their own projects.

9. When and how do you start plans for site marketing?

When the client is ready, basically. Again, this process really goes hand in hand with our work with the client team. In a previous project for Miller Freeman, Inc., for example, we were asked to design two Web sites in an incredibly short amount of time, and then were invited back one week after launch to complement the two extremely successful sites with ad campaigns. Web to print, all with the same design partners — that's what we love to provide our clients with. Impact Design provides this seamless crossover between all media — something we're very proud of.

10. How has site marketing changed, and is it possible to predict future Web marketing directions?

I'll leave this one out. If you have to have an answer to it, let us know.

JEFFREY ZELDMAN, CREATIVE DIRECTOR, JEFFREY ZELDMAN PRESENTS

1. How does the typical client/designer relationship differ with Web work than with other design work, or does it differ at all?

I come from an advertising background, rather than from the world of design.

Initially (in 1995), the client/designer relationship was balanced more in the designer's favor than it is in other creative service industries, for the simple reason that the Web was new, and clients were intimidated. The Webmaker was seen as a guru, initiated into sacred mysteries beyond the client's understanding; the designer thus had greater permission to say "No." For example, "No, I can't do that; we don't have the bandwidth" could make a client's bad idea go away.

Of course, *I* never pulled any stunts like that.

And clients, like everyone else, are much more Web-savvy these days.

2. How do you define a client's Web needs and set goals for the Web site?

My commercial sites tend to be created for entertainment clients: movie companies and so on. The site's structure will thus come out of story and character. For instance, http://www.analyzethis.com is the site for a Mafia-meets-psychiatry comedy, so we created a section where you could interact with a virtual shrink, a wiseguy's map of NYC, and so on. http://www.batman-robin.com, for the Warner Bros. flick *Batman and Robin*, revolved around multiple characters, because a larger-than-ever assortment of villains and heroes characterized the (then-upcoming) film. Each character got his/her own URL, and all copy on each character's site was written in that character's tone of voice.

For The Web Standards Project (http://www.webstandards.org/), the goal was to create a memorable "brand image" for a protest by a group of high-level Web developers. The brand image was needed because the protest was somewhat technical in nature, and would therefore be hard to grasp without something to "hold onto."

I've written at greater length about these things in my forum for Webmakers, A List Apart (http://www.alistapart.com/), specifically at these locations:

- http://www.alistapart.com/stories/branding/ (Brand That Site!)
- http://www.alistapart.com/stories/writing/ (Writing for the Web)

3. Once you understand a client's needs and wishes, how do you translate this into a coherent Web site?

Can't analyze the creative process, but the goal is to find a memorable, unique, and appropriate overall brand image for the client's product — or find a Web-appropriate translation of an existing brand image.

This brand image must drive the navigation and structure, the graphic design, the writing/content, and the behavior/programming of the site. These elements must work together to further the overall brand identity.

This brand ID need not be a metaphor, but it must be articulate, extensible, coherent, and consistent.

I present this idea to the client, then we work together to determine what materials must be on the site. I go away and determine how to filter these materials to the proposed identity. If it's a good fit (if the brand identity is working), these things often solve themselves creatively rather quickly. Larger areas and navigation can then be structured.

4. How do you set checkpoints for Web work and keep to a schedule?

(Sigh.) I never sleep.

5. Administratively, how do you keep track of Web projects, and what mechanisms do you use for keeping the client up to date on work in progress?

No fixed plan — I just stay in constant contact with my clients, constantly apprising them of where we are and what we are doing, and showing them certain things when appropriate.

6. When is a site ready for launch?

Two months after it launches.

7. When do you start planning for the maintenance of a site?

When we start planning the file structure, at the very beginning of the process. A complex file structure locks you in to a fixed object. A simple and fluid structure enables you, or others, to make changes. From painful experience, we've learned to figure these things out right from the start.

8. How active are clients in site maintenance, and do clients require training to play a more active role?

This process is still very rough. I have no wisdom on the subject.

9. When and how do you start plans for site marketing?

As we are finishing up.

Generally, entertainment sites are marketed by the clients themselves. Other sites we market in the traditional time-tested ways: word of mouth, networking, opt-in mailing lists, search engine listings, banner swaps, and so on.

10. How has site marketing changed, and is it possible to predict future Web marketing directions?

10.15

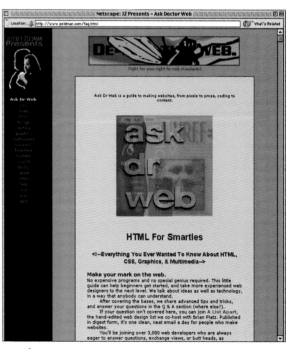

10.16

It is sometimes possible to know that a trend will die. For instance, it was obvious to us that Push would die. We expect the RealPlayer to stick around. We're not as sanguine about bubble viewing plug-ins. Some things are obvious. But it is impossible to truly predict anything in this volatile medium. Two years ago, who would have thought Netscape's browser would be seriously humbled by Microsoft Internet Explorer?

10.17

© 1997 Copyright Adjacency, Inc. (www.adj.com)

ANDREW SATHER, CREATIVE DIRECTOR AND CEO, ADJACENCY

1. How does the typical client/designer relationship differ with Web work than with other design work, or does it differ at all?

It differs from other design work in the way that it touches upon client's core business processes. Much more like business, brand, design, and IT consulting rolled into one. Because of that, the up-front work is exaggerated. There's more time interviewing clients to determine the key business requirements of what you're going to do. Up to a third of the entire time spent on the project is on the groundwork before starting the design. You're building an application, not just designing. Design is just one part of the process.

2. How do you define a client's Web needs and set goals for the Web site?

The first thing we do is sit down with the clients and try to interview the key stakeholders within the organization and determine what they perceive the needs to be. We analyze those and look for opportunities to map them to the Internet or in some cases use Internet technology to fundamentally change or streamline those processes. Then we think and come up with what we believe a proposed strategy should be and all the components of that. We present this, and the client decides what we move forward with.

3. Once you understand a client's needs and wishes, how do you translate this into a coherent Web site?

By combining strategy, design, and technology in a way that creates something that's beautiful, usable, brand appropriate, and powerful.

4. How do you set checkpoints for Web work and keep to a schedule?

The same way any designer or applications developer would. Create a very detailed timeline, note things that are dependent on other things. The biggest challenge is that, unlike other graphic designs, you very often have technical requirements and as much or more text than any print job. Managing yourself internally as well as the client and their delivery of material is very important. When you're designing a 30,000-page Web site, you have to collect all the materials and resources in a timely manner.

5. Administratively, how do you keep track of Web projects, and what mechanisms do you use for keeping the client up to date on work in progress?

We use MS Project internally. We have account managers and project managers who are both involved in owning that document and keeping people to task to meet it. With some clients we'll actually share that document. We have a very involved extranet, the Adjacency Client Extranet (ACE), which we use to manage a timeline, track and facilitate communications with the client, present and archive design directions as they evolve, and preview the actual work in progress. The beautiful thing about what we do, unlike some print firms, is it is our medium. You have to FedEx prints and proofs, but our clients have 24-hour, seven-day-a-week global access to the actual work in progress.

6. When is a site ready for launch?

After it's been thoroughly QA'd. QA responsibilities are spread out throughout our departments. We also have dedicated QA people, and project managers have ultimate responsibility. The site's ready to go live when we and the client sign off on it. More often than not, it's on schedule. It launches on time.

7. When do you start planning for the maintenance of a site?

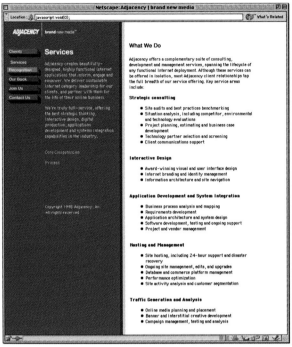

10.18

Before we've even designed or programmed it. It needs to be part of the strategy, scalable, and maintainable. We and our clients like to make it so that most of our sites are maintainable by the client, at least for daily updates—which also frees us up to work on ongoing enhancement and strategy development. We also develop an awful lot of very user-friendly WYSIWYG site editing tools for our clients. It makes it so that they don't need to learn to use HTML or database programming to maintain their site.

8. How active are clients in site maintenance, and do clients require training to play a more active role?

Very and yes, but hopefully as little training as possible. Just like good Web site design, good Web maintenance tool design will result in something that is intuitive and easy to use. But it also depends on the clients. Some clients have us do every single thing. It depends on how much they want to do and how frequently they want their site changed.

9. When and how do you start plans for site marketing?

A very top-level component of that is done up front. More of the details solidify in the last half of the development cycle. Sometimes we'll go live with a campaign to drive traffic to that site. The client's PR machine has to do that. Sometimes we'll do a soft launch, run them for a couple of weeks, let the traffic scale up, and then really hit them hard. Especially when the client is doing the maintenance, it gives them a chance to ramp up gradually instead of trying to swim in a tsunami.

10. How has site marketing changed, and is it possible to predict future Web marketing directions?

It really depends on the client. The greatest marketing of the Web occurs, not necessarily with a brilliant banner ad campaign with millions of impressions, but very often simply as a result of the strength of the site or the Web application itself. Example: We did some work a long time ago for Fleischmann's Yeast. Does that sound exciting? It was an amazingly successful site. In the first two weeks, it outstripped Patagonia, Land Rover, Specialized, and Roller Blade, who were at that time our four highest traffic sites. All that happened was we got a couple of mentions of the day.

We try to build sites that empower users and enable them to do things they can't do any other way or anywhere else. In the case of Fleischmann's Yeast, we developed an enormous online baking information resource with a huge recipe database. People went there and used it and were blown away by how useful it was, then they'd e-mail to their friends—a virus marketing tool—the e-mail contains the URL back to the site.

Word of mouth is the biggest factor very often. A lot of people make fluffy, useless sites with an equally fluffy banner ad campaign with top-notch placement, and they wonder why people aren't coming back to their site. Tricking people to come to a site once is not very hard. But giving them the value to come back every week is much more difficult. We have 40,000 active users for the PowerBar site that return on average every ten days. That's the power of the Web. You can create a site that's so cool that it creates for itself a cult following. We could do it with a site about yeast and with a site about candy bars. It's even easier with Apple or Nordstrom, where there already is a cult following.

INDEX

continued

ABOUT THE AUTHOR

Clay Andres has been a freelance computer journalist for more than a dozen years, during which time he has written seven books. He is a former contributing editor to *MacWEEK* magazine and has written scores of articles on everything from object technology and ISDN to spreadsheets and graphic design. At the same time, Andres has written white papers and other technical marketing materials for many corporate clients, including IBM, Apple, Xerox, and Adobe. Andres is also a cofounder of Interactive Arts & Engineering, a Web design and Internet consultancy.

In former incarnations, Clay was a programmer and computer center manager. But before that, he was a student of architecture and still spends a large fraction of his time as a graphic designer, typographer, and self-proclaimed Web architect. His book design for *Illustrator Illuminated* was a finalist for the prestigious Benjamin Franklin Book Design Award.

Clay lives in northwestern Connecticut with a wife, three sons, and a corgi.

COLOPHON

This book was produced electronically in Foster City, California. Microsoft Word 97 was used for word processing; design and layout were produced using QuarkXPress 4.04 and Adobe Photoshop 5 on Power Macintosh computers. The typeface families used are Minion, Myriad Multiple Master, Prestige Elite, Symbol, Trajan, and Zapf Dingbats.

Acquisitions Editor: Michael Roney
Development Editor: Katharine Dvorak
Technical Editor: Dennis Cohen
Copy Editor: Ami Knox
Permissions Editor: Jesse Simko
Project Coordinator: Tom Debolski
Book Designer: Margery Cantor
Cover Art: Peter Kowaleszyn, Murder by Design/Image Poetry
Production: York Graphic Services
Proofreading and Indexing: York Production Services

my2cents.idgbooks.com

Register This Book — And Win!

Visit **http://my2cents.idgbooks.com** to register this book and we'll automatically enter you in our fantastic monthly prize giveaway. It's also your opportunity to give us feedback: let us know what you thought of this book and how you would like to see other topics covered.

Discover IDG Books Online!

The IDG Books Online Web site is your online resource for tackling technology — at home and at the office. Frequently updated, the IDG Books Online Web site features exclusive software, insider information, online books, and live events!

10 Productive & Career-Enhancing Things You Can Do at www.idgbooks.com

- Nab source code for your own programming projects.

- Download software.

- Read Web exclusives: special articles and book excerpts by IDG Books Worldwide authors.

- Take advantage of resources to help you advance your career as a Novell or Microsoft professional.

- Buy IDG Books Worldwide titles or find a convenient bookstore that carries them.

- Register your book and win a prize.

- Chat live online with authors.

- Sign up for regular e-mail updates about our latest books.

- Suggest a book you'd like to read or write.

- Give us your 2¢ about our books and about our Web site.

You say you're not on the Web yet? It's easy to get started with IDG Books' *Discover the Internet,* available at local retailers everywhere.